Open Marxism 4

Also available

Open Marxism

1. Dialectics and History
Edited by Werner Bonefeld, Richard Gunn and Kosmas Psychopedis

2. Theory and Practice
Edited by Werner Bonefeld, Richard Gunn and Kosmas Psychopedis

3. Emancipating Marx
Edited by Werner Bonefeld, Richard Gunn, John Holloway
and Kosmas Psychopedis

Open Marxism 4

Against a Closing World

Edited by Ana Cecilia Dinerstein, Alfonso García Vela,
Edith González and John Holloway

Foreword by Werner Bonefeld

"ALFONSO VÉLEZ PLIEGO"

Instituto de Ciencias Sociales y Humanidades
Benemérita Universidad Autónoma de Puebla

First published 2020 by Pluto Press
345 Archway Road, London N6 5AA

www.plutobooks.com

British Library Cataloguing in Publication Data
A catalogue record for this book is available from the British Library

ISBN   978 0 7453 4024 1   Hardback
ISBN   978 0 7453 4025 8   Paperback
ISBN   978 1 7868 0541 6   PDF eBook
ISBN   978 1 7868 0543 0   Kindle eBook
ISBN   978 1 7868 0542 3   EPUB eBook

Typeset by Stanford DTP Services, Northampton, England

Contents

PART III: DEMOCRACY, REVOLUTION AND EMANCIPATION

Foreword

Werner Bonefeld

The previous three volumes of *Open Marxism* were published between 1992 and 1995. What a time that was! The Soviet Empire had collapsed, and with great fanfare capitalism was duly celebrated as not only victorious but also as the epitome of civilisation that had now been confirmed as history's end – as if history maintains a class of dispossessed producers of surplus value in the service of vast wealth. 'History' does not pursue its own ends and it does not assert itself in the interests of bourgeois civilisation, morality and profitability. 'History' does not make society. Nor does it take sides. History as it actually unfolded was no history in any meaningful sense. It does not unfold. It is rather that, in the pursuit of their own interests, definite human beings make history, just as they make society. What eventually unfolded is what endures in the present. History was truly made in the late 1980s and early 1990s. About this there is no doubt.

Amidst the fanfare, the debt crisis of the 1980s had started to move from the global South to the global North, from the crash of 1987 via the third global recession in less than 20 years in the early 1990s to the various currency crises, including those of the British Pound and the Mexican Peso in 1992 and 1994 respectively. The Peso crisis coincided with the uprising of the Zapatistas in 1994. Then there was the emergence of China as a world power, founded on a labour economy that combined, and continues to combine, authoritarian government with the provision of cheap labour and disciplined labour relations. It was the time of the first Gulf War, the mere posturing of deadly might in search of a global enemy that was needed to secure the domestic containment of the 'querulous rabble', as Hegel put it when he remarked on how a successful war can check domestic unrest and consolidate the power of the state at home.

Since the early 1990s, with the passing into oblivion of the Soviet Empire, the entire edifice of Marxism-Leninism has crumbled. It had served as the official doctrine and the source of legitimation for state socialism and its various derivative ideologies that found expression in Gramscian or Althusserian Eurocommunism or in the manifold sectarian organisations that proclaimed their allegiance to Trotsky, Lenin's military commander and suppressor of the Kronstadt uprising of 1921, and bearer of an anti-Stalinist Lenin. Although these traditions continue to force themselves onto the critique of political economy, their history has come to an end. They no longer provide the ideological foundation for what is now yesterday's idea of the forward march of state socialism. To be sure, some still believe in the revolutionary party as a means of socialist transformation. Yet, in reality, the party is no more – it had in fact been a mirage for a long time. It died in Spain during the Civil War and during the show trails in Stalinist Russia, and its morbid foundation perished finally in either 1953 or 1956, or indeed 1968. Like Jeremy Corbyn in the United Kingdom, Jean-Luc Mélenchon in France is just a ghost of yesterday. Neither is a Chávez or a Maduro, or indeed an Ortega – and that is a relief. Both Corbyn and Mélenchon seek political power for the sake of justice in an unjust world. Instead of the critique of political economy, the endeavour now is to moralise, and lament by way of political philosophy conceptions of well-being.

In distinction, the *Open Marxism* volumes did not argue for justice in an unjust world by means of Leninist forms of state socialist planning of a labour economy or of social democratic reforms of a capitalist labour economy through progressive schemes of taxation and just ideas for redistribution. Nor did they argue in favour of hegemonic strategies for the achievement of political power on behalf of the many. They did not endorse the state as the institution of institutions. Rather, they understood that the production and realisation of surplus value is the purpose of capital and that the state is the political form of that purpose. The contributors to those volumes also understood that world market competition compels each nation state to achieve competitive labour markets, which are the condition for achieving a measure of social integration. The politics of competitiveness, sound money, fiscal prudence, enhanced labour productivity, belong to a system of wealth that sustains the welfare of workers on the condition that their labour yields a profit. In this system of wealth, the profitability of labour is a means not only of avoiding bankruptcy. It is also a means of sustaining the employment of labour, allowing workers to maintain access to the means of subsistence through wage income.

There is a fate far worse than being an exploited worker, and that is to be an unexploitable worker. If labour power cannot be traded, what else can be sold to make a living and achieve a connection to the means of subsistence? First, the producers of surplus value, dispossessed sellers of labour power, are free to struggle to make ends meet. Their struggle belongs to the conceptuality of capitalist wealth – that is, money that yields more money. In this conception of wealth, the satisfaction of human needs is a mere sideshow. What counts is the time of money. What counts therefore is the valorisation of value through the extraction of surplus value. There is no time to spare. Time is money. And then suddenly society finds itself put back into a state of momentary barbarism; it appears as if famine, a universal war of devastation, had cut off the supply of every means of subsistence to the class that works for its supper. Second, the understanding of the mysterious character of an equivalent exchange between unequal values, of money that yields more money, lies in the concept of surplus value. There is the purchase of labour power, and then the consumption of labour that produces a total value that is greater than the value of labour power. The equivalent exchange relations are thus founded on the class relationship between the buyers of labour power and the producers of surplus value. This social relationship, which entails a history of suffering, vanishes in its economic appearance as an exchange between one quantity of money and another.

Contrary to a whole history of Marxist thought, class struggle is not something positive. Rather, it suffuses the capitalist social relations and drives them forward. Class struggle does not follow some abstract idea. Nor does it express some ontologically privileged position of the working class, according to which it is the driving force of historical progress as the traditions of state socialism saw it. Rather, it is a struggle for access to the means of subsistence. It is a struggle to make ends meet and a struggle for human significance, for life-time, and for human warmth and for affection. There is no doubt that the demand for a politics of justice recognises the suffering of the dispossessed. Political commitment towards the betterment of the conditions of the working class is absolutely necessary – it civilises society's treatment of its workers. Nevertheless, the critique of class society does not find its positive resolution in the achievement of fair and just exchange relations between the sellers of labour power and the consumers of labour. What is a fair wage? Is it not the old dodge of the charitable alternative to the employer from hell, who nevertheless also pays his labourers with the monetised surplus value he previously extracted from them? The critique of class society finds its positive resolution only in a society in which the progress of the 'muck of ages' has come to an end.

The *Open Marxism* volumes of the 1990s saw themselves as a contribution to the attempt at freeing the critique of the capitalist labour economy from the dogmatic embrace of the bright-side view that it is an irrationally organised labour economy. In this view, state socialism is superior to capitalism because it was assumed to be a rationally organised labour economy, based on conscious planning by public authority. The anticapitalism of central economic planning – or, in today's flat enunciation of Negri and Hardt's term the multitude, the politics for the many – is entirely abstract in its critique of labour economy. In fact, it presents the theology of anticapitalism – one that looks on the bright side in the belief that progress will be made upon the taking of government by the party of labour. Anticapitalist theology does not grasp capitalist society. It mystifies it. What is capitalist wealth, what belongs to its concept, how is it produced and what is its dynamic, what holds sway in its concept and what therefore is its conceptuality? Only a reified consciousness can declare that it is in possession of the requisite knowledge and technical expertise for regulating capitalism in the interests of the class that works. The *Open Marxism* volumes sought to reassert the critique of capitalist social relations as a critique of political economy, of both labour economy and the principle of political power – at least that was the critical intention.

The earlier volumes were also an intervention to free Marx from the 'perverters of historical materialism', as Adorno had characterised the doctrinal Marxists in *Negative Dialectics*. For this to happen, looking on the bright side is not an option. Rather, it entails an attempt at thinking in and through the conceptuality of capitalist wealth, which asserts itself as an independent subject behind the backs of acting social individuals that nevertheless, and critically so, endow it with a consciousness and a will through their social practice. In the absence of such an attempt at understanding the conceptuality of real economic abstractions, the struggle of the working class, which belongs to the concept of capital and sustains its progress, will not be understood. Instead, it will either be romanticised as alienated labour in revolt or viewed, with moralising righteousness, as an electoral resource.

The said purpose of the attempt at freeing Marx from the orthodox ritualization of the labour economy was not in any case novel. In fact, it could look back onto a distinguished history that included the council communism of, for example, Pannekoek, Gorter and Mattick; the work of Karl Korsch; the critical theory of Adorno, Horkheimer, Benjamin and Marcuse; the Yugoslav Praxis Group; Axelos's open Marxism; the Situationist International; the critical Marxist tradition in Latin America associated with Bolivar Echeverría, Sánchez Vázquez, Schwarz and Arantes; the state derivation debate of, amongst others, Gerstenberger, Blanke, Neußüss, and von Braunmühl; the *neue Marx Lektüre* of, amongst others, Backhaus, Reichelt and Schmidt; the autonomous Marxism of, amongst others, Dalla Costa, Federici, Caffentzis, Tronti, Negri, Cleaver and Bologna; and, in the context of the British-based Conference of Socialist Economists from which it emerged, the works of especially Simon Clarke and John Holloway about value, class and state. Clarke's critique of structuralist Marxism, especially the works of Lévi-Strauss, Althusser and Poulantzas, and his contributions to state theory and value-form analysis, were fundamental in the immediate context of the early 1990s.

The title *Open Marxism* derived from the work of Johannes Agnoli, a Professor of the Critique of Politics at the Free University of Berlin. His contribution to the heterodox Marxist tradition focused the critique of political economy as a subversive critique of the economic categories, the philosophical concepts, the moral values and the political institutions, including the form of the state, of bourgeois society. The direct link between the title of the *Open Marxism* volumes and Agnoli is the title of a book that he published with Ernest Mandel in 1980: *Offener Marxismus: Ein Gespräch* über *Dogmen, Orthodoxie & die Häresie der Realität* (Open Marxism: A Discussion about Doctrines, Orthodoxy & the Heresy of Reality). The choice of the *Open Marxism* title was not about paying homage to Johannes Agnoli as the foremost subversive thinker of his time. It was programmatic.

The much too long delayed publication of this fourth volume of *Open Marxism* does not require contextualisation. Nothing is as it was and everything is just the same. We live in a time of terror and we live in a time of war. The so-called elite has become a racket, which it in fact had been all along. Antisemitism is back *en vogue* as both the socialism of fools and as the expression of thoughtless resentment and nationalist paranoia. Racism is as pervasive as it always was – as enemy within and without. Gender has become liberal. Feminism no longer disintegrates society as it once promised. The so-called clash of civilisations is unrelenting in its inexorable attack on the promise of freedom. Even the talk about socialism in one country has made a comeback without a sense of purpose – first because there can be none, second because there is none, and third because there never was one. The political blowback of the crisis of 2008 has been intense and relentless: Austerity. Precariat. Profitability. Rate of growth. Price competitiveness. What is so different from the early 1990s, however, is that capitalism as a term of critical inquiry has vanished; it has disappeared from contemporary analysis. The *Zeitgeist* identifies neoliberalism as the object of critique. As a consequence, the past no longer comes alive in the critique of contemporary conditions. Instead, it appears as a counterfoil of imagined civility to today's much-criticised neoliberal world. The critique of neoliberalism conjures up a time in which money did not yield more money but was rather put to work for growth and jobs. Illusion dominates reality. The spectre of society without memory is truly frightening.

While the first three volumes of *Open Marxism* sought to free Marx from the dogmatic perverters of historical materialism, it seems to me that the purpose of this fourth volume is to bring back centre-stage the critique of capitalism, in part to re-establish in a (self-)critical and open manner what the neoliberal *Zeitgeist* disavows, and in part also to think afresh of what it means to say no. On the one hand, there is the preponderance of the object – society as a real abstraction that manifests itself behind the backs of the acting social subjects – and, on the other hand, there is the spontaneity of society as subject – a subject of its own objective dialectics of the forces and relations of production, but a subject nevertheless.

Hope is the true idealism in a world that asserts itself behind the backs of the acting subjects, mere personifications of the economic categories. What is the objective truth of the economic thing? The given world of economic compulsion requires the active intervention of the thinking subject for its comprehension, in order to release the truth which it contains. For Adorno, the most eloquent elements of Kant's *Critique of Pure Reason*, its truth content, are the 'wounds which the conflict in the theory leaves behind' (Adorno 1965: 84). The promise of utopia lies in the 'breaks' (*Brüche*) in its logic and in the gaps in its systematic unity. These cracks, as Holloway refers to them in *Crack Capitalism* (2010), disclose the 'traces' (Bloch) of utopia already experienced in the present.

Only in these 'traces' is there 'hope of ever coming across genuine and just reality' (Adorno 1973: 325). Idealism is the true realism – to the science of economic objectivity, the glimpse of what could be appears as a mere metaphysical distraction.

The point of *Open Marxism* is to interpret the preponderance of society as economic object – not to reject it abstractly and wilfully. Rather, the point of interpretation is to disclose its truth content. Only society as subject has the capacity for deciphering and for refusing to accept the logic that holds sway in the economic object. Non-conformity is the signature of society as subject. However, this does not mean that the truth content lies in the universality of the human being as the hidden secret of the economic world, as Backhaus (2005) suggests. The point is rather to enter into society as economic object, to think in and through it, in order to establish its social nature – 'to develop from the actual, given relations of life the forms in which these have been apotheosized' (Marx 1990: 484, fn. 4). The primacy of interpretation is not a substitute for praxis but a preventative against a false praxis and thus a precondition for change.

Let me conclude with reference to Adorno's *Negative Dialectics* because it contains the memory of Auschwitz. Adorno reformulates Kant's categorical imperative into the principle 'to arrange one's thoughts and actions so that Auschwitz will not repeat itself, so that nothing similar will happen' (1990: 365). Society as object does nothing. It does not maim, kill and gas. 'It is man, rather, the real, living man who does all that', and, in so doing, bestows society as object with a deadly will (paraphrasing Marx, as cited in *Negative Dialectics*). Finally, and however debased as personifications of real economic abstractions, 'there would be nothing without individuals and their spontaneities' (Adorno 1990: 304). Hope dies last.

York

26 March 2019

References

Adorno, T. W. (1965) *Noten zur Literatur*, Vol. 3, Berlin: Suhrkamp.

Adorno, T. W. (1973) 'Die Aktualität der Philosophie', *Gesammelte Werke*, Vol. 1, Berlin: Suhrkamp.

Adorno, T. W. (1990) *Negative Dialectics*, London: Routledge.

Backhaus, H. (2005) 'Some Aspects of Marx's Concept of Critique in the Context of his Economic-Philosophical Theory', in W. Bonefeld and K. Psychopedis (eds), *Human Dignity: Social Autonomy and the Critique of Capitalism*, Aldershot: Ashgate.

Holloway, J. (2010) *Crack Capitalism*, London: Pluto Press.

Marx, K. (1990) *Capital*, Vol. 1, London: Penguin.

Acknowledgements

We would like to thank Anna-Maeve Holloway wholeheartedly for her fine work of translation of several of the chapters of this volume (Chapters 3, 5, 6, 7, 9 and 10 from Spanish, and Chapter 8 from Greek). The book would not have been possible without her dedication. We also express our warmest thanks to the Instituto de Ciencias Sociales y Humanidades 'Alfonso Vélez Pliego' of the Benemérita Universidad Autónoma de Puebla for supporting the costs of translation.

Introduction: Open Marxism Against a Closing World

Ana Cecilia Dinerstein, Alfonso García Vela,
Edith González and John Holloway

We write against a closing of the world. Walls are going up around us. The wall on the USA border with Mexico, the walls that UK Brexiteers would build, the walls being constructed by left and right nationalisms all over the world: walls of exclusion, of borders, often walls of hatred, walls of pain. Intellectually and academically too, walls are going up around us. In the universities (where the four of us work), the walls of academic correctness are growing bigger: the pressures of competition, insecurity and the precarity of academic work, combined with quality assurance committees, lists of indexed journals and quantitative criteria of assessment, make it harder, especially for students and young academics, to write what they want to write. To say what they want to say. The disciplines of the social sciences are becoming just that: disciplines. While resistance struggles continue and expand outside academic walls, critical thought is being squeezed out of the universities, reframed in innocuous forms or simply sidelined. Gradually, often without us noticing it, critical terms become taboo. They become 'durty words' (Brunetta and O'Shea 2018). Increasingly, these durty words begin to be whispered, until they fall out of use altogether. 'Revolution' is the most obvious one, but also 'class struggle', and 'capital' too. The more atrocious the barbarity of patriarchal and colonial capitalism becomes, the less we can name it.

Radical thought has not come to an end though. Not at all. The critique of capital exists. But it survives mainly in the shadow of the criticism of the *forms of expression* of capital: authoritarianism, neoliberalism, the financialisation of the economy, policy failure, the crisis of representative democracy, etc. We write against the closure of the world, then, because we see a danger in some of the present struggles today: that we *only* demand regulation, job creation, distributive justice, transparent democracy, etc. In our view, these criticisms and demands are necessary and important but they are incomplete without a critique of capital (see González, in this volume). With the intensification of the fetishisation of social relations, emancipation looks like a ghost that everyone laughs at. Talking about emancipation becomes simply absurd. The idea of a 'society where "the development of each is the condition for the development of all"' (see Gunn and Wilding, in this volume) seems meaningless. In recent years, and particularly since the financial crisis of 2008, capital has become simultaneously more abstract and more aggressive. Neo-fascism, war, xenophobia, feminicide, racism, ecocide, and repression against all resistances around the world – you name it – signal a world enclosed by walls. This is now a world 'without a Front' (Bloch cited by Amsler 2016: 26). Instead of 'being the place of becoming of "the world, of world process"' (Bloch cited by Amsler 2016: 26), a *world without a front* is a world where hope is constantly diminished, misinterpreted as fantasy or optimism, or dismissed for building castles in the air when we need to discuss the 'urgency' of today's world crisis (see Dinerstein, in this volume). Is there no way out? The institutional left offers an alternative: 'Vote for us'. But is this institutional hope a real alternative? Or it is a way to save capitalism from itself? (Holloway, Nasioka and Doulos 2019). The alternative offered by institutional hope is a short-term promise of 'controlling' capitalists and producing a capitalism with a human face, for the many. But how? When trying to answer this simple question, institutional hope collapses against the walls of a reality where the frenetic logic of capital and the command of money over life prevails. For us, as Bonefeld suggests in his Foreword to this volume, 'looking on the bright side is not an option'.

Marxism is an insolent word. But to retain its insolence, it must constantly be reinvented. It must spit against the horrors of capitalism but, to do that, it must also reject the closed dogmas of its own tradition. The notion of open Marxism has been outlined in the introduction to *Open Marxism 1* (Bonefeld et al. 1992a). The term appeared for the first time in 1980, in the publication of a debate between Johannes Agnoli and Ernst Mandel about Marx's critique of political economy titled *Offener Marxismus*. *Offener Marxismus* became a project of opening up the categories of Marxist thought, and more (see Bonefeld's Foreword). Open Marxism was set up as a new form of understanding the categories developed by Marx, especially in *Capital*, not as predetermined laws but as conceptualisations of class struggle(s). Against the old dichotomy of class struggle and laws of capitalist development, open Marxism challenged Marxists, radical intellectuals and activists to explore money, capital, the state, the law, and so on, as forms of struggle from above and, therefore, open to resistance and rebellion. A key aspect of open Marxism is then to negate *both* capitalist society as well as the dogmatic closure of its categories. The focus is on critique, a critique that investigates the internal contradictions of capital which assert themselves as both theory and struggle. As the editors of *Open Marxism 1* stated in their introduction, 'critique is open in as much as it involves a reciprocal interrelation between the categories of theory [which interrogates practice] and of practice [which constitutes the framework for critique]' (Bonefeld et al. 1992a: xi).

The open Marxists' critique has had a substantial impact on the rethinking of Marxism in the twenty-first century, especially but not exclusively in Europe and Latin America, and several books have emerged from the approach,[1] which has generated many reviews, debates and criticisms. These range from general evaluations of the open Marxist interpretations of Marx's theory, theory of the state, global capital and class struggle, critical theory, social form and human praxis.[2]

This volume continues the work initiated by open Marxism in the 1990s. Its aims are no different from the previous three volumes: to (re)think how to break the descent into barbarism; to break capital by venturing through a theoretical exploration to free the critique of capitalist labour economy from economic dogmas (see Bonefeld's Foreword); to open up to the movement of struggle and to understand itself as part of that movement. That, for us, is the project of open Marxism, and is why we are presenting this collection of essays as the fourth volume of *Open Marxism*. We regard Marxism as an emancipatory theory, a theory of struggle, rather than as an objective analysis of capitalist domination. As John Holloway highlights elsewhere, 'to speak of struggle is to speak of the openness of social development; to think of Marxism as a theory of struggle is to think of Marxist categories as open categories, categories which conceptualise the openness of society' (1993: 76). To Marx, '[t]he critique of social forms ... amounts to a critique of economic categories on a human basis and it does so by returning the constituted forms of the economic categories to "relations between humans"' (Bonefeld in Bieler et al. 2006: 178). We endorse what the editors of *Open Marxism 2* two expressed in their introduction:

> the openness of categories – an openness on to practice – obtains as a reflexive critique of ideologies and social phenomena, which, for

their part, exist as moments of historically asserted forms of class struggle ... Open Marxism insists on the antagonistic nature of social existence. This being so, the Marxist understanding of a unity of theory and praxis entails *not* the theoretical suppression of class struggle, but the invocation of class struggle as the movement of the contradiction in which capital, itself, consists. (Bonefeld, Gunn and Psychopedis 1992b: xi and xii)

Openness means openness of categories, of debates, of our hearts, of spaces for critique, of fronts of political possibility (Amsler 2016; Dinerstein, in this volume).

This fourth volume of *Open Marxism* gives fresh impetus to the intertwining of theoretical discussion and radical, anticapitalist practice with a selection of authors that we consciously sought to include: not only the established names associated with open Marxism but also a new wave or second generation of open Marxists. The fact that this new generation includes a high proportion of women and Latin Americans says much about the way that rebellion and rebellious thought have been moving in recent years. Our aim is that open Marxism should be open to the changing flows of struggle, although it must be admitted that the reference lists of the various chapters remain heavily dominated by white men.

The contributions to this volume were inspired by the broad idea of 'open Marxism against a closing world', but the authors were left free to decide how to contribute to it. This editorial decision responds to the aim to discover and present to the reader some of the open Marxists' theoretical developments and political concerns of the past two decades. We have grouped the eleven chapters that follow around three main subjects: open Marxism and critical theory (Part I); global capital, the nation state and the capitalist crisis (Part II); and democracy, revolution and emancipation (Part III).

In past decades, there has been a renewed interest from journalists, academics and activists in exploring the meaning and the authority of Marx's work today. Yet, as Hudis and Anderson highlight in their introduction to Dunayevskaya's *Selected Writings on the Dialectic in Hegel and Marx*, 'one surprising feature of much of the current return to Marx ... is the relative silence on Hegel and the dialectic' (2002: xv). In the opening essay of this collection, Richard Gunn and Adrian Wilding return to Hegel to recover the *revolutionary* notion of 'mutual recognition' as theorised by Marx and – before him – Hegel. Gunn and Wilding argue that the recuperation of the notion of mutual recognition is one of the ways to renew an 'open' Marxism in the twentieth century. For them, recognition can become a unifying theoretical and uniting principle of the Left. By exploring Marx's discussion of the term against the setting of Hegel's *Phenomenology of Spirit*, the authors underline the common revolutionary impulse of both Marx and Hegel, and how they uncover the contradictory forms which recognition takes on in a world of domination and institutional alienation.

One of the central concerns of open Marxism has been, and still is, Marx's notion of the unity between theory and praxis. Following Bonefeld et al., Marxist orthodoxy takes this unity as 'referring to the "field of application" … and is reflected in the separation between the logic of capital, on the one hand, and social practice, in the other' (Bonefeld et al. 1995: 2). The next four contributions by Ana Cecilia Dinerstein, Alfonso García Vela, Mario Schäbel and Frederick Harry Pitts speak to this problematic in different ways, addressing the contributions of Theodor W. Adorno, Ernst Bloch, open Marxism and the New Reading of Marx (NRM) to the theorisation of the relation between object(ivity) and subject(ivity) in our understanding of radical change. In Chapter 2, Ana C. Dinerstein re-evaluates the place of the theoretical in today's praxis. By pointing to the sphere of social reproduction as the 'site' of both new forms of class struggle and the renewal of critical theory, Dinerstein argues that critical theory today should be based on Bloch's philosophy of hope. Despite the critical theorist's fear of the positivisation of social struggles, Dinerstein argues that the fight against barbarism is not only possible but *already exists* in the form of struggles for alternative forms of life. In a context of the crisis of social reproduction, these struggles should not be regarded as *positive*: they are *critical affirmations* that affirm life as a form of negating a totality of destruction *in a 'contradictory' manner* (see Gunn 1994). To her, while Adorno's negative dialectics (Adorno 1995) remarkably prevents dialectical closure of the capitalist totality from taking place *theoretically*, negative dialectics cannot open onto a 'world with Front' *in practice*. And this is what is needed today.

Alfonso García Vela opens his chapter with the assertion that open Marxism does enable us to overcome the positive conceptualisation of dialectics, totality and emancipation typical of orthodox Marxism, with practical relevance for anticapitalist struggles. However, referring mainly to John Holloway's work, he claims that open Marxism has not yet solved the problem of the separation between subject and object, between structure and struggle. He points to what he calls the open Marxist's 'subjectivist' position, which conceives of the object only as a mode of existence of the subject. This, argues García Vela, can be regarded as a voluntarist perspective on emancipation. According to the author, this contrasts with Adorno's primacy of the object which contests the subjectivism of modern thought and therefore opens the possibility of rethinking the dichotomy between structure and struggle beyond subjectivism, without relapsing into the objectivist position represented by structuralism. Also, for García Vela, the transformation of the world requires the self-reflection of critical thought, because critical thought is not separated from capitalist society but emanates from it. An important aspect of Adorno's negative dialectics is that it calls to the self-reflection of thinking. So, if the critical theory of open Marxism wants to contribute to changing the world it must undertake self-reflection. Otherwise, it runs the risk of its reification.

In Chapter 4, Frederick Harry Pitts highlights open Marxism's critical contribution to value-form analysis. To be sure, orthodox economics cannot grasp the real problem of the expansion of 'money as command' (Cleaver 1996), because their 'abstract abstractions' try to 'get rid of contradictions in definitions' in such a way that economic categories do not explicate 'the phenomenon from which the economic abstraction comes' (Ilyenkov 2008: 243, 103). Open Marxists follow Marx in his critique of 'abstract' or 'formal' abstractions, and work with determinate abstractions insofar as they embody the contradictions of the real movement of struggle. As Gunn suggests, 'if it is a "theory of" anything, Marxism is a *theory of contradiction*' (1994: 53). 'Without contradiction', argues Bonefeld, 'inhuman forces like Capital and Money, are naturalised and the economy becomes something superior, unmanageable, as existing above us, like God' (2016: 235). Pitts's assessment of open Marxism's contribution to value-form analysis makes exactly this point: while for the NRM 'the validity of economic categories such as labour and value does not hold in abstraction from society as whole', for open Marxism value is a historical – contradictory – process based on class struggle. To Pitts, while both open Marxism and the NRM offer a 'radically open and non-dogmatic unfinished project', open Marxism should be valued for having restated the centrality of class struggle at the core of the NRM's 'monetary' theory of value.

In Chapter 5, Mario Schäbel also discusses the work of the NRM, exploring its synergies with open Marxism. However, his focus is on the association of open Marxism with Adorno's negative dialectics. Schäbel enquires whether open Marxists can be regarded as the successors of Adorno's critical theory or not. His analysis suggests that open Marxism can *only* be considered an offspring of the Frankfurt School in connection to Herbert Marcuse's subjective idealism rather than Adorno's critical materialism, the latter having been embraced by scholars of the NRM. Unlike Pitts, Schäbel does not regard either open Marxism's rejection of the *primacy* of the object over the subject, or its restatement of class struggle at the core of the analysis of capital and the value-form, as contributions that could 'fix' the NRM's 'objective' analysis of capital. To Schäbel, open Marxism's closeness to Marcuse's critical theory, rather than Adorno's, risks replacing 'the dogmatic and one-sided materialism of orthodox Marxism with an equally dogmatic and one-sided idealism based on granting the subject absolute primacy in the context of the dialectical unity of subject and object'.

The next two chapters offer innovative critical approaches to two of the traditional concerns of open Marxism: global capital and the state, and the crisis of the accumulation of capital. In Chapter 6, Sagrario Anta Martínez joins those who have challenged the adequacy of Marx's notion of primitive accumulation today (Dalla Costa 1995; Harvey 2005; Bonefeld 2008; De Angelis 2008), particularly when the context is the possibly terminal crisis of capital (see Ortlieb 2008; Kurz 2010). She suggests that as a 'system of social organisation' capitalism does not ensure the reproduction of the human life, but quite the opposite: it is destroying the sources of social reproduction, and therefore leading to a crisis of the latter (see Dinerstein, in this volume). Anta Martínez offers the term 'terminary accumulation', as opposed to primitive accumulation, to suggest that, in the current global situation, talk of primitive accumulation is simply anachronistic. With 'terminary accumulation' in mind, she then explores the antagonism between capital and life and the limits of the former as a form of social organisation. In Chapter 7, Rodrigo Pascual and Luciana Ghiotto examine the established idea in the discipline of International Political Economy (IPE) that the state possesses territorial foundations, while capital maintains itself as global, free and non-territorial. Their analysis – which connects open Marxism's recent contributions to long-term debates about the relation between the state, multinational corporations and imperialism – demonstrates that the realist perspective in IPE embraces this partition, which is based on the analysis of the two moments in the process of accumulation of capital: production, which requires territoriality, and circulation, which does not. However, Pascual and Ghiotto challenge this separation and argue that territoriality and non-territoriality are not attributes of the state and capital respectively, but a result of class antagonism. Territoriality and globality imprint a tension in the domain of class exploitation, and this can only be resolved temporarily within the territorial contours of the State.

The third and final part of the book concerns democracy, revolution and emancipation. In Chapter 8, Katherina Nasioka traces the effects of the capitalist crisis since the 1970s, and the shifts that are observed in class struggle as a result of this ongoing crisis. She argues that the anticapitalist struggle today displays two mutually contradicting dynamics which reflect the intensity of the capitalist crisis and the sharpening of contradictions in the capital *relation*. On the one hand, the twentieth-century's dominant form of political organisation of the working class, hegemonised by the labour movement and guided by the Leninist canon, is hard to assert in the present-day context. On the other hand, the contemporary struggles against capital, which are defensive in most cases, are often fought in the name of 'we, the workers', looking for class unity in those categories that have built the identity of the labour movement in the past, e.g. the nation, the state. Therefore, while organisation based on the working class is debilitated, the lack of class unity is challenging the prospect of revolution. Nasioka asks, then: how can new struggles be translated into a political prospect that goes *against-and-beyond* capitalist society? In Chapter 9, Sergio Tischler might provide a plausible response to Nasioka by bringing the case of the Zapatista movement (Chiapas, Mexico) into the discussion of revolution today.[3] Tischler suggests that Zapatismo has not been a simple revolutionary movement of a local character, but has implied a shaking of contemporary revolutionary thought on such fundamental issues as the relationship between Marxism and the revolution today. Zapatismo offers a critique of the Leninist canon of revolution, that is, of the revolutionary subject conceived typically from the perspectives of vanguard and hegemony. The relevance of the Zapatistas' autonomy lies in it being a *practical criticism* of the idea of the vertical and state-centric subject of the anticapitalist transformation. Through the images and practice of

Zapatismo, a space and a political-conceptual process was opened that can lead to a re-conceptualisation of the anticapitalist struggle.

In Chapter 10, Edith González starts with a critical reflection on the place that democracy occupies in left thinking today. She is concerned about a shift that has taken place in that thinking from revolution to democracy, and the political consequences that this bears for any process of emancipation. González argues that democracy has become the central theme in both critical analyses of the past decade and in social movements and grassroots political discourse and practice. To be sure, Occupy Wall Street and social movements in Argentina have become symbols of resistance against capitalism. These movements have reinvented radical democracy by means of a new 'horizontalism' (Sitrin 2006; 2012). They are regarded as agents of the prefiguration of a new democracy (Brissette 2013; Teivainen 2016). But are these movements aware of the limits of the use of the concept of 'democracy' without a critique of capital? To González, the equality that democracy can promise in a capitalist society is, in fact, an abstraction of inequality. Therefore, the question is: 'what is the power of the anticapitalist "democratic" struggle without a critique of capital?' The concept of capital, argues John Holloway in the final chapter of the book, is crucial for understanding the present situation of the world. Here, Holloway engages with the categorisation of his open Marxist approach as being 'subjectivist' (see Schäbel and García Vela, in this volume). Using 'the train' as a metaphor for the inherently expansive and destructive nature of capital, Holloway claims that capital is not a pure object for the domination of the subject. Rather, capital 'is a struggle'. It is clear that we have produced 'the train', he argues; that is, the train is a 'social construct', and it became 'objectified' as the dominant form of social relations 'through bloody struggles'. Capital has its own rules. However, the problem starts when we 'understand capital simply as a form of domination (as capital-logicians and New Readers of Marx tend to do)'. Holloway suggests that while the 'primacy of the object' characterises capital, *it is precisely that which we must break.* There is a dissonance in the relation between subject and object: 'The presence of the object within the subject has been much emphasised, but what interests us more is the destructive force of the subject within the object, the presence of the subject in-against-and-beyond the object as its crisis.'

References

Adorno, T. W. (2000) *Introduction to Sociology*, Cambridge: Polity Press.

Adorno, T. W. (1995) *Negative Dialectics*, London: Continuum.

Amsler, S. (2016) 'Learning Hope: An Epistemology of Possibility for Advanced Capitalist Society', in A. C. Dinerstein (ed.), *Social Sciences for An-Other Politics: Women Theorising without Parachutes*, Basingstoke: Palgrave Macmillan, 19–32.

Best, B., Bonefeld, W. and O'Kane, C. (eds) (2018) *The Sage Handbook of Frankfurt School Critical Theory*, 3 vols, London: Sage.

Bieler, A. and Morton, A. (2003) 'Globalisation, the State and Class Struggle: A "Critical Economy" Engagement with Open Marxism', *British Journal of Politics and International Relations* 5(4): 467–99.

Bieler, A., Bonefeld, W., Burnham, P. and Morton, A. (2006) *Global Restructuring, State, Capital and Labour: Contesting Neo-Gramscian Perspectives*, Basingstoke: Palgrave Macmillan.

Boldyrev, I. (2015) *Ernst Bloch and his Contemporaries: Locating Utopian Messianism Today*, London: Bloomsbury.

Bonefeld, W. (2008) 'The Permanence of Primitive Accumulation: Commodity Fetishism and Social Constitution', in W. Bonefeld (ed.), *Subverting the Present, Imagining the Future*, New York: Autonomedia, 51–66.

Bonefeld, W. (2010) 'Abstract Labour: Against its Nature and on its Time', *Capital & Class* 34(2): 257–76.

Bonefeld, W. (2014) *Critical Theory and the Critique of Political Economy: On Subversion and Negative Reason*, London: Bloomsbury.

Bonefeld, W. (2016) 'Bringing Critical Theory Back in at a Time of Misery: Three Beginnings Without Conclusion', *Capital & Class* 40(2): 233–44.

Bonefeld, W. and Holloway, J. (eds) (1995) *Global Capital, National State and the Politics of Money*, Basingstoke: Palgrave Macmillan.

Bonefeld, W. and Psychopedis, K. (2005) *Human Dignity: Social Autonomy and the Critique of Capitalism*, New York: Routledge.

Bonefeld, W. and Tischler, S. (2002) *What is to be Done? Leninism, Anti-Leninist Marxism and the Question of Revolution Today*, New York: Routledge.

Bonefeld, W., Holloway, J. and Tischler, S. (eds) (2005) *Marxismo Abierto. Una visión Europea y Latinoamericana*, Vol. 2, Buenos Aires/Puebla: Ediciones Herramienta & Universidad Benemérita Autónoma de Puebla.

Bonefeld, W., Gunn, R. and Psychopedis K. (eds) (1992a) *Open Marxism 1*, London: Pluto Press.

Bonefeld, W., Gunn, R. and Psychopedis, K. (eds) (1992b) *Open Marxism 2*, London: Pluto Press.

Bonefeld, W., Gunn, R., Holloway, J. and Psychopedis, K. (eds) (1995) *Open Marxism 3*, London: Pluto Press.

Brissette, E. (2013) 'Prefiguring the Realm of Freedom at Occupy Oakland', *Rethinking Marxism* 25(2): 218–27.

Bruff, I. (2009) 'The Totalisation of Human Social Practice: Open Marxists and Capitalist Social Relations, Foucauldians and Power Relations', *The British Journal of Politics and International Relations* 11: 332–51.

Brunetta, V. and O'Shea, K. (eds) (2018) *Durty Words*, Limerick: Durty Books.

Clarke, S. (ed.) (1991) *The State Debate*, Basingstoke: Macmillan.

Cleaver, H. (1996) 'The Subversion of Money-as-Command in the Current Crisis', in W. Bonefeld and J. Holloway (eds), *Global Capital, National State and the Politics of Money*, Basingstoke: Palgrave Macmillan, 141–77.

Dalla Costa, M. (1995) 'Capitalism and Reproduction', in W. Bonefeld, R. Gunn, J. Holloway and K. Psychopedis (eds), *Open Marxism 3*, London: Pluto Press, 7–16.

De Angelis, M. (2008) 'Marx and Primitive Accumulation: The Continuous Character of Capital's Enclosures', in W. Bonefeld (ed.), *Subverting the Present, Imagining the Future*, New York: Autonomedia, 27–50.

Dinerstein, A. C. (2012) 'Interstitial Revolution: The Explosive Fusion of Negativity and Hope', *Capital & Class* 36(3): 513–32.

Dinerstein, A. C. (2015) *The Politics of Autonomy in Latin America: The Art of Organising Hope*, Basingstoke: Palgrave.

Dinerstein, A. C. (ed.) (2016) *Social Sciences for An-Other Politics: Women Theorising without Parachutes*, Basingstoke: Palgrave Macmillan.

Dinerstein, A. C. (2018) 'John Holloway: A Theory of Interstitial Revolution', in B. Best, W. Bonefeld and C. O'Kane (eds), *The Sage Handbook of Frankfurt School Critical Theory*, London: Sage, 533–49.

Dinerstein, A. C. and Neary, M. (eds) (2002) *The Labour Debate*, New York: Routledge.

Dinerstein, A. C. and Pitts, F. H. (2018) 'From Post-work to Post-capitalism? Discussing the Basic Income and Struggles for Alternative Forms of Social Reproduction', *Journal of Labor & Society* 21(4): 471–91.

Dönmez P. E. and Sutton, A. (2016) 'Revisiting the Debate on Open Marxist Perspectives', *The British Journal of Politics and International Relations* 18(3): 688–705.

Eden, D. (2012) *Autonomy: Capitalism, Class and Politics*, London: Routledge.

Grollios, V. (2017) *Negativity and Democracy: Marxism and the Critical Theory Tradition*, New York: Routledge.

Grosfoguel, R. (2009) 'Izquierdas e Izquierdas Otras: Entre el Proyecto de la izquierda eurocéntrica y el Proyecto transmoderno de las nuevas izquierdas decoloniales', *Tabula Rasa* 11: 9–29.

Gunn, R. (1994) 'Marxism and Contradiction', *Common Sense* 15: 53–9, https://commonsensejournal.org.uk/1994/04/01/issue-15.

Harvey, D. (2005) *The New Imperialism*, Oxford: Oxford University Press.

Holloway, J. (1993) 'Open Marxism, History and Class Struggle', *Common Sense* 13: 76–86.

Holloway, J. (1994) 'The Relevance of Marxism Today', *Common Sense* 15: 38–42.

Holloway, J. (2002) *Change the World Without Taking Power: The Meaning of Revolution Today*, London: Pluto Press.

Holloway, J. (2010) *Crack Capitalism*. London: Pluto Press.

Holloway, J., Matamoros, F. and Tischler, S. (eds) (2009) *Negativity and Revolution: Adorno and Political Activism*, London: Pluto Press.

Holloway, J., Nasioka, K. and Doulos, P. (eds) (2019) *Beyond Crisis: After the Collapse of the Institutional Hope, What?*, San Francisco: PM Press.

Hudis, P. and Anderson, K. L. (2002) 'Introduction: Raya Dunayevskaya's Concept of Dialectic', in R. Dunayevskaya, *The Power of Negativity: Selected Writings on the Dialectic in Hegel and Marx*, ed. P. Hudis and K. Anderson, Lanham: Lexington Books, xv–xlii.

Ilyenkov, E. V. (2008 [1960]) *The Dialectics of the Abstract and the Concrete in Marx's Capital*, New Delhi: Aakar Books.

Khasnabish, A. (2008) *Zapatismo Beyond Borders: New Imaginations of Political Possibilities*, Toronto: University of Toronto Press.

Kiciloff, A. and Starosta, G. (2011) 'On Value and Abstract Labour: A Reply to Werner Bonefeld', *Capital & Class* 35(2): 295–305.

Kurz, R. (2010) 'On the Current Global Economic Crisis: Questions and Answers', in N. Larsen, M. Nilges, J. Robinson and N. Brown (eds) (2014) *Marxism and the Critique of Value*, Chicago: MCM', 321–56.

Mandel, E. and Agnoli, J. (1980) *Offener Marxismus – Ein Gespräch über Dogmen, Orthodoxie and die Häresie der Realität*. Frankfurt: Campus.

Mignolo, W. (2002) 'The Zapatistas' Theoretical Revolution: Its Historical, Ethical, and Political Consequences', *Review – Fernand Braudel Center* 25(3): 245–75.

Moir, C. (2018) 'In Defence of Speculative Materialism', *Historical Materialism* 1. Online Article, 1–33, doi:10.1163/1569206X-00001609.

Ortlieb, C. P. (2008) 'A Contradiction Between Matter and Form: On the Significance of the Production of Relative Surplus Value in the Dynamic of Terminal Crisis', in N. Larsen, M. Nilges, J. Robinson and N. Brown (eds) (2014) *Marxism and the Critique of Value*, Chicago: MCM', 77–122.

Sitrin, M. (ed.) (2006) *Horizontalism: Voices of Popular Power in Argentina*, Oakland, CA and Edinburgh: AK Press.

Sitrin, M. (2012) *Everyday Revolutions: Horizontalism and Autonomy in Argentina*, London and New York: Zed Books.

Susen, S. (2012) '"Open Marxism" Against and Beyond the "Great Enclosure"? Reflections on How (Not) to Crack Capitalism', *Journal of Classical Sociology* 12(2): 281–331.

Teivainen, T. (2016) 'Occupy Representation and Democratise Prefiguration: Speaking for Others in Global Justice Movements', *Capital & Class* 40(1): 19–36.

Tsolakis, A. (2010) 'Opening up Open Marxist Theories of the State: A Historical Materialist Critique', *The British Journal of Politics and International Relations* 12: 387–407.

Notes

1. Among them, Best, Bonefeld and O'Kane 2018; Bonefeld and Tischler 2002; Bonefeld, Holloway and Tischler 2005; Bonefeld 2014; Dinerstein and Neary 2002; Dinerstein 2015, 2016; Holloway 2002, 2010; Holloway, Matamoros and Tischler 2009; Bonefeld and Psychopedis 2005.

2. Bieler and Morton 2003; Bruff 2009; Dönmez and Sutton 2016; Tsolakis 2010; Grollios 2017; Kiciloff and Starosta 2011; Eden 2012; Dinerstein 2012, 2018; Susen 2012; several authors in *Historical Materialism* 13(4), 2005; several authors in *Capital & Class* 29(1), 2005; and several authors in *Herramienta* (2002) available at www.herramienta.com.ar/articulo.php?id=34.

3. On the Zapatista's *theoretical revolution* see also Grosfoguel 2009; Khasnabish 2008; and Mignolo 2002, among others.

PART I

OPEN MARXISM AND CRITICAL THEORY

1

Recognition and Revolution

Richard Gunn and Adrian Wilding

How might an open Marxist school of thought be developed? The authors of the present chapter are keen readers of Hegel (1770–1831) and of 'German Idealism' more generally. It strikes us that themes highlighted by open Marxism echo a strand of thought in Hegel's *Phenomenology of Spirit* (1807).[1] In pointing to this strand, which is central to our recent work, we underline a continuity between Hegel and Marx. Stated differently, we attempt to renew what is referred to as 'Left' or 'Young' Hegelianism – which has become all but moribund in neoliberal years.

Marxism has traditionally aimed at emancipation – or, to quote Marx's words, a society where 'the development of each is the condition for the development of all' (Marx and Engels 1976b: 506). In the present chapter, we argue that the form of society which Marx seeks to establish is a form which has roots in Hegel's *Phenomenology of Spirit*. It is well known that Marx started his intellectual life as a Young Hegelian – the Young Hegelians being theorists of the 1830s and 1840s who emphasised emancipatory strands in Hegel's work. In a number of early writings, Marx criticised the Young Hegelians.[2] It may be just as important to say, however, that he always remained faithful to Young Hegelian ideas.

The key idea which concerns us here is 'recognition'. In Hegel's *Phenomenology of Spirit*, although not in his later and more conservative *Philosophy of Right* (1821), the term 'mutual recognition' has overtones of the freedom and self-determination at which the French Revolution of 1789 aimed. In a society where recognition is 'mutual' – or, to use an alternative term, 'reciprocal' – freedom is not alienated or contradicted. Where recognition is denied, freedom is denied for its part. A society where there is mutual recognition is one where individuals see or acknowledge one another's freedom. Where mutual recognition is present, freedom obtains.

Why, it may be asked, bring 'recognition' into the picture? Why not merely say that Marx favours social relations of an emancipatory kind? One answer is that 'pure' or 'mutual' recognition is linked to a recipro-cal to-and-fro process of interaction that Hegel's *Phenomenology* does its best to explain (see Hegel 1977: 111–12). It is important, we think, to highlight this process: to-and-fro interaction is part of what emancipa-tion entails.

A second answer is that 'recognition' – and, thence, recognition which is mutual – is a term that has not merely a cognitive but a constitutive force. That is to say: the way that individuals are 'seen' or recognised makes them who and what they are. When individuals are recognised as self-determining, therefore, their self-determination is accentuated. They become self-determining through the process of recognition that Hegel describes. Individuals who are mutually recognitive do not merely sit alongside one another. They cast one another's self-determination into relief.

A further reason for talking about 'recognition' is political: in emanci-patory political projects, recognition as set out in Hegel's *Phenomenology* and in Marx is a much-foregrounded theme. In, for example, an 'alterna-tive' cooperative – and we are thinking of a cooperative of a 'prefigurative' kind[3] – much energy goes into experimentation. Experimentation with what? The answer which suggests itself is: 'experimentation with forms of recognition'. It is, of course, possible to reply: 'experimentation with social relations'. Such a reply, however, tells us little about the content of the relations in question. It is, we suggest, mutual recognition that provides the *detail* of emancipation which radical theory (including Marxism) often merely sketches. Moreover, by introducing 'recognition' into our conceptual picture, we find a term that highlights an activity which, from the seventeenth century onwards, radicals have regarded as key.[4] The notion of *mutual* or to-and-fro recognition embodies the form of society which, for generations, revolutionaries sought to achieve.

It is true that, amongst orthodox or DIAMAT-style Marxists, 'recog-nition' has not found favour either as a theoretical term or a practical concern. One reason for this is that, for the decades of the Soviet Union's pre-eminence, Marxism was gripped by the 'base/superstruc-ture' metaphor.[5] If everything in society must be allocated to a 'base' or a 'superstructure', recognition is superstructural to say the least. When open Marxism breaks with economistic and 'base/superstructure' dogmatism and focuses instead on everyday and grassroots issues (see

Gunn 2017), the way is clear to give 'recognition' a central place. This done, a central aim of revolutionary activity is moved to the centre of theory's stage.

Hegel on Recognition

In the present chapter, considerations of time and space prevent us from considering Hegel's work in a systematic fashion. Elsewhere, we have written on Hegel and given the *Phenomenology* and its discussion of 'Lord' and 'Bondsman' (the so-called 'Master-Slave dialectic') an emphatic place.[6] Here, our concern is with Marx – whom we regard not as a theorist of base and superstructure but as a theorist of recognition.

Whilst not attempting a detailed discussion of Hegel, our article cannot avoid drawing Hegelian issues into play. When Hegel wrote his *Phenomenology*, the French Revolution of 1789 struck him as an event that paved the way to emancipation. French Revolutionary emancipation seemed to him the practical basis on which truthful thought (or 'science', in Hegel's meaning of the term) – for example the 'science' of the *Phenomenology* itself – rests.[7] In chapters IV and, especially, VI of the *Phenomenology*, Hegel traces an outline of European history from the Ancient Greek *polis* to the French Revolution of his own day. Each phase of this history represents a distinctive pattern of recognition; this history ends with the French Revolution, when mutual recognition or non-alienated recognition is attained.

At this point, some detail regarding the *Phenomenology* is unavoidable. Although the French Revolution is, for the Hegel of 1806–7, the event which brings mutual recognition into being, the section of the book headed 'Absolute Freedom and Terror', wherein the events of the Revolution are discussed, is no straightforward triumphalist text. Hegel's starting point is that, in the Revolutionary crowd, 'each [individual], undivided from the whole, always does everything, and what appears as done by the whole is the direct and conscious deed of each' (1977: 357). This formulation echoes a phrase used by Hegel when he first introduces the idea of mutual recognition. There, he envisages a situation where there is an '"I" that is "We" and "We" that is "I"' (1977: 110). Hegel's return to this vocabulary of reciprocity at the end of his outline of European history allows us to see what the French Revolution has achieved. In effect, mutual recognition makes its first appearance on the streets of Revolutionary Paris. Hegel's claim in the passage cited above is that Revolutionary freedom and mutual recognition are one and the same thing. He is aware, of course, that crowd activity is unstable and evanescent: the problem faced by the Revolution is to give mutual recognition a lasting being. The difficulty faced by the French Revolution is that attempts to instantiate mutual recognition contradict mutual recognition itself. When the Revolution turns to the 'universal work' of constitution building, for instance, it sets up a social structure that stands over against the individual and alienates freedom once again.[8] What Hegel terms 'deeds proper' (1977: 359) – by which he understands military ventures – contradict and alienate freedom in a novel way. When, finally, the Revolution turns to state Terror, the contradiction is evident: 'The sole work and deed of universal freedom is ... *death*' (1977: 360). It would be fair to say that, although the French Revolution has brought the principle of mutual recognition into being, it has not shown how mutual recognition can be instantiated in a stable way. For the Hegel of the *Phenomenology*, the problems of mutual recognition *lie out ahead*. They represent problems for the present and future, as the Young Hegelians and Marx saw.

A further detailed point which deserves emphasis here concerns the course of history. We have suggested that, for the Hegel of the *Phenomenology*, historical periods are *patterns of recognition*. The point we wish to emphasise is that these patterns are, without exception, patterns of contradictory – or, to state the point differently, patterns of alienated or contradicted – recognition. Only at the end of the *Phenomenology*'s historical narrative does recognition exist in an uncontradicted – which is to say, a mutual – way. When the Hegel of the *Phenomenology* writes of contradictory or contradicted recognition, what contradictions – what sorts of contradiction – does he have in mind? We pause to clarify this point because it has a bearing on Marx's claims.

One form of contradiction that the *Phenomenology* envisages is what Hegel terms 'one-sided and unequal' recognition (1977: 116). The most famous example of this is the recognition that obtains between a Lord (*Herr*) and a Bondsman (*Knecht*). Recognition that is 'one-sided and unequal' is contradictory in that it undermines itself. It undermines itself because a Lord depends on recognition by a Bondsman – and yet he, the Lord, denies that the Bondsman is capable of recognition. From the Lord's point of view, the Bondsman is beneath contempt. A relation of domination (*Herrschaft*), Hegel tells us – and the implications of this are considerable – is not just reprehensible but self-defeating, a tower built on sand.

In the *Phenomenology*, 'one-sided and unequal' recognition is a key form that contradictory recognition takes. But there is a second form, and it is important to acknowledge this because it too reappears in Marx's work. This form of contradictory recognition is recognition that goes forward in terms of role definitions, which the *Phenomenology* regards as inscribed in social institutions. Social institutions – Hegel's phrase is '*geistige Massen*' (see Hegel 1977: 300, 356–7) – stand over against individuals. In relation to social institutions, an individual can only lead an alienated life. An individual who is recognised only in terms of social role definitions is divided against him- or herself: the part of the individual included in the role definition (the 'universal' part) is socially acknowledged but the multifaceted remainder of the individual (the 'particular' part) falls out of account. The individual is not acknowledged as a coherent and self-determining being. Individuals defined by roles and the institutions which generate them are not free in and through one another. In a world of institutions, individuals no longer cast each other's self-determination into relief.

This second form of contradictory recognition is taken up by Marx when he refers to, and criticises, 'ökonomischen Charaktermasken' (1975a: 114). It is implied when, in the *Grundrisse*, Marx declares that, in a market, individuals 'recognize one another as proprietors' (1973: 243). Unless the *Phenomenology*'s second form of contradictory recognition is borne in mind, passages such as that just cited can send one on a hunt for tacit aspects of mutual recognition in capitalist market relations.[9] As we show later, no such potentially reformist motifs are present in Marx's thought.

Whilst on the subject of details in Hegel, it is important to underline the difference between recognition which exists in the course of history – or, as Marx phrases the point, in the history 'of all hitherto existing society' (Marx and Engels 1976b: 482) – and recognition in a mutual and, so to say, post-historical world.[10] The difference is that between recognition which is alienated and recognition where a self-determining and emancipatory perspective is restored. Exploring this difference, we come upon a point that is not merely one of detail but is essential to our claims. We have suggested that mutual recognition has a to-and-fro and interactive dynamic. It is, we propose, analogous to a good conversation – by which we mean a conversation that is open to all comers and which follows the subject matter wherever it leads. If the conversation is restricted by external requirements – for example, requirements on which this or that social institution or social role insists – it ceases to be 'good'. It ceases to be a 'conversation'. It becomes an empty ritual propping up the power structure that the social role or institution serves. Stating this point in slightly different terms: if recognition is to be mutual, and to have a to-and-fro dynamic, it must (just as a 'good' conversation must follow the subject matter where it leads) be answerable to nothing but itself. If recognition is to have a structure, the structure must be its own. It must be 'unstructured' – not in the sense that it is chaotic or random but in the sense that it gives its dynamic to itself. In this sense, we readily admit that our view of recognition is anarchistic.

Marx on Recognition

Just as recognition is at the core of Hegel's thought, so too is it a theme which runs through Marx's thinking and makes sense of a diverse range of his concerns. Of course, to argue that Marx is a thinker of recognition is, in Marxist terms, unorthodox. Due to longstanding prejudices, the concept of recognition has an 'unmarxist' ring. At best, recognition features at the edges of discussions of the topic of alienation; at worst it is assumed to belong to the Hegelian baggage supposedly jettisoned by the 'mature' Marx. A further prejudice blocks the way to a recognitive reading of Marx, namely the tendency to view his relationship to Hegel through the lens of the 'Critique of the *Philosophy of Right*' and to overlook the influence of Hegel's earlier and – as we have argued – more radical *Phenomenology of Spirit*. We suggest that Marx was fully aware of the revolutionary implications of the *Phenomenology*'s discussion of recognition and that it remained a touchstone throughout his life. Hegel's and Marx's views of recognition run parallel.

Thus a reader who has an image of recognition as a 'bourgeois' category must set aside his or her preconceptions when encountering Marx's writings. Marx's view is much more subtle. Recognition is indeed a category upon which bourgeois thinkers and other apologists for capitalism have called, but when understood consistently it is a category which explodes the bourgeois worldview. Marx, we believe, takes up Hegel's challenge to expose the contradictory patterns of recognition of his day and to conceive a mutually recognitive existence that would solve these contradictions.

Space forbids a thorough discussion of Marx on recognition here.[11] Instead we sketch a selection of his most relevant texts. We begin with his *Comments on James Mill*, a text dating from the same year as the *Paris Manuscripts* (1844) and which deals with the relationship between creditor and debtor. What strikes a reader of this short text is how closely the language of Marx's discussion of creditor and debtor follows that of Hegel's treatment of Lord and Bondsman. The relation of creditor to debtor displays the same contradictory mix of 'independence' (*Selbständigkeit*) and 'dependence' (*Unselbstständigkeit*) which features in Hegel's discussion. As with Lord and Bondsman, each of the 'terms' of the creditor-debtor relation are individuals who are determined by that relation. What Marx calls the 'bond' of debt defines (subjectively, morally) the creditor and particularly the debtor, whose 'creditworthiness' comes to exhaust his or her identity (Marx 1975b: 263). The creditor, Marx says, is 'recognised' solely in terms of his ability to repay:

> On the man without credit is pronounced not only the simple judgment that he is poor, but in addition a pejorative moral judgment that he possesses no trust, no recognition [*Anerkennung*], and therefore is a social pariah, a bad man, and in addition to his privation, the poor man undergoes this humiliation and the humiliating necessity of having to ask the rich man for credit. (1975b: 264, translation modified)

To seek or offer credit, Marx notes, involves not mutual recognition but 'mutual dissimulation, hypocrisy and sanctimoniousness'. The 'mutual complementing' of an individual's freedom that Hegelian recognition involved has here become 'mutual plundering'. The relation between creditor and debtor has become one of 'mutual servitude' (*wechselseitige Knechtschaft*) to money. And just as the relation of Lord and Bondsman proved a house of cards, so this pattern of one-sided recognition is highly unstable: what if the debtor defaults on his or her debt?[12]

Marx's concern in this short text is not just with credit as a recognitive relation but with political economists' (here, specifically, James Mill's) attempt to justify the credit system and thus a key pillar of capitalism at large. In political economy (today one could say in 'neoliberal' thinking) we go through the looking glass into a world where human dependence appears as independence and humiliation appears as dignity. Political economy presents the capitalist market as the epitome of freedom and equality, as 'the highest recognition of man' (Marx 1975b: 264),[13] but it is really a world where individuality and morality have become 'counterfeited' and 'man himself transformed into money'. In the topsy-turvy world of political economy, contradictory recognition is able to masquerade as mutual recognition.

The form of Marx's critique of contradictory recognition is thus one appropriate to a social world that has become *inverted*, where everything is other than it seems. To this extent Marx does not simply turn Hegel (who is supposedly 'standing on his head') the 'right way up' (cf. Marx 1976: 103). Rather, he works with the same notion of an 'inverted world' (*verkehrte Welt*) of contradictory recognition that Hegel had already depicted.[14] That contradictory recognition creates an 'inverted world' can be seen in the numerous references in Marx's *Comments on James Mill* to the 'semblance' (*Schein*) of mutual trust and mutual recognition in the relation between creditor and debtor (see esp. Marx 1975b: 263). Following Hegel, Marx realises that where contradictory recognition prevails, morality necessarily appears in hypocritical guise. It is with reason that bourgeois morality hides its own essence. The credit system can only appear as mutual recognition in a world where everything is upside down.

When we turn to what later works such as *Grundrisse* (1857–8) and *Capital* (1867) have to say about recognition it becomes clear that there is no radical change in Marx's outlook – only a change of emphasis. *Grundrisse* and *Capital* share the aim of the *Comments on James Mill* in exposing varieties of contradictory recognition. Where the *Comments* focused on the recognitive inequality between (and alienated social roles of) creditor and debtor, *Grundrisse* exposes the contradictory recognition involved in exchange between 'proprietors'. In order for individuals to 'recognize one another reciprocally as proprietors' (Marx 1973: 243) they must first recognise each other as legally free. This means that 'no one seizes hold of another's property by force. Each divests himself of his property voluntarily' (1973: 243). As Marx immediately points out, such recognition of each other's freedom is mere semblance: a 'surface process, beneath which, however, in the depths, entirely different processes go on, in which this apparent individual equality and liberty disappear' (1973: 247). Once we look behind the appearance of proprietors or persons exchanging on free and equal terms, when we look instead at capital and labour (their 'prerequisite'), then this 'equality and freedom … prove to be inequality and unfreedom' (1973: 248–9).[15]

The reasons for this are laid bare in *Capital*. There the premise of commodity exchange is shown to be the systematic exploitation of the labourer by the capitalist. In *Capital* a relation of recognitive inequality thus takes centre stage. That work's most famous step leads beyond political economy – with its focus on the realm of exchange, 'where everything takes place on the surface' and where 'liberty, equality, property and Bentham' (Marx 1976: 280) are watchwords – into the 'hidden abode of production', where social relations take a very different form:

> When we leave this sphere of simple circulation or the exchange of commodities, which furnishes the 'free-trader vulgaris' with his views, his concepts and the standard by which he judges the society of capital and wage labour, a certain change takes place, or so it appears, in the physiognomy of our dramatis personae. He who was previously the money-owner now strides in front as capitalist; the possessor of labour-power follows as his labourer. The one smirks self-importantly and is intent on business; the other is timid and holds back, like one who has brought his own hide to market and now has nothing to expect but – a tanning (Marx 1976: 280).

As with the credit system, Marx reveals an apparent relation of equality to be shot through with contradiction; freedom for one is unfreedom for another. The realm of exchange, as with the credit system, presents the semblance of mutual recognition between 'persons', behind which lies a very different reality: the actuality of exploitation – that is, contradictory recognition. Capitalist exploitation is an instance of domination (*Herrschaft*) precisely in Hegel's sense.[16]

That the exploitation of worker by capitalist involves Hegelian 'one-sided and unequal recognition' should now be clear. But Marx is just as concerned with what we termed the second form of Hegelian contradictory recognition, namely that involved in social role-definitions. Capitalist and labourer, Marx's later works tell us, are 'personifications' – they are 'embodiments' or 'incarnations' or 'bearers' (he tries out various metaphors) of particular class relations and interests (Marx 1976: 92). The capitalist *just is* capital personified; only as such does he become 'respectable' (1976: 739). Likewise, the worker *just is* labour personified: lacking means of production, owning only the capacity to work, he or she has become wholly fungible: 'abstract labour'. Both capitalist and worker are thus 'machines' or 'cogs' in a 'social mechanism' (1976: 742,

739) – their roles following inevitably from the institution of the capitalist market. To be labour or capital personified is to be an abstraction, all
one's individual characteristics bracketed out and one's many-sidedness
reduced to a single generalisation. It is to wear a 'character mask'
(*Charaktermaske*) (Marx 1975a: 114).

In the light of what we have said about recognition, the radicality
of Marx's line of thinking becomes clear. One implication is that he
cannot simply be siding with the category of labour. A class is a pole
of a one-sided and unequal recognitive relation. It involves, moreover,
role-definitional recognition: to be a 'worker', to be a 'member' of the
'working class', is to be recognised in a contradictory way. Such a recognitive identity is something to be thrown off rather than celebrated. Hints
of this radical line of thought were already present in the *Comments on
James Mill* where Marx opposes 'life' to 'labour' (1975b: 278). They
reappear in Marx's later works where communism is construed not in
productivist terms but as a wholly new 'self-conscious activity'. As the
Grundrisse describes it: 'the development of the rich individuality which
is all-sided in its production as in its consumption, and whose labour
also therefore appears no longer as labour, but as the full development of
activity itself' (Marx 1973: 325).[17]

A reader unaware of the recognitive theme running through Marx's
work can easily be led astray and seek his view of social 'reality' (as
opposed to mere semblance) in the realm of production. On the
contrary, as *Capital* indicates, individuals in such a realm still wear masks
('*personae*' in its original Greek meaning) and 'personification' remains
a guise. Just as capitalism appears as voluntary exchange between con-
tracting 'persons', so 'worker' and 'capitalist' are not just classes but
abstractions which misrecognise (and thus alienate) the individuals concerned.[18] By implication – and the point is far-reaching – such
abstractions are incompatible with an emancipated world. Communism,
as Marx conceives it, is not a reversal in the hierarchy of capitalist and
worker but the detonation of these roles.[19]

On the rare but intriguing occasions when Marx pictures communist
existence, it is with reason that he portrays it as a condition free from
social roles and institutions, such as a division of labour (see e.g. Marx
and Engels 1976a: 47). Thus *Capital* looks beyond the world of commodities to 'an association of free men' (Marx 1976: 171) – one where 'the
full and free development of every individual forms the ruling principle'
(1976: 739) – while *The Communist Manifesto* envisages 'an associa-

tion, in which the free development of each is the condition for the free development of all' (Marx and Engels 1976b: 506). Such a condition, in which individuals are free through (and not in spite of) their relations with others, is, we suggest, none other than what Hegel understood by 'mutual recognition'.

At the start of this section we mentioned the need to discard a prejudice – that recognition is a bourgeois ideal. Have we justified our case for recognition being a revolutionary rather than an affirmative category? Does Marx really adopt mutual recognition as a guiding principle or does he simply expose its hypocritical use by political economy? Our response is that the two possibilities are not exclusive. When Marx criticises 'political economic recognition' – that between creditor and debtor or that between owners of commodities – he is implicitly opposing to it a form of recognition that would be more than merely formal, illusory and hypocritical. Marx is a critic not of recognition but of the semblance of mutual recognition where its opposite in fact prevails. His works – and here no break between the 'young' and the 'mature' Marx is to be found – expose the reversal of equality and freedom into their opposite, of mutual recognition into contradictory recognition. To criticise this inversion, as Marx does, is implicitly to uphold mutual recognition as a value. Only from such a standpoint – even if only an implicit standpoint, a 'view from nowhere', so to say – can one so criticise. Mutual recognition becomes for Marx (as it was for Hegel) the measure by which its own reversal into contradictory recognition can be judged. Marx's critique rests upon no other values than the mutual recognition which capitalism in its very essence undermines.[20]

Recognition and Revolution

Is a remodelling of Marx and Marxism along the lines that we have sketched plausible? The history of ideas certainly suggests that it is. When Hegelians in the decades after Hegel's death divided into Right Hegelian (or Old Hegelian) and Left Hegelian (or Young Hegelian) schools,[21] the *Phenomenology*'s notion of mutual recognition became for the latter an image of emancipation. Edgar Bauer, for example, looked towards a 'free community' which would be self-conscious and, at the same time, 'beyond the state' (cited in Stepelevich 1983: 273–4). Max Stirner's *The Ego and His Own* championed a 'new freedom' which would encompass particularity and involve more than 'freedom from' (cited in Stepelevich

1983: 339, 343). Our suggestion that Marx models his notion of an emancipated society on Hegel's notion of mutual recognition fits directly with the spirit of the young Marx's times. Marx began his revolutionary life as a Young Hegelian and, despite his exile to London, remained faithful to his earlier ideas. He is famous for having broken with Young Hegelianism. He should, instead, be famous for having consistently upheld Young Hegelian and Left Hegelian emancipatory ideas.

A more detailed survey of Marx's works would, we suggest, offer yet more evidence that he, like Hegel, is a theorist of recognition. Viewed in this light, the image of Marx changes dramatically, with equally dramatic political implications. When one construes Marx's claims about capitalist social relations as claims about recognition, their contradictory character is thrown more sharply into relief; when one views Marx's comments on communism as claims about mutual recognition, the depth of his vision of freedom-through-others becomes clearer. Just as Hegel's *Phenomenology* traces a contradictory history of domination, so Marx's work aims to 'overthrow all relations in which man is a debased, enslaved, forsaken, despicable being' (Marx and Engels 1975: 182).[22] Marxism aims, in other words, at the abolition of all relations of contradictory recognition.

Such an aim could not be more topical or urgent. A focus on recognition becomes ever more germane in a time when numerous left-wing revolutionary movements across the globe have realised the dangers of reproducing domination and institutional alienation within their own structures. What today's left-wing struggles show above all is a rejection of hierarchical forms of organisation in favour of prefiguration (Gunn and Wilding 2014a). That at which struggle aims – for Marx 'the full and free development of every individual' – is also to be nurtured in the struggle itself. What is at stake in choosing prefiguration over the democratic centralism of past movements is, we suggest, mutual recognition.

Once revolution is seen in terms of recognition, fresh perspectives appear. The attempt made in today's revolutionary movements to develop radically egalitarian, directly democratic ('horizontal') forms of organisation, through the fostering of solidarity and mutual aid and the foregrounding of self-education, are so many attempts to build a mutually recognitive 'home' for 'struggle outwards'.[23]

To a participant in a revolutionary struggle (just as for a theorist of open Marxism) questions about glimmers of a self-determining future are all important. What matters above all else, and before all else, is that mutual recognition – the life and interaction in and through which freedom may be sustained – exists in a tangible and directly experiential way. If mutual recognition is present, there is a future to revolution. If mutual recognition is absent, or sacrificed to a more-or-less-distant strategic goal, the revolution has lost its way. A revolution, if it is to count as such, must start as it intends to go on. Once revolution cools the white heat of mutually recognitive interaction, a future of hierarchical and role-definitional alienation points towards a grey and grim infinity. If, by contrast, a mutually recognitive 'home' is sustained, revolution – whatever violence may be hurled against it – retains its rationale. 'Struggle outwards' becomes possible because the goal of revolution remains in play.

References

Bloch, E. (2006) *Traces*, trans. A. Nassar, Stanford: Stanford University Press.
Cleaver, H. (2000) *Reading Capital Politically*, 2nd edition, Leeds and Edinburgh: Antithesis/AK Press.
Cleaver, H. (2017) *Rupturing the Dialectic*, Oakland: P. M. Press.
Dinerstein, A. (2015) *The Politics of Autonomy: The Art of Organising Hope*, Basingstoke: Palgrave Macmillan.
Federici, S. (2008) *Revolution at Point Zero*, Oakland: PM Press.
Gunn, R. (2015), *Lo que usted siempre quiso saber sobre Hegel y no se atrevió a preguntar*, Buenos Aires: Herramienta.
Gunn, R. (2017) 'On Open Marxism', paper presented at the Conference '25 Years of Open Marxism', Benemérita Universidad Autónoma de Puebla, 16 October.
Gunn, R. and Wilding, A. (2012) 'Holloway, La Boétie, Hegel', *Journal of Classical Sociology* 12(2).
Gunn, R. and Wilding, A. (2013) 'Revolutionary or Less-than-Revolutionary Recognition', www.academia.edu/4098673/Revolutionary_or_Less-than-Revolutionary_Recognition.
Gunn, R. and Wilding, A. (2014a) 'Recognition Contradicted', *South Atlantic Quarterly* 113 (Spring).
Gunn, R. and Wilding, A. (2014b) 'Marx and Recognition', at www.richard-gunn.com/marx-and-marxism.
Hardt, M. and Negri, A. (2017) *Assembly*, Oxford: Oxford University Press.
Hegel, G. W. F. (1977) *Phenomenology of Spirit*, trans. A. V. Miller, Oxford: Clarendon Press.
Holloway, J. (2010) *Crack Capitalism*, London: Pluto Press.
Honneth, A. (2014) *Freedom's Right*, Cambridge: Polity Press.
Hook, S. (1962) *From Hegel to Marx*, Ann Arbor: University of Michigan Press.
McLellan, D. (1980) *The Young Hegelians and Karl Marx*, London: Macmillan.

Marom, Y. and Klein, N. (2012) 'Why Now? What Next? A Conversation about Occupy Wall Street', *The Nation* (9 January), www.thenation.com/article/ why-now-whats-next-naomi-klein-and-yotam-marom-conversation-about-occupy-wall-street.

Marx, K. (1973) *Grundrisse*, Harmondsworth: Penguin.

Marx, K. (1975a) *Kapital*, Vol. I, in K. Marx and F. Engels, *Werke*, Vol. 23, Berlin: Dietz Verlag.

Marx, K. (1975b) 'Excerpts from James Mill's *Elements of Political Economy*', in *Early Writings*, Harmondsworth: Penguin.

Marx, K. (1976) *Capital*, Vol. 1, trans. B. Fowkes, Harmondsworth: Penguin.

Marx, K. (1971) *A Contribution to the Critique of Political Economy*, London: Lawrence and Wishart.

Marx, K. and Engels, F. (1975) *Collected Works*, Vol. 3, London: Lawrence and Wishart.

Marx, K. and Engels, F. (1976a) *Collected Works*, Vol. 5, London: Lawrence and Wishart.

Marx, K. and Engels, F. (1976b) *Collected Works*, Vol. 6, London: Lawrence and Wishart.

Reichelt, H. (2005) 'Social Reality as Appearance: Some Notes on Marx's Conception of Reality', in W. Bonefeld and K. Psychopedis (eds), *Human Dignity: Social Autonomy and the Critique of Capitalism*, Farnham: Ashgate.

Renault, E. (2012) 'The Early Marx and Hegel: The Young-Hegelian Mediation', https://marxandphilosophy.org.uk/wp-content/uploads/2018/01/renault 2012.doc.

Smith, N. (ed.) (1984) *A Collection of Ranter Writings from the Seventeenth Century*, London: Junction Books.

Stepelevich, L. S. (ed.) (1983) *The Young Hegelians: An Anthology*, Cambridge: Cambridge University Press.

Toews, J. E. (1980) *Hegelianism*, Cambridge: Cambridge University Press.

Wilding, A. (2013) 'The Problem with Normative Reconstruction', www. academia.edu/5115504/The_Problem_With_Normative_Reconstruction.

Wilding, A., Gunn, R., Smith, R. C., Fuchs, C. and Ott, M. (2015) 'Occupy and Prefiguration: A Roundtable Discussion', www.richard-gunn.com/politics.

Winstanley, G. (1973) *The Law of Freedom and Other Writings*, ed. C. Hill, Harmondsworth: Penguin.

Notes

1. A general characterisation of open Marxism is attempted in Gunn 2017.
2. For an English-language reader, Stepelevich 1983 is a useful source. McLellan 1980 is a further standard text.
3. On 'prefiguration', or seeking to anticipate the social relations that one wishes to realise, see Wilding et al. 2015, and Dinerstein 2015.

4. See, for example, Winstanley 1973. For a further useful collection of seventeenth-century writings, see Smith 1984. Winstanley's Diggers and Abiezer Coppe's Ranters wrote and acted in 'prefigurative' terms.

5. See Marx 1971 and particularly Maurice Dobb's editorial comment on p. 16.

6. See, for example, Hegel 1977: 119, and Gunn and Wilding 2013. A book-length statement of our views, *Revolutionary Recognition*, is forthcoming.

7. For a discussion of 'science' as a unity of theory and practice, see Gunn 2015: Ch. 5.

8. On 'universal work', see Hegel 1977: 357.

9. As is Axel Honneth in his *Freedom's Right* (2014, originally published 2011). For a critique see Wilding 2013.

10. In his recent *Rupturing the Dialectic*, Harry Cleaver draws attention to this difference or distinction (see Cleaver 2017: 110, n. 5). We are grateful to Cleaver for his perceptive reading.

11. That thorough discussion is to be found in Gunn and Wilding 2014b.

12. On the face of it, both Hegel and Marx echo La Boétie's idea of a domination that rests solely on – and is as fragile as – the consent of the subjugated. Nevertheless, important differences exist between La Boétie, Hegel and Marx on the issue of domination. See Gunn and Wilding 2012.

13. In the *Economic and Philosophical Manuscripts*, written in the same year, Marx writes that even when capitalist economies are booming and wages rising, the worker 'declines[s] to a mere machine, a bondsman (*Knecht*) of capital' (Marx and Engels 1975: 238, translation modified).

14. For Hegel on the 'inverted world', see 1977: 97–8.

15. What in the early work appears as moral inversion appears in the late work as a '*Lichtbild*'. Marx's metaphor comes from early photography: just as a photographic slide inverts reality, so capitalism presents a world through the looking glass (Marx 1973: 249). On Marx (like Hegel) as theorist of the '*verkehrte Welt*', see Reichelt 2005.

16. Capital's 'domination' (*Herrschaft*) over labour is a common motif in *Das Kapital* (see Marx 1975a: 386, 390, 526, 645, 648, 765), and though on occasion Marx contrasts it with 'immediate relations of domination and servitude (*unmittelbaren Herrschafts- und Knechtschaftsverhältnissen*)' (1975a: 93, 354) it is clear he means by this that capitalist domination, in contrast to other modes of production, is highly *mediated* – it is exerted not so much by a particular Lord (as in feudalism or slavery) as by the Lordship of capital as such.

17. Marx's critique of labour is taken up in Holloway 2010: 87–99, and Cleaver 2000: 127–31.

18. Marx notes drily that he by no means depicts the capitalist 'in a rosy light'. But it seems to us he could have added the same about the worker, since both roles involve misrecognition. Of course one role is more 'comfortably' misrecognised, comfortably alienated, than the other. For further discussion of Marx on class see Gunn and Wilding 2014b.

19. Cf. Ernst Bloch: 'The proletariat is the only class which does not want to be one ... [Thus] every kind of *Proletkult* is false, and a bourgeois infection' (2006: 18).
20. A point we take to be consistent with the claim of the *Economic and Philosophical Manuscripts*, that 'we have proceeded from the premises of political economy. We have accepted its language and laws ... On the basis of political economy itself, in its own words, we have shown that the worker sinks to the level of a commodity and becomes indeed the most wretched of commodities' (Marx and Engels 1975: 270).
21. The lengthy literature on Hegelianism in the years after Hegel's death includes Hook 1962 and Toews 1980. Renault 2012 offers a fresh consideration.
22. Such relations are today no less ubiquitous than in Marx's time. As Silvia Federici notes, 'Along with impoverishment, unemployment, overwork, homelessness, and debt has gone the increasing criminalisation of the working class, through a mass incarceration policy recalling the seventeenth-century Grand Confinement, and the formation of an *ex-lege* proletariat made of undocumented immigrant workers, students defaulting loans, producers or sellers of illicit goods, sex workers. It is a multitude of proletarians, existing and labouring in the shadow, reminding us that the production of populations without rights – slaves, indentured servants, peons, convicts, sans papiers – remains a structural necessity of capitalist accumulation' (Federici 2008: 105).
23. The term comes from Marom 2012. A contrasting view is to be found in Hardt and Negri's *Assembly* (2017) which, despite its many strengths, shows a reluctance to jettison the institutions which – we have argued – inherently contradict recognition. The point, we contend, is to *sustain* mutual recognition without *institutionalising* it.

2

A Critical Theory of Hope:
Critical Affirmations Beyond Fear

Ana Cecilia Dinerstein

Expectation, hope, intention towards possibility that has still not become, this is not only a basic feature of human consciousness, but concretely corrected and grasped, a basic determination within objective reality as a whole. Since Marx, no research into truth and no realistic judgement is possible at all which will be able to avoid the subjective and objective hope-contents of the world without paying the penalty of triviality or reaching a dead-end. *Philosophy will have conscience of tomorrow, commitment to the future, knowledge of hope, or it will have no more knowledge* (Ernst Bloch 1986: 7, italics in the original).

Does critical theory truly belong with radical praxis today?[1] Bonefeld (2016) rightly suggests that 'we must bring critical theory back in at a time of misery'. In this chapter, I argue that this theory should be Ernst Bloch's critical philosophy *of hope*, rather than Theodor W. Adorno's negative dialectics. Critique, Postone reminds us, 'should be contextualized, that is it should see itself as historically situated ... to be able to explain the possibility of its own existence' (Postone 2007: 109, my translation). This means that 'it is necessary to reconstruct a critique adequate to the form of capitalism today' (2007: 111, my translation). We must rethink critical theory from within the contemporary historical context. My exploration into a critical theory of hope is based on the urgent need to grasp the utopian content of present (class) struggles around social reproduction, at a time of crisis and destruction. While Adorno's critical theory is important insofar as it prevents dialectical closure from taking place, it cannot inform the prefigurative struggles that are taking place at the grassroots in the context of today's capitalist crisis. I establish a connection between the social struggles around issues of social reproduction and Ernst Bloch's critical philosophy of hope, and name present struggles as 'critical affirmations', to distinguish them from positive praxis. I suggest that both critical affirmations and Bloch's critical theory can articulate the utopian dimension of radical praxis, without compromising negativity, beyond fear.

Crisis, Social Reproduction and Life Struggles

The financial crisis of 2008 exposed once again the fact that capitalism is crisis-ridden (Clarke 1994: 280), but it also revealed the crisis of the social reproduction of life mediated by money-capital. While 'capitalist development has always been *unsustainable* because of its *human impact*' (Dalla Costa 1995: 11, italics in the original), the present crisis, with its 'austerity' 'solutions', accompanied by authoritarian strategies of domination, is penetrating every corner of the social domain to the point that the fulfilment of basic needs such as water, food, shelter, that sustain the reproduction of life, has been compromised. Understood in this broad way the crisis of social reproduction has displaced class struggles onto the social realm (Dinerstein and Pitts 2018). As Zechner and Hansen (2015) suggest, this is 'a crisis and widespread vulnerability ... that has opened an incredible number of struggles around social, economic resources and survival, which have put the struggle for life at their center: [e]veryday life, bodily survival, and collective life: the problem of human needs touches most in the crisis'.

The term 'survival strategies', frequently deployed to describe the social struggles of 'the poor', designates the hardship suffered by individuals, families and entire communities and their struggle to access 'crude and material things without which no refined and spiritual things could exist' (Benjamin 1999: 246)' (Bonefeld 2016: 241). In fact, these are class/labour struggles. Social reproduction feminists offer a complex understanding of class based on Marx to argue for a broader understanding of the working class beyond a definition based on having a job (Bhattacharya 2017). If one considers production and social reproduction as a totality, as Marx did, it becomes apparent that the struggles around social reproduction address the 'conditions of possibility of labor-power' and the 'manner in which labor power is biologically, socially and generationally reproduced' (Ferguson and McNally 2015), without which capitalist work would not exist. Thus, social reproduction struggles –

such as struggles around food, land, care, education, water, housing – are 'instances of class struggle' (Dinerstein and Pitts 2018).

The general crisis of social reproduction provides the context for a renewal of utopia today (Dinerstein 2017a). Struggles in this context are dedicated to creating non-capitalist forms of food production and consumption, cooperative housing, water systems, land and rural reform, health and care, radical pedagogies, together with the artistic, ethical, aesthetical cultural transformation of social relations, at the grassroots of the world. They are creating surplus possibilities, embodied critiques, radical knowledges and alternative organisations. Yet, this utopian dimension of present mobilisations is not reflected in critical theory writings and discussions, with exceptions. I deal with this silence about the utopian element of present struggles since it holds the clue to both an understanding of class struggle and the renewal of critical theory.

Positive Autonomism or Critical Affirmations?

The process of communising, inventing, exploring, creating, contradicting, which I have termed elsewhere 'the art organising hope' (Dinerstein 2015) is affirmative in the sense that it is shielding life – albeit in a non-religious and non-transcendental manner – by attempting to create other possible ways of living in common. The problem for open Marxism and critical theory is how to theorise this affirmative praxis as a theory of struggle (see the Introduction to this volume). If the misery of the world today has fostered an *affirmative praxis* against barbarism that is opening a 'world with a front' (Bloch 1986), the question is can critical theory understand it? In the edited collection that revitalised Adorno as the theorist of resistance today (Holloway, Matamoros and Tischler 2009), Holloway establishes a clear-cut distinction between positive and negative autonomism. He rejects the former and embraces the latter: while positive autonomism is classificatory and 'flirts with progressive governments', negative autonomism 'pushes against and beyond all identities, part of the budding and flowering of useful creative-doing. The distinction matters politically' (Holloway 2009b: 99).

In this chapter I use the term 'critical affirmations' to name the struggles around social reproduction because they are *affirming life as a form of negation*, with, against and beyond, capital (Dinerstein 2017b). I wish to establish a clear distinction between positive autonomism and critical affirmations in order to recognise the radical potential of the latter for radical change. The first difference is that, while positive autonomism accepts reality as it is, and accommodates to the political process, critical affirmations negate that reality and affirm a new reality without compromising negation. The second difference, connected to the first, is that positive autonomism eliminates the contradiction that exists between the compulsion to reproduce life through money and the need to abolish money to live – while critical affirmations encounter and navigate this contradiction. The third difference between positive praxis and critical affirmations is that only in the latter we find a real commitment to *possibility* and an anticipation of the Novum that awaits in the reality of the *not yet* (Bloch 1986 [1959]).

My point is that, generally speaking, critical theory finds it difficult to engage with the affirmative dimension of struggles, and this is symptomatic of a theory characterised by a *fear of the positivisation* of resistance, i.e. of the state's triumph over revolt. In the case of Adorno, as Coole suggests, despite his insistence that 'constellations' were not supposed to be only 'thought experiments, but also incite practical negations ... Adorno does not elaborate on this sense of praxis' (Coole 2000: 179). He thought that there is 'a need for a "practice that fights barbarism" and yet ... there can be no such practice' (Bonefeld 2016: 239–40). For Adorno, capitalism is an objective totality which is constantly reproduced by subjects. The existence of this totality is a 'necessity', because 'totality is inherently connected with the phenomenon of fetishism, of reification', in a system of commodity production (Grollios 2017: 132). A reified totality cannot be fought directly by means of political or social activism. Today, Bonefeld argues, 'Barbarism cannot be fought in a direct and immediate manner: what really does it mean to struggle against money, resist the movement of coins, combat the law of economic value, oppose capitalist profit, and fight poverty in a system of social reproduction that contains the pauper in its conception of wealth?' (Bonefeld 2016: 239–40).

This is a paralysing 'theoretical' position leading to a political stalemate underpinned by 'exalted despair' (Bloch 2009). On the one hand, insofar as capitalism is a totality, the possibility of transforming the world only exists 'as a complete, all-encompassing transformation of the status quo' (Boldyrev 2015: 172). On the other hand, to do so would mean to be 'part of a process of perversion and fetishisation of the idea of revolutionary change' (Tischler 2009: 109). While totalising revolutionary change is unfeasible, the patchy transformation of the world would defeat hope altogether. Surely this leads to a condition that Adorno termed a 'blocked state': 'a condition as much intellectual as social in which every attempt to change society radically seems closed off' (Wilding 2009: 27). With the publication of *Change the World Without Taking Power* (2002) and *Crack Capitalism* (2010), Holloway unblocked critical theory. His notion of the 'crack' produced a synergy between negativity and hope (Dinerstein 2012). The 'crack' is an inspirational term that designates negative praxis, struggle, openness and movement and already belongs to the social activist's vocabulary of resistance. The cracks: 'clash with the logic of the state, the homogenisation of time, the fetishism of commodities and money', which, 'at the same time ... signal the assertion of another type of (anti-capitalist) human activity: *doing*' (Dinerstein 2012: 522). But, as I have argued elsewhere, I believe it was Holloway's longstanding engagement with Bloch's philosophy that enabled him to conceptualise the utopian and imaginative aspects of social struggles as 'cracks': 'Cracks are "fissures" that offer "[a] thousand answers to the question of revolution"' (Holloway 2002: 4)' (Dinerstein 2018: 545). In the conceptualisation of the cracks and interstitial revolution, paraphrasing Bloch, there is not fear, but hope.

Hope: Theorising Possibility, Opening Fronts

Ernst Bloch was not fearful of theorising *possibility*. His critical philosophy is all about possibility. Daly suggests that in Bloch's critical philosophy 'humanity is conceived as ... a challenge to become, not as a given, and this means that no actual assumption concerning the content of being can be made' (Daly 2013: 172). The 'discovery' of the content of possibility is not passive but active (Bloch 1971: 21). We are compelled to move outwards and forwards by our own needs and lacks in search for their fulfilment. Far from the means of salvation or religion, Bloch speaks about hope as an explosion of human force that:

> presents itself as the continual Not-Yet of true human possession. It is an aspect of the quest for meaning, and, far from drugging the hunger for meaning (and with it the non-meaning of death) with any opium of the people in the form of dreamed up compensation in another world, it fills it with the food of restless labor, working away, unswerving and incorrupt, to gain a true awareness and genuine satisfaction of man's Utopian needs. (Bloch 2009: 248)

To Bloch, then, hope is key for the revolutionary transformation of the world. The latter could not occur without hope (Boldyrev 2015). Bloch's idea of a revolutionary transformation is neither teleological nor eschatological: it is an uncertain concrete praxis, without transcendence. The critical theory of hope rejects what Bloch termed 'a world without Front': 'Marx's work', he argues, 'marks the turning-point in the process of concrete venturing beyond becoming conscious. But around this point deeply ingrained habits of thinking cling to a world without Front … The desiderium, the only honest attribute of all men, is unexplored' (Bloch 1986: 5). The world without Front is a 'political ontology' or 'mode of being' where, according to Amsler, 'there is no space of or location from which to enunciate or engage in responses to "badly existing" realities in order to alter them because these realities do not include "unfinished material" or "open dimensions" in people or things' (Bloch cited by Amsler 2016: 25).

Against a 'world without front', Bloch offers the 'ontology of Not-Yet-Being', which opens onto a world 'with Front'. The Front is not, of course, a 'physical location', but *the site of the not-yet* (Amsler 2016: 25). The Front is where 'the Unbecome is located and seeks to articulate itself' (Bloch 1986: 199). The struggles around social reproduction are altering 'badly existing realities' and opening up possibility at the *front* of praxis. But we must learn and educate hope (*docta spes*), in order to be able to throw ourselves 'actively into what is becoming to which [we] belong' (Bloch 1986: 3).

The Utopian Character of Material Reality: Discarding Subjectivism

The anticipatory consciousness of the not yet is not ideological or idealist, but it is connected to the *material* dimension of reality that inhabits the present one. Hope is *not* merely a projection of reason, a 'mental creation' of human thought, *but an expression of what is really possible* (Bronner 1997: 177, emphasis added). The claim that changing the world *is always* possible is based on the recognition of the material content of the world and it informs the ontology and epistemology of Bloch's philosophy: his speculative materialism (Moir 2018b).

Boldyrev highlights that 'Bloch was hostile towards "subjectivist" theories, he takes hope to be the very affect that links subjective aspirations with objective tendencies, directing a human being not just to his future psychological state but to a future world as well' (Boldyrev 2015:

33). The subjective in Bloch's philosophy is not subjective as in 'the will of subject', but in the sense of the *lack* that resides in the matter of the world; that is, utopia is not subjective but resides in matter itself, Bloch argued, 'and human beings, as matter become-conscious, are capable of realising it' (Moir 2018b: 2). Critical theorists and John Holloway have paid little attention to this significant aspect of Bloch's philosophy, which I am exploring now to contest generalised allegations of 'subjectivism' in relation to open Marxism (see García Vela and Schäbel, in this volume).

For both Bloch and Adorno 'utopian thinking is implied in all critical thought'; both agree that 'utopia's key function is its capacity for critique' (Moir 2018a: x). But Adorno's criticism of Bloch's alleged utopianism (which disagreed with Adorno's negative dialectics) was unjustified: Bloch's concept of utopia is not *utopianist*. It is indissolubly connected with a historical materialist conception of history and a material under-standing of the world (Moir 2018b). Interestingly, it is not only that utopia is material but that 'material reality is utopian in the sense of being literally not (yet) "there" in a finished form' (Moir 2018a: 201). The pos-sibility of utopia lies in the material reality of the world. Matter, in Bloch's 'speculative materialism' (Moir 2018b), means being-in-possibility. This is far removed from subjectivist and voluntarist approaches to utopia and radical change. Bloch's materialism is utterly corporeal and connected to the human emotions (Grollios 2017: 221), so it stands also against Habermas' unfounded charge of Bloch being a 'romantic philosopher' (Grollios 2017: 222; Moir 2018a, 2018b).

Concrete Utopia and a Critical Theory of Hope

Ruth Levitas highlights Bloch's significant distinction between concrete and abstract utopia (Levitas 1997). Bloch criticised utopian thought that was not anticipatory (Levitas 2008: 43). Concrete utopia is a process at work that involves 'no transcendence' (Bloch 1971: 41); it is concrete precisely because it is a non-predetermined praxis. It is the product of the contingent transformative activity of human labour (Bloch 2009: xix). Bloch does not transport utopia into the future, because when this happens, he argues, 'not only I am not there, but utopia itself is also not with itself' (Bloch in Adorno, Bloch and Krüger 1975: 3). Utopia is not a 'thought' as existing in the future, but is a 'praxis-oriented category' (Levitas 1997: 70). The *not yet* is not understood as 'something expected according to its "disposition" in reduced form, as if encapsulated' – which would be a 'backward interpretation of Not-Yet [that] would suppress or fail to understand precisely the dialectical leap into the New' (Bloch 1986: 1373) – but in connection to the *Novum*. 'It is through the *Novum* that we orient ourselves and reshape the inconstruable question about the nature of human existence in concrete ways so that we can see more clearly the direction of utopia' (Zipes 1988: xxxvii).

Social struggles and autonomous organising are re-exploring fundamental practical questions: What are the possibilities of articulating other forms of social reproduction of life beyond the world of money-value-capital? How can we challenge the power of a self-expansive abstraction? How do we deal with the paradox and navigate the contradictions that exist between the fact that the reproduction of human life is mediated by money-capital (while working for a wage and earning money is becoming increasingly difficult, if not impossible), and the need to destroy a system where social reproduction is mediated by the most abstract power of capitalist property: money? The search for answers to these questions is the starting point for the reinvention of utopia. This is an eminently concrete starting point, from which to search for *alternative* forms of social reproduction, against and beyond money-capital. This utopian praxis contains an *experiential critique* of patriarchal and colonial capitalist society, a critique which is rooted in everyday life, in the body, in social relations and in communal practices. Critical affirmations are prefigurative, for they challenge the demarcations of reality and engage with the reality of the not yet (Bloch 1986: 146).

To search for forms of life does not entail a 'positive' praxis as opposed to negative praxis. Critical affirmations are antagonistic and contradictory forms of negativity that by exploring and affirming alternatives open up 'fronts of political possibility' (Amsler 2016). When we say *No* (see Holloway 2015), we venture beyond to realise an undefined *lack* (which Bloch calls 'the not'), e.g. dignity. The lack of dignity is not really *a lack*. Since there cannot be nothing, the lack of dignity, its absence, is not *just* an absence, but it is material that is *unrealised*. For a critical theory of hope, the possibility of negation depends on the ability to understand reality as being full of *unrealised materiality* that is already on its way when negation takes place, and therefore constitutes the material of concrete utopia. We do not really search for what we lack: we search to realise what is experienced as a 'lack', but the possibility of its realisation is already latent in the present material of reality. Dignity is already possible. We must realise it. As Bloch claims: 'in all events, Utopia is to be found essentially in the determinate negation of that which merely is, and in as much as it concretely discloses what is as false, it always points at the same time to that which should be' (Bloch cited by Neupert-Doppler 2018: 726).

Should the critical theorist be concerned with the risk of positivisation that all social struggles are exposed to? No, because such concern is not only unjustified but also leads to fear, frustration and to the 'blocked state'. The problem is practical and political and cannot be theorised a priori. The risk that concrete utopias can be assimilated into the logics of capital is real. What is important to acknowledge is that class struggle and utopia praxis are *mediated*: the law, money, the state, the trade unions, ideology, are *forms* of social relations through which capitalist social relations obtain (Dinerstein 2015). These mediations are 'form processes' (Holloway 2010: 168). They are then criss-crossed by class struggle, and therefore prone to crisis. Crises produce moments of 'de-mediation' (Bonefeld 1987), for instance a financial crisis or a crisis of the state, which are instances of de-fetishisation when capitalist mediations cannot hide their true fetishising character. In those moments, the space for autonomous organising opens wide because the possibility of appropriation of resistance seems difficult (Dinerstein 2015: 70). De-mediation reveals the existing struggle over the *forms of* mediations.

Beyond Fear: Translation as Struggle

The question in my view is not 'how we can avoid mediations?', e.g. the state, but how do we theorise 'translation'? That is, how are the capitalist mediations oppressing, repressing, integrating, legalising, prohibiting, ignoring, our radical struggles by translating them into positive rebellions? Is it possible to articulate non-capitalistic forms of mediation? These questions are politically relevant because, after a crisis, when the capitalist mediations are restored and their true fetishising and oppressive nature is, once again, obscured, we can empirically observe the makeover of those mediations and of our struggles (if they have not been obliterated altogether) in the form of, say, a new piece of legislation, a new allocated budget, a new policy programme, a new governmental department, a new steering committee. We will feel defeated. Or not.

Bloch argued that hope must be disappointable: 'hope is not confidence. If it could not be disappointable, it would not be hope' (Bloch

1988: 16–17). He expressed his political experience marked by the defeat of the German revolution in 1918 and Nazism. But critical affirmations produce excess. The clue resides in understanding *translation* 'as struggle' (Vázquez 2011: 41) in a way that the question of *untranslatability* can become politically relevant: what are the signs, ideas, horizons, practices, dreams, elements, that have remained 'untranslatable, outside the scope of translation? What is excluded from its movement of incorporation?' (Vázquez 2011: 36). The critical theory of hope emphasises the signifi- cance of Marx's method for discovering the potential of class struggles to produce radical change, that is to create an excess that is untranslat- able into the grammar of capital (Dinerstein 2015). Bloch's philosophy enables us to explore the politics of social reproduction *in the key of hope*.

Excess, I suggest, is not defined by the 'non-identity ... between the objective force of accumulation and the subjective mis-fitting of ourselves' (Holloway, in this volume): it is defined by what Bloch calls a *utopian surplus*, i.e. 'an expression of the still unfulfilled desire for utopia and the anticipatory consciousness of its possibility' (Moir 2018a: 207). But with a caveat. In the utopian surplus of non-western and indige- nous resistance, such as the Chiapas communities governed by the Zapatistas (see Tischler, in this volume), the utopian surplus is inevita- bly mediated by traditions, customs and habits that have been oppressed since time immemorial by colonial powers and capitalist democracies (Dinerstein 2015). Why does this matter? Because here the defence of the past constitutes *a form of resistance* (Aubry 2003), mobilised with political imagination in a new fashion (Khasnabish 2008: 51). While the Zapatistas exercise self-government by engaging with ancestral Mayan traditions, habits and customs, they also claim 'we are united by the imagination, by creativity, by tomorrow' (Subcomandante Insurgent Marcos in Ponce de León 2001: 167).

Critical theory of hope focuses on the utopian surplus brought about by critical affirmations and their concrete utopias. As we can see, estab- lishing a clear difference between positivisation and critical affirmation is of crucial political importance for a critical theory of hope, which aims to belong with today's class struggles by recognising the affirma- tive potential of concrete utopia. Without this differentiation, negativity becomes an abstract critique, detached from the real movement of class struggle, historically unspecific. There is also a risk that such critique will oppress the experiential critique offered by subaltern struggles, imposing a Eurocentric and male-dominated philosophy on them.

If critical theorists decide to engage with the question of hope and utopia, as some do, they should leave the fear positivisation behind. In the 'dreamlessness in regard to the future ... there is fear, not hope; and instead of an understanding of the future as the greater dimension of the present ... there is only an anti-climax' (Bloch 1971: 32–3). In the end, we are all 'located in our own blind spot' (Bloch 2000: 200). We do not know. The 'inconstruable' question might never be posed. But, following Gunn, 'the relation of the present to its future is what contradiction brings to light. *I am and am not myself* (Gunn 1994: 55). We *are still not*.

References

Adorno, T. W. (1995) *Negative Dialectics*, New York: Continuum.
Adorno, T. W., Bloch, E. and Krüger, H. (1975) 'Something's Missing. A Discussion Between Ernst Bloch and Theodor W. Adorno on the Contradictions of Utopian Longing', in Bloch, E. (ed.), *The Utopian Function of Art and Literature: Selected Essays*, Cambridge, MA: MIT Press, 1–17.
Amsler, S. (2016) 'Learning Hope: An Epistemology of Possibility for Advanced Capitalist Society', in A. C. Dinerstein (ed.), *Social Sciences for An-Other Politics: Women Theorising without Parachutes*, Basingstoke: Palgrave Macmillan, 19–32.
Aubry, A. (2003) 'Autonomy in the San Andrés Accords: Expression and Fulfilment of a New Federal Pact', in J. Rus, R. Hernandez Castillo and S. Mattiace (eds), *Mayan Lives, Mayan Utopias: The Indigenous Peoples of Chiapas and the Zapatista Rebellion*, Oxford: Rowman & Littlefield, 219–42.
Benjamin, W. (1999) 'Theses on the Philosophy of History', in *Illuminations: Essays and Selections*, London: Pimlico, 245–55.
Bhattacharya, T. (2017) 'How Not to Skip Class: Social Reproduction of Labor and the Global Working Class', in T. Bhattacharya (ed.), *Social Reproduction Theory*, London: Pluto Press, 68–93.
Bloch, E. (1971) *On Karl Marx*, New York: Herder and Herder.
Bloch, E. (1986 [1959]) *The Principle of Hope*, Cambridge, MA: MIT Press.
Bloch, E. (1988) *The Utopian Function of Art and Literature: Selected Essays*, trans. J. Zipes and F. Mecklenburg, Cambridge, MA: MIT Press.
Bloch, E. (1998) 'Can Hope Be Disappointed?', in *Literary Essays*, Stanford: Stanford University Press, 339–45.
Bloch, E. (2000 [1918]) *The Spirit of Utopia*, Stanford: Stanford University Press.
Bloch, E. (2009 [1972]) *Atheism in Christianity*, London: Verso.
Boldyrev, I. (2015) *Ernst Bloch and his Contemporaries: Locating Utopian Messianism Today*, London: Bloomsbury.
Bonefeld, W. (1987) 'Marxism and the Concept of Mediation', *Common Sense* 2: 67–72, https://commonsensejournal.org.uk/1987/07/01/issue-two.

Bonefeld, W. (2009) 'Emancipatory Praxis and Conceptuality in Adorno', in J. Holloway, P. F. Matamoros and S. Tischler (eds), *Negativity and Revolution: Adorno and Political Activism*, London: Pluto Press, 122–47.

Bonefeld, W. (2013) 'Antagonism and Negative Critique: An Interview', *ViewPoint Magazine*, www.viewpointmag.com/2013/09/15/antagonism-and-negative-critique-an-interview/September 15.

Bonefeld, W. (2016) 'Bringing Critical Theory Back in at a Time of Misery: Three Beginnings Without Conclusion', *Capital & Class* 40(2): 233–44.

Bronner, S. (1997) 'Utopian Projections: In Memory of Ernst Bloch', in J. O. Daniel and T. Moylan (eds), *Not Yet: Reconsidering Ernst Bloch*, London: Verso, 165–74.

Clarke, S. (1994) *Marx's Theory of Crisis*, Basingstoke: Macmillan.

Coole, D. (2000) *Negativity and Politics: Dionysus and Dialectics from Kant to Poststructuralism*, London: Routledge.

Dalla Costa, M. R. (1995) 'Capitalism and Reproduction', in W. Bonefeld, R. Gunn, J. Holloway and K. Psychopedis (eds), *Open Marxism 3*, London: Pluto Press, 7–15.

Daly, F. (2013) 'The Zero Point: Encountering the Dark Emptiness of Nothingness', in P. Thompson and S. Žižek (eds), *The Privatization of Hope: Ernst Bloch and the Future of Utopia*, Durham, NC: Duke University Press, 164–202.

Dinerstein, A. C. (2012) 'Interstitial Revolution: On the Explosive Fusion of Negativity and Hope', *Capital & Class* 36(3): 513–32.

Dinerstein, A. C. (2015) *Autonomy in Latin America: The Art of Organising Hope*, Basingstoke: Palgrave Macmillan.

Dinerstein, A. C. (2016) 'The Radical Subject and its Critical Theory. An Introduction', in A. C. Dinerstein (ed.), *Social Sciences for An-Other Politics: Women Theorising without Parachutes*, Basingstoke: Palgrave Macmillan, 1–18.

Dinerstein, A. C. (2017a) 'Concrete Utopia: Reproducing Life in, Against and Beyond the Open Veins of Capital', Public Seminar, New York: New School Social Research, www.publicseminar.org/2017/12/concrete-utopia.

Dinerstein, A. C. (2017b) Keynote: 'Afirmación como negatividad. La otra teoría crítica' (Affirmation as Negation: The Other Critical Theory), Symposium for the 25th Anniversary of Open Marxism, Institute for Humanities and Social Sciences, Benemérita Autonomous University of Puebla, Puebla, 16–19 October.

Dinerstein, A. C. (2018) 'John Holloway: The Theory of Interstitial Revolution', in B. Best, W. Bonefeld and C. O'Kane (eds), *The Sage Handbook of Frankfurt School Critical Theory*, London: Sage, 533–49.

Dinerstein, A. C. and Pitts, F. H. (2018) 'From Post-work to Post-capitalism? Discussing the Basic Income and Struggles for Alternative Forms of Social Reproduction', *Journal of Labor & Society* 21(4): 471–49.

Ferguson, S. and McNally, D. (2015) 'Social Reproduction Beyond Intersectionality: An Interview', *Viewpoint Magazine*, https://viewpointmag.com/2015/10/31/social-reproduction-beyond-intersectionality-an-interview-with-sue-ferguson-and-david-mcnally.

Grollios, V. (2017) *Negativity and Democracy: Marxism and the Critical Theory Tradition*, New York: Routledge.

Gunn, R. (1987) 'Marxism and Mediation', *Common Sense* 2: 57–66, https://commonsensejournal.org.uk/1987/07/01/issue-two.

Gunn, R. (1994) 'Marxism and Contradiction', *Common Sense* 15, https://commonsensejournal.org.uk/1994/04/01/issue-15.

Holloway, J. (2002) *Change the World Without Taking Power: The Meaning of Revolution Today*, London: Pluto Press.

Holloway, J. (2009a) 'Why Adorno?', in J. Holloway, F. Matamoros and S. Tischler (eds), *Negativity and Revolution: Adorno and Political Activism*, London: Pluto Press, 12–17.

Holloway, J. (2009b) 'Negative and Positive Autonomism. Or Why Adorno? Part 2', in J. Holloway, F. Matamoros and S. Tischler (eds), *Negativity and Revolution: Adorno and Political Activism*, London: Pluto Press, 95–100.

Holloway, J. (2010) *Crack Capitalism*, London: Pluto Press.

Holloway, J. (2015) 'No, No, No', *Roar Magazine*, Issue 0, https://roarmag.org/magazine/john-holloway-no-no-no.

Holloway, J., Matamoros, F. and Tischler, S. (2009) (eds) *Negativity and Revolution: Adorno and Political Activism*, London: Pluto Press.

Khasnabish, A. (2008) *Zapatismo Beyond Borders: New Imaginations of Political Possibilities*, Toronto: University of Toronto Press.

Levitas, R. (1997) 'Educated Hope: Ernst Bloch on Abstract and Concrete Utopia', in J. O. Daniel and T. Moylan (eds), *Not Yet: Reconsidering Ernst Bloch*, London: Verso.

Levitas, R. (2008) 'Pragmatism, Utopia and Anti-Utopia', *Critical Horizons* 9(1): 42–59.

Moir, C. (2018a) 'Ernst Bloch: The Principle of Hope', in B. Best, W. Bonefeld and C. O'Kane (eds), *The Sage Handbook of Frankfurt School Critical Theory*, London: Sage, 199–215.

Moir, C. (2018b) 'In Defence of Speculative Materialism', *Historical Materialism*, online article, 1–33, doi:10.1163/1569206X-00001609.

Neupert-Doppler, A. (2018) 'Critical Theory and Utopian Thought', in B. Best, W. Bonefeld and C. O'Kane (eds), *The Sage Handbook of Frankfurt School Critical Theory*, London: Sage, 714–33.

Ponce de León, J. (ed.) (2001) *Our Word Is Our Weapon: Selected Writings from Subcomandante Marcos*, New York: Seven Stories Press.

Postone, M. (2007) *Marx Reloaded. Repensar la Teoría Crítica del Capitalismo*, ed. A. Riesco Sánz and J. García López, Madrid: Bifurcaciones, Traficantes de Sueños.

Tischler, S. (2009) 'Adorno: The Conceptual Prison of the Subject, Political Fetishism and Class Struggle', in J. Holloway, F. Matamoros and S. Tischler (eds), *Negativity and Revolution: Adorno and Political Activism*, London: Pluto Press, 103–21.

Vázquez, R. (2011) 'Translation as Erasure: Thoughts on Modernity's Epistemic Violence', *Journal of Historical Sociology* 24: 27–44.

Wilding, A. (2009) 'Pied Pipers and Polymaths: Adorno's Critique of Praxisism', in J. Holloway, F. Matamoros and S. Tischler (eds), *Negativity and Revolution: Adorno and Political Activism*, London: Pluto Press, 18–38.

Zechner, M. and Hansen, B. R. (2015) 'Building Power in a Crisis of Social Reproduction', *Roar Magazine*, https://roarmag.org/magazine/building-power-crisis-social-reproduction.

Zipes, J. (1988) 'Introduction: Toward a Realization of Anticipatory Illumination', in E. Bloch (ed.), *The Utopian Function of Art and Literature: Selected Essays*, trans. J. Zipes and F. Mecklenburg, London: MIT Press, xi–xliii.

Notes

1. I am grateful to Sarah Amsler, Werner Bonefeld, Edith González and Richard Gunn for their suggestions on earlier versions of this chapter. Many thanks also to the participants in the following events for their passion, enthusiasm and insightful comments on earlier drafts and related papers: the Symposium for the 25th Anniversary of Open Marxism, Institute for Humanities and Social Sciences, Benemérita Autonomous University of Puebla, Puebla, 16–19 October 2017; the Seminar 'Subjectivity and Critical Theory', Institute for Humanities and Social Sciences, Benemérita Autonomous University of Puebla, Puebla; the Conference 'Ernst Bloch and the Marxist Legacy', University of Warsaw, June 16–17, 2018; the Public Debate 'Critical Theory Today: Conversation with John Holloway', Standing Seminar for Critical Theory, University of Bath, 11 October 2018; the 2018 Summer School 'The Art of Organising Hope', organised by CESDER-PRODES A.C. and UCIRed in Zautla, 22–29 July; and the Alternative Summit, 'The Art of Organising Hope: New Narratives for Europe', Ghent, November 2018, with special mention to Dominique Willaert, Sara Vilardo and Matthias Velle (from the Victoria Deluxe Artist Organisation, Ghent).

3

Objectivity and Critical Theory: Debating Open Marxism

Alfonso García Vela

For John Holloway

> Thought need not be content with its own legality; without aban-
> doning it, we can think against our thought, and if it were possible to
> define dialectics, this would be a definition worth suggesting (Adorno
> 2007: 141).

Open Marxism opened up to Adorno's critical theory mainly to develop
anticapitalist thought and posit an anti-identitarian conception of emancipatory theory and practice. The pivot of this opening was – and still
is – Adorno's major work: *Negative Dialectics*. It must be emphasised
that Adorno's idea of negation has sparked debate amongst the representatives of open Marxism but, at the same time, has also allowed for
the overcoming of positive conceptions of dialectics, totality and emancipation that have characterised traditional Marxism. In this sense,
open Marxism has sought to place the non-identical, contradiction, at
the centre of its theoretical and practical perspective. However, as we
shall show in the first section of this chapter, there is still an underlying
identity in the theoretical and practical perspective of open Marxism,
one that can be considered fundamental: the identity between subject
and object. We believe such identity leads the representatives of open
Marxism into the trap of an arguably absolute subjectivism. This means
that the object is identified with the subject, implying an absolute primacy
of the subject and the understanding of Marx's critique as a *reductio ad
hominem*; the political consequence of this is voluntarism. We acknowledge the existence of different approaches amongst the representatives of
open Marxism – which we cannot analyse in the present chapter for lack
of space – but we do believe its overall theoretical framework is based on
the identity of subject and object.

Adorno's critical theory is grounded on the negation of such identity. Nevertheless, my goal is not to prove the existence of irreconcilable differences between Adorno's theorising and open Marxism; it is to take a new approach to the purpose of positing an anti-identitarian conception of theory and practice and to go deeper into negative thought. For this we must open up the critical theory of open Marxism and reveal its fundamental limitations; to this end, we shall also analyse elements of *Negative Dialectics*. Mario Schäbel (in this volume) also criticises open Marxism for giving in to absolute subjectivism. According to Schäbel, open Marxism is essentially a subjective idealism, for it dissolves the object within the subject dialectically. Even in its formulation of the unity-in-separation between subject and object, open Marxism performs a theoretical process that ultimately turns subject and object into one and the same, transforming their unity-in-separation into a unity-in-identity. On this I agree with Schäbel; however, unlike him, I will try to show that this subjectivism has been socially constituted. As we shall see, subjectivism is not an exclusive feature of open Marxism; it is part of a tendency in modern theorising that is linked to capitalist society.

It must be clarified that I do not intend to negate the subjective moment of emancipation and fall into the trap of objectivism. I am well aware of the fact that the transformation of the world requires 'the will to confront the possibility of humanity's total annihilation that capitalist society entails and not be simple spectators of the destruction'.[1] In this sense, I applaud open Marxism's general project as an attempt to reclaim the value of the subject, its dignity and rebelliousness, in a world that negates it even in thought. Nevertheless, beyond will power, the transformation of the world requires the self-reflection of critical thought. At this point, 'thinking against itself' is essential: this is a fundamental part of negative dialectics. This allows us to go beyond self-criticism and break with the ideal of an absolute principle, be it subject or object. Furthermore, in this chapter I will show that the principle of identity is present in Holloway's theoretical and political contribution. Rather than perceiving this as an essential weakness in Holloway's theorising or in that of open Marxism, we must keep in mind that thought is not separate from society, but emanates from it. In other words, thought is socially constituted. That is why, for Adorno, 'to think is to identify' (2007: 5). However, the task of critical theory is not to renounce thought, but to dissolve the identity that constitutes thought itself.

One of the main theses in Adorno's critical theory is that modern thinking is essentially characterised by the primacy of the subject; without this premise, one cannot understand what Adorno describes as his purpose in the Preface to *Negative Dialectics*. In the second part of this chapter we shall see that, for Adorno, the different variants of modern thought such as idealism, ontology and positivism are, ultimately, subjective thinking. Adorno tried to ground the primacy of the subject in modern thinking socially and historically; for him, it is the result of the reification of society in an objectivity that is alienated from men. In other words, there is a prevailing tendency in theorising to reduce objectivity more and more to the subject, a tendency that exists against the backdrop of reification. In the present essay I will argue that this tendency can also be found in critical thought. From this perspective, we can say that the fundamental characteristic of traditional Marxism is the primacy of the subject as the expression of identity.

In the third section of this chapter I will argue that Adorno's critique of modern thinking led to the elaboration of his theory of the 'primacy of the object' in *Negative Dialectics*. This has been the cause of heated debates; however, I believe the primacy of the object is not the negation of a subjective participation or an idea of objectivity that amounts to the disappearance of the subject. It is Adorno's attempt to break the spell of identity that contains the primacy of the subject; furthermore, it seeks to eliminate the hierarchy of the subject over the object and vice versa. It is the way in which Adorno tries to overcome the identity of subject and object, and the step that allows dialectics to become materialist. Finally, I will show that a tension exists within open Marxism or, perhaps, an aporia. On the one hand, it sets out to overcome the subject-object duality through identity, with the political intention of giving concrete human beings the power to self-emancipate. On the other hand, it wishes to place the non-identical at the centre of its theoretical and practical perspective in order to go beyond the principle of identity. It seems to me that this tension entails the possibility of overcoming the principle of identity that underlies open Marxism. Generally speaking, our outlook can be understood as an 'in-against-and-beyond open Marxism'.[2]

Subject, Emancipation and Identity

The critical theory of open Marxism is a very important effort to overcome the classic dichotomy between subject and object which, in terms of social categories, can be expressed as the relation between 'objectivity and struggle' or 'structure and action'. From the time of the state derivation debate, in the 1970s, Holloway criticised Joachim Hirsch for the dualist perspective that his state derivation implied. For Hirsch, capital's objective laws are on one side and class struggle on the other. More recently, Bonefeld (2004a, 2004b) criticised structuralism, Moishe Postone's critique of value and Antoni Negri's autonomism for this same dualist perspective. While taking into account the dissimilarities between the different interpretations of Marxism, Holloway and Bonefeld argue they all make the fundamental mistake of considering that capitalist society is divided between an objective framework of general social determinations (structure, laws) and the subjectivity that is inherent in this framework of objective domination. Given that it is objectivity that is ultimately prioritised in order to establish the conditions that are crucial for class struggle, this would be one of the main features of a traditional Marxist theory. Thus, traditional Marxism assumes objective domination as the starting point from which to think the transformation of the world, underestimating the force of the subject as an internal con-tradiction within capital. The political consequence of this is the need for a party or vanguard to liberate the subject from objective domina-tion and to lead class struggle; this political perspective was represented by Leninism and went into crisis in the twentieth century. Orthodox Marxism is a more radical expression of Marxist traditional theory for it considers itself a positive science that aims at discovering the objective laws of capitalist society. Open Marxism emphatically rejects any type of scientism, both in classical sociology and within Marxism, and claims that Marx's theorising is scientific in a different way: 'it criticises positive science, and at its core lies not society understood as an object that is neutrally and impartially (objectively) interpreted by science, but class struggle' (Bonnet, Holloway and Tischler 2005: 1).

According to Holloway and Bonefeld, the fundamental error of the different Marxist interpretations lies in the fact that they accept what is apparent as real and conceptualise it as something objective, that is, external to the subject. And they do so even if the argument claims that human practice constitutes the objective structure of society, for this argument ultimately leads to the autonomy of structure against human practice. Traditional Marxism considers that social relations in capital-ism have become almost completely autonomous from the subject and have constituted an objectivity that is alienated from human beings.

According to open Marxism, this autonomy is not the product of social objectivism or capitalism, but an inverted image projected by the fetish-ised forms of social relations. Thus, the objective is understood as the mode of existence of the subject, and society as an objectification of this very subject (Bonefeld 2009; Holloway 2005). Moreover, the representatives of open Marxism pursue the analysis of subjectivity from human practice and class struggle, for the latter are both moments of subjectivity. For Holloway, the objective laws of capitalism are nothing but the movement of class struggle; for Bonefeld, social structures are a product of the alienated existence of human practice. From this viewpoint, the subject is the epicentre of the theoretical perspective and the starting point for thinking of emancipation.

According to Holloway (1995, 2005), the world can only be understood in subjective terms. Therefore, the starting point for Holloway's theoretical and practical reflection in *Change the World Without Taking Power*, his major publication, is the 'scream', which means opposition, negativity, the struggle of the subject that rebels against domination and shouts 'basta-enough' or 'No'. This critical theory starts from the immediate, emotional and living subject, a subject that has the strength to bring out the possibilities of emancipation from within. The consciousness that rebels is born out of the 'scream' and not out of something conceptual as Lenin or Lukács claimed; Holloway's starting point is the irrational. This perspective differs significantly from the Marxist tradition that has been characterised by embracing reason – apparently capable of knowing and dominating everything – as the starting point of critique. Capitalist domination is of a rational nature; therefore, it can be conceptually expressed as laws and structures. This is the starting point for traditional Marxism, a beginning that assumes the domination of the subject. For Holloway, critical reflection must begin from the immediate subject that screams and rebels; it is a starting point that emphasises the crisis and the possibilities of breaking capitalism. On the contrary, to begin theoretically from domination – that is, to begin with reason – obscures the fragility of capitalism and leads to a theory of domination that incorporates the crisis and rupture produced by the subject as moments of the same social domination. In Holloway's open Marxism, the irrational is enormously relevant as the effort to understand that which is not identical to reason: the scream is the non-identical, it is the irrational moment that is not assimilated by capitalism nor subsumed by concepts such as structure, laws or objectivity.

Arguably, open Marxism is the effort to assert the value of the subject, of its dignity and rebelliousness in a world that negates it even in thought. The subject negates and weakens itself in conceptually placing objectivity before itself and its struggle. It is against this that open Marxism rebels, against the process of conceptual reification that establishes an objectivity or an autonomous structure from which the subject and class struggle are derived. Such a critical theory leads to what Marxism has traditionally ignored or relegated to second place: the capacity of humans to stop producing capitalism. Open Marxism acknowledges that there is still strength in the subject; it acknowledges the human capacity for self-emancipation and, therefore, tries to liberate class struggle from the party and the vanguards once and for all. However, from where we are standing the main problem with open Marxism is that it falls into a subjectivism we would call absolute, and the political consequence is voluntarism. Indeed, one of the objectives of Holloway's theoretical reflection is to show that 'there is no object, there is only a subject' (1995: 171). However, beyond theoretical analysis, it is a political intervention that seeks to give power to the subject, the power to emancipate itself and crack capitalism. It is a movement that starts from the non-identical, the scream of negation that helplessly confronts the objectivity of capitalism. For Holloway, nevertheless, Marxist theory shows that social objectivity is the product of the power of human practice which, in capitalism, is negated by the objectivity of the world. In other words, the object negates the subject but never ceases to be a subject. Therefore:

> Society is nothing but subjectivity and its objectification, it follows that subjectivity (practice) is the only possible starting point for the comprehension of society, that the understanding of society is a process of tracing the (objectifying) forms of our own subjectivity – a path which is totally closed by the notion of 'scientific objectivity'. The world can only be understood subjectively, critically, negatively, from below (Holloway 1995: 172).

Moreover, in *Change the World Without Taking Power*, Holloway points out:

> We are the only reality, the only creative force. There is nothing but us, nothing but our negativity. The essential claim of Marxism, that which distinguishes it from other varieties of radical theory, is its claim to

dissolve all externality. The core of its attack against 'them' is to show that 'they' depend on us because 'they' are continually created by us. We, the powerless, are all-powerful (2005: 176).

For Holloway, critical reflection breaks with the objectivist interpretations of society and discovers the subjectivity behind all objectivity; it is essentially a critique *ad hominem*. Open Marxism interprets Marx's critique as a *reductio ad hominem*,[3] a 'critique that attacks objectivity and shows that it is a projection of subjectivity' (Holloway and Löwy 2003: 20). It is an effort to substantiate once and for all the social world in the subject and, just like idealism, it turns truth into a subject.[4] However, unlike idealism, it presents the category of the subject expressed fundamentally by the materialist category of class struggle. In this sense, the truth is class struggle, a general principle prevailing in society as a whole. This idea was intended to open up society as a process but it ended up in closure, in that it became a general and absolute principle.

To show that the object is indeed the subject goes beyond overcoming the subject-object dichotomy; as we have said, it has a political purpose. For Holloway, 'the scream of the powerless victim, heard through the ears of Marxist theory, becomes the scream of the all-powerful subject' (1995: 171).[5] In other words, the goal is to transform the 'all-powerful subject' that has the will and the power to struggle and break all objective frontiers. Like Marx, Holloway seeks to transform powerlessness into power, but the theoretical deployment of this transformation falls victim to identity: the identity between subject and object. Only through identity can we reach an 'all-powerful subject' that can, in itself, transform the world on pure will. 'Stop making capitalism' is at the core of Holloway's theory of emancipation:

This is the pivot of our somersault, its centre of levity. The doing that we pitch against labour is the struggle to open each moment, to assert our own determination against all pre-determination, against all objective laws of development. We are presented with a pre-existing capitalism that dictates that we must act in certain ways, and to this we reply 'no, there is no pre-existing capitalism, there is only the capitalism that we make today, or do not make'. And we choose not to make it (2010: 254).

Although there is an undeniable will to change the world in Holloway's theorising, the dialectic movement that began with the non-identical concludes in identity. One could say that it is ultimately a movement that negates in order to assert (the subject). Dinerstein (2017) adopts a similar perspective in arguing that Marxism, as a theory of struggle, is a movement that negates all that exists so as to affirm life and the subaltern subjects. As a result of her critique of the principle of negativity, Dinerstein has acknowledged the dialectic movement that underlies open Marxism. Thus, the negative is the foundation that makes the affirmative possible and, as a result, the non-identical turns into its opposite.

Open Marxism certainly distances us from Marxist objectivism and scientism and shows us the subjective moment of emancipation. However, at the centre of this theory lies an identitarian interpretation of the subject-object relation that leads straight into absolute subjectivism; in Adorno's (2017) words, we escape Scylla and fall into Charybdis. We must take into consideration that open Marxism has tried to bring forward an anti-identitarian conception of critical thinking through Adorno's negative dialectics, giving it the possibility of breaking with the positive conceptions of dialectics, totality and human emancipation that have characterised traditional Marxism. In this sense, there is a tension within open Marxism. On the one hand, it wants to overcome the subject-object duality through an identity, with the political purpose of giving the power to specific human beings so that they can self-emancipate. On the other hand, it continues along the path opened by Adorno's non-identity in arguing that 'non-identity breaks identity and paves the way for the creation of something new. The movement of non-identity is the movement of creativity' (Holloway, Matamoros and Tischler 2009: 8). Furthermore, Bonefeld points out that:

> Adorno's negative dialectics has to be studied, especially in miserable times. Its courageous delivery of the concept of bourgeois society operates like the proverbial mole which, according to Marx, prepares for the revolution by tunneling through the defences. The mole is a philosophical mole. Once its work is done, the mole departs (2009: 144).

Our goal is to follow the path of non-identity and to rethink an open Marxism that will not conclude in postulating an identity. That was the original plan of Horkheimer and Adorno: to break with the identity of subject and object.[6] We are aware of the fact that, if this identity is broken, we shall have to ask ourselves once again about the potential of the subject to self-emancipate. However, we strongly believe that if open Marxism wants to contribute to changing the world it must reflect on itself: 'negative dialectics calls for the self-reflection of thinking, the tangible implication is that if thinking is to be true – if it is to be true today, in any case – it must also be a thinking against itself' (Adorno 2007: 365). 'Thinking against itself' does not amount to self-criticism. For Adorno, it is to give thinking the shape of something interrupted, discontinuous, and not of a positive, unbreakable deductive coherence that emerges from an 'absolute principle' in an unconditional continuity. To reject the 'absolute primacy of the subject' is not to render self-emancipation impossible; this possibility remains on the table even in the harsh times we live in, when fascism is once again gaining momentum in the world. As we shall see in what follows, for Adorno, to reject the supremacy of the object is not to give up; it is, in fact, to reject the world's reification.

Negative Dialectics and the Critique of the Subject

In the Preface to *Negative Dialectics*, Adorno formulates one of the most important tasks of his critical theory: 'To use the strength of the subject to break through the fallacy of constitutive subjectivity' (2007: xx). This complex and ambiguous phrase encompasses one of the central theses in Adorno's theorising: modern thought is essentially characterised by the primacy of the subject. Ultimately, and despite their differences, all major variants of modern thinking such as idealism, Heidegger's ontology and positivism are subjective thinking. And, for Adorno, the subject amounts to identity.[7]

The primacy of the subject is the theoretical effort to establish or justify the existence of the object through a subjective unity, and expresses the thought that identifies, that renders equal all that is unequal and is characteristic of bourgeois society. According to Adorno, the subject and the object condition each other mutually and cannot be reduced to a pure identity of one or the other. And here the question arises: in what sense is positivism subjective if it is, in principle, anti-subjectivist? Generally speaking, Adorno (1977b, 1977c) argues that positivism grounds the objectivity of knowledge on the methods of research and not on what is being researched, and the methods of research are based on the subject;

therefore, positivism does not detach itself from the subjectivism it believes itself to have overcome, and its objectivity is mere appearance. Adorno did not reject objectivity as such; he criticised the apparent objectivity of positivism and its idea of objectivity, where facts are interpreted as something existing in itself, an objectivity whose constitution has been erased.[8]

Adorno argues that Heideggerian ontology appears to be a philosophical project that 'has escaped the captivity of subjectivity' (2019: 101). However, the model of being in Heidegger's theorising is the reduction of the subject to pure essence; Heidegger's being is a subjective being. In this sense, Adorno points out that it is no coincidence 'that Heidegger falls back on precisely the latest plan for a subjective ontology produced by western thinking: the existentialist philosophy of Soren Kierkegaard' (1977a: 123). Adorno (2008) posits the thesis that idealism has not been overcome and still subsists in different forms of theorising. Furthermore, in idealism the subject proclaims itself as the master and creator of all things, this being the fallacy of constitutive subjectivity or the myth of the subject that produces everything with superiority; the primacy of the subject results in the domination of nature, which in turn involves the domination of men.[9]

In *Eclipse of Reason*, Horkheimer also criticised the demand for maintaining critical philosophy's principle of *reductio ad hominem* from Kant, a principle according to which 'the fundamental traits and categories of our understanding of the world depend on subjective factors. Awareness of the task of tracing concepts back to their subjective origins must be present in each step of defining the object. This applies to basic ideas, such as fact, event, thing, object, nature; no less than to psychological or sociological relations' (2004: 63). According to Horkheimer, the subjectification produced in capitalist society gives the subject power over nature but at the same time condemns it, given that, in participating in the oppression of nature, the subject at the same time participates in the oppression of its internal nature. For Adorno and Horkheimer, the human effort of emancipation from nature results in a type of social domination that leads to the subjugation of the external and internal nature of humans.

Adorno tried to socially and historically ground the primacy of the subject in modern thinking; to him it is the result of the reification of society in an objectivity that is alienated from men; that is, 'the more individuals are in affect degraded into functions within the societal totality as they are connected up to the system, the more the person pure and simple, as a principle, is consoled and exalted with the attributes of creative power, absolute rule, and spirit' (1998: 248). In other words, the primacy of subjectivity is an unconscious reaction of individuals before the power of the objective social relations that engulf them.

For Adorno (1977d, 2017), the more anonymous and alien the relations of domination are, the more unbearable it is for the subject to experience its own impotence. Therefore, thinking will tend towards a higher subjectivity. At the same time, the desperate self-exaltation of the subject stands in the way of its self-reflection. Generally speaking, the rise of subjectivity in theorising and the reification of the world are correlated. This proximity clarifies the relation between the different variants of modern thought and capitalist society in critical terms. At this point, it must be clarified that Adorno does not consider social relations in capitalism as completely autonomous from the subject, as having produced an objectivity that constitutes human beings this way. This presupposition would be a mistake, as would assuming the existence of a subjectivity as the non-reified content of an objective form. For Adorno, 'the belief that the object can be made to coincide entirely with the subject, that the object really is the subject, is itself false; it is simply not the case ... the pure subject presupposes objectivity, just as, conversely, objectivity presupposes subjectivity' (2001: 218). Therefore, there is no absolute principle: neither subject nor object. Both moments are determined respectively and cannot be reduced to one another: they are mutually produced. As we shall see in what follows, this is developed in the Adornian theory of the primacy of the object. It is my belief that this theory allows for the overcoming of objectivism and subjectivism in critical thought.

Objectivity and Critical Theory

One of the central themes in *Negative Dialectics* is what Adorno calls the 'primacy of the object'; negative dialectics cannot exist without it. The primacy of the object is not an inversion of the primacy of the subject or a superior alternative; rather, it is 'the corrective to the subjective reduction' and the step that allows dialectics to become materialist (1998: 250; 2007). Importantly, the primacy of the object is not 'the denial of a subjective share' or an idea of objectivity as the mere disappearance of the subject. Neither is it a relapse of traditional Marxism in considering social objectivity as absolute and underestimating the force of the subject. On the contrary, negative dialectics is the acknowledgement of this force; according to Adorno, 'the objectivity of dialectical cognition needs not less subjectivity, but more' (2007: 40).

The Adornian theory of the primacy of the object is of enormous complexity and depth, both in materialist and philosophical terms. We would even say it is the attempt to break with the spell of identity that the primacy of the subject involves. Furthermore, it tries to eliminate the hierarchy of the subject over the object and vice versa. It is, in itself, the rupture of hierarchy[10] – even if its name, paradoxically, seems to express the opposite. A crucial element for understanding the primacy of the object is its conception as the 'corrective' of subjective reduction. According to Adorno, the primacy of the subject is not something completely false, it is only a half-truth that turns false when established as an absolute principle: the principle of the subject that produces everything and can also stop doing so by an act of will. The primacy of the object corrects this and is valid only in its interrelation with the subject, not as a new absolute principle. In this sense, as Schäbel (in this volume) points out, the primacy of the object must be understood in critical terms: as the critical primacy of the object, for it does not want to suggest a different original principle.

The primacy of the object is the understanding that the subject is mediated by social objectivity, an objectivity that constitutes individual consciousness. It is the force of the objective that prevails in subjects and hinders their will but does not eliminate it. Volition is still possible, for the subject is a mediation of the object. Adorno (2007) acknowledges that, in capitalism, human practice has produced a social objectivity that is independent from particular subjects to a certain extent and rules over them universally, preventing their becoming subjects. It is an objectivity that must be abolished; this too makes the primacy of the object critical.

We believe it is this social objectivity that Postone (2003) has very perceptively named structures of social relations constituted by a type of objectifying practice, social structures that produce some sort of domination with abstract and impersonal characteristics. However, Postone erred in comparing objectified social relations to a Subject that has a dynamic of its own and is independent of particular subjects; that is, an automatic Subject that represents Marx's category of capital. In other words, in Postone's critical theory it is not human beings or the proletariat who are the subject, but capital interpreted as a historical Subject in the Hegelian sense. From a different point of view, Postone identifies the object with a subject and his objectivist shift amounts to absolute subjectivism. It is a return to the transcendental subject, albeit with a materialist tone.

As we have seen, there is a prevailing tendency in theorising to reduce objectivity more and more to the subject, a tendency that exists against the backdrop of reification: it is the Adornian thesis that idealism still subsists in different forms of thought and, we might add, even in critical thought. For Adorno the primacy of the subject is the universal rule of domination, and the critical-primacy-of-the-object accounts for the fact that 'the subject is never quite the subject, and the object never quite the object; and yet the two are not pieced out of any third that transcends them' (2007: 175; 2008). Subject and object are mutually produced; this way, human beings produce society and society produces them. Paraphrasing Adorno, we can say that the primacy of the object transcends the critical understanding of open Marxism as *reductio ad hominem*, in completing it inversely as *reductio hominis*, which is 'an insight into the delusion of the subject that will style itself as absolute. The subject is the late form of the myth, and yet the equal of its oldest form' (2007: 186). Likewise, the primacy of the object opens up the possibility of thinking of the dualism of subject and object without concluding in the identity of one or the other. Therefore, it transcends subjectivism and objectivism, while Marxism traditionally tends to position itself at either of these poles.

Finally, the essential characteristic of traditional Marxism is not that it assumes objective domination as the starting point from which to think the transformation of the world and underestimates the force of the subject as contradiction, as open Marxism argues; nor that it has a trans-historical interpretation of labour at its core, in Postone's terms (2003). Both critical perspectives have their moment of truth. However, the fundamental trait of a traditional Marxism is the principle of identity, a principle that must be overcome if we want to attain a radically different critical theory. Adorno's negative dialectics is the effort to overcome this principle through the force of the subject. Furthermore, to renounce the affirmation of an 'all-powerful' subject does not create the need for a party or vanguard again, since the latter are, just like the 'all-powerful' subject, expressions of identity. Therefore, the question that lies before us concerns the possibility of a human emancipation that is driven by the force of negation, of the non-identical and of a thought that can express this possibility without absolute principles, without identity.

References

Adorno, T. W. (1977a) 'The Actuality of Philosophy', *Telos* 31: 120–33.

Adorno, T. W. (1977b) 'Introduction', in T. W. Adorno et al. (eds), *The Positivist Dispute in German Sociology*, London: Heinemann.

Adorno, T. W. (1977c) 'Sociology and Empirical Research', in T. W. Adorno et al. (eds), *The Positivist Dispute in German Sociology*, London: Heinemann.

Adorno, T. W. (1977d) *Terminología filosófica* (Philosophical Terminology), Vol. 2, Madrid: Taurus.

Adorno, T. W. (1998) *Critical Models: Interventions and Catchwords*, New York: Columbia University Press.

Adorno, T. W. (2001) *Kant´s Critique of Pure Reason*, Stanford: Stanford University Press.

Adorno, T. W. (2007) *Negative Dialectics*, London: Continuum.

Adorno, T. W. (2008) *Lectures on Negative Dialectics: Fragments of a Lecture Course 1965/1966*, Cambridge: Polity Press.

Adorno, T. W. (2015) *Filosofía y sociología* (Philosophy and Sociology), Buenos Aires: Eterna Cadencia.

Adorno, T. W. (2017), *An Introduction to Dialectics*, Cambridge: Polity Press.

Adorno, T. W. (2019) *Ontology and Dialectics*, Cambridge: Polity Press.

Bonefeld, W. (2004a) 'On Postone's Courageous but Unsuccessful Attempt to Banish the Class Antagonism from the Critique of Political Economy', *Historical Materialism* 12(3): 103–24.

Bonefeld, W. (2004b) 'The Principle of Hope in Human Emancipation: On Holloway', *Herramienta* 25: 197–208.

Bonefeld, W. (2009) 'Emancipatory Praxis and Conceptuality in Adorno', in J. Holloway, F. Matamoros and S. Tischler (eds), *Negativity and Revolution: Adorno and Political Activism*, London: Pluto Press, 122–47.

Bonefeld, W. (2013) *La razón corrosiva: una crítica al Estado y al capital* (Corrosive Reason: A Critique of the State and Capital), Buenos Aires: Herramienta.

Bonnet, A., Holloway, J. and Tischler, S. (eds) (2005) *Marxismo abierto. Una visión europea y latinoamericana* (Open Marxism: A European and Latin American Perspective), Buenos Aires: *Herramienta* and Universidad Autónoma de Puebla.

Dimópulos, M. (2013) 'Prólogo', in T. W. Adorno, *Introducción a la dialéctica* (Introduction to Dialectics), Buenos Aires: Eterna Cadencia.

Dinerstein, A. C. (2017) 'Afirmación como negatividad. Abriendo espacios para otra Teoría Crítica' (Affirmation as Negativity: Opening Up Spaces for Another Critical Theory), Paper presented at the Colloquium 25 Years of Open Marxism: Reflections on Critical Theory and Revolutionary Praxis, Puebla, Mexico, 16–18 October.

Hegel, G. (2018) *The Phenomenology of Spirit*, Cambridge: Cambridge University Press.

Holloway, J. (1994) *Marxismo, Estado y Capital* (Marxism, State and Capital), Buenos Aires: Editorial Tierra de Fuego.

Holloway, J. (1995) 'From Scream of Refusal to Scream of Power: The Centrality of Work', in W. Bonefeld, R. Gunn, J. Holloway and K. Psychopedis (eds), *Open Marxism 3*, London: Pluto Press, 155–81.

Holloway, J. (2005) *Change the World Without Taking Power*, London: Pluto Press.

Holloway, J. (2010) *Crack Capitalism*, London: Pluto Press.

Holloway, J. and Löwy, M. (2003) 'Intercambio entre Michael Löwy y John Holloway', *Bajo el Volcán* 3(6): 13–25.

Holloway, J., Matamoros, F. and Tischler, S. (2009) 'Negativity and Revolution: Adorno and Political Activism', in J. Holloway, F. Matamoros and S. Tischler (eds), *Negativity and Revolution: Adorno and Political Activism*, London: Pluto Press, 3–11.

Horkheimer, M. (2004) *Eclipse of Reason*, London: Continuum.

Postone, M. (2003) *Time, Labor and Social Domination: A Reinterpretation of Marx's Critical Theory*, Cambridge: Cambridge University Press.

Notes

1. Many thanks to John Holloway.
2. Many thanks to Panagiotis Doulos, Mario Schäbel and Roberto Longoni for the discussions held.
3. On this, Bonefeld writes: 'What about Marx's concept of critique? He argued that critique has to demonstrate *ad hominem*. Critique is about the conditions of Man, and therewith also her dignity and possibilities. Critique has to develop the congealed social forms, the world of things, from definite social relations. Its task is to show that the forms of capital are constituted by – and subsist through – definite human social relations' (2013: 28–9).
4. According to Adorno (2017) idealism ultimately shows that the truth is the subject. Adorno's assertion is based on the Preface to *The Phenomenology of Spirit*, where Hegel writes 'In my view, which must be justified by the exposition of the system itself, everything hangs on grasping and expressing the true not just as substance but just as much as subject' (2018: 12).
5. In various of his works, Holloway explicitly or implicitly presents the notion of the subject as 'all-powerful'. Another example is the essay 'We Are the Only Gods: From the Critique of Heaven to Critique on Earth' (Holloway 1994).
6. Dimópulos points out that Horkheimer wrote a letter to Adorno in 1949 which read as follows: 'men must force men to force nature, or else nature will force men. This is the concept of society. Our specific task is to acknowledge it with precision in its conditionings without, however, the spirit postulated by Hegel.' According to Dimópulos 'the program could be outlined in a short sentence: the spirit must be taken away from Hegel or, even better, the identity of subject and object must be broken' (2013: 15–18).

7. According to Adorno, 'given that identity is formed in self-conservation, one could argue that the subject itself is somehow a latent principle of identity' (1977d: 62).

8. For Adorno, 'in the newest forms of positivism there is a modest subjectivism of sorts; it can, however, be shown that precisely these last criteria are in fact criteria of a mere subjectivity' (2015: 211).

9. Just like Adorno, Horkheimer argues that 'domination of nature involves domination of man' (2004: 64).

10. According to Adorno: 'it is not the purpose of critical thought to place the object on the orphaned royal throne once occupied by the subject. On that throne the object would be nothing but an idol. The purpose of critical thought is to abolish the hierarchy' (2007: 181).

4

Value-Form Theory, Open Marxism and the New Reading of Marx

Frederick Harry Pitts

This chapter charts the theory of the value-form found in, on the one hand, the New Reading of Marx (NRM), and, on the other, Open Marxism (OM). The latter is in part an outgrowth of the former, insofar as both launch a complementary overhaul of how we think about the relationship between value, labour and capitalist society. But it also marks a critical contribution, accompanying the NRM's stress on the social form of value with a stern emphasis on the concrete antagonistic social relations of class society that serve to constitute value and are contained not only logically but historically within it. By moving critically within the latter, OM helps restate the centrality of class struggle at the core of the NRM's 'monetary' theory of value, facilitating an understanding of the forces that intervene in the struggle with, against, despite and beyond the value-form.

This has produced mutual criticisms and creative tensions between NRM and OM, leading to the complementarity of the one with the other. By bringing an understanding of the constitution of abstract social forms in continuing concrete forms of human practice and domination, OM suggests that the unfolding of the value-form as presented in Marx's *Capital* is not simply a logical derivation but a historical process based in the forceful dispossession and separation of individuals from the means of reproducing their conditions of living in order to create a class of wage labourers. It also suggests that behind the apparent 'non-empirical reality' of value lie antagonistic social relations that have a real-life efficacy mediated in abstract social forms. In this, OM's critique of the NRM is also what affords the possibility of its complementarity with, and extension of, the latter.

Value-form Theory

Many applications of and debates around Marxian value theory within the study of work and economic life focus myopically on labour and production as the central sites of both inquiry and contention within the capitalist circuit. Moreover, changes in capitalism are extrapolated from changes in the immediate content taken by labour within production. But the social-form analysis broadens this and makes for a perspective more circumspect about the possibility of reading off wider changes when the essential social forms of capitalist society carry over. As Moishe Postone points out, there is a common perspective uniting, on one hand, those who 'maintain that the labor theory of value had been valid in the past', but not today (for critiques see Pitts 2018a, 2018b), and, on the other hand, those who maintain an attachment to the traditional labour theory of value that 'reduce[s] everything to the amount of labor-time ... that went into it'. In neither is value seen as something more than production, as a 'historically specific form of wealth' (Postone and Brennan 2009: 320).

Value-form theory, meanwhile, proposes that a fixation on labour alone is insufficient to grasp what really makes capitalism tick as a historically specific mode of organising production and exchange, and cannot constitute a basis on which to either rule out or rule in epochal shifts in its character. It therefore trumps analyses that narrowly restrict themselves to the sphere of production, missing the social relations that foreground labour and the social forms assumed by its results, whilst also circumventing the pitfall of seeing 'free labour' everywhere, collapsing the distinction between production and circulation, and in so doing erasing any sense of the determination of labour as wage labour. This, we suggest, leads to either reducing the analysis or expanding it to breaking point. As two leading variants of value-form theory, OM and the NRM offer possible routes out by means of what Diane Elson (1979) once called a 'value theory of labour'.

Value-form approaches to the Marxian theory of value have their roots in the mature economic works of Marx, but differ in important ways from orthodox, traditionalist approaches to his output, redressing the disproportionate emphasis placed upon the value-producing properties of labour in favour of a perspective that foregrounds the abstract process of *social validation* which renders labour productive of value, and, in turn, the concrete antagonistic social relations that undergird this. The New

Reading of Marx focuses primarily on the first, open Marxism primarily on the second. Together, their Frankfurt School-inflected reading of Marx's *Capital* emphasises the status of Marx's theory as a critical theory of society rather than a positivistic economic account (Bellofiore and Riva 2015; see also Pitts 2017).

The New Reading of Marx

The New Reading of Marx is best expressed in work by Marxian theoreticians such as Michael Heinrich (2012), who can broadly be described as holding a broadly 'monetary' theory of value. Inspired by the readings of Marx given in the work of I. I. Rubin (1972) and originating in the work of Helmut Reichelt (2005) and Hans-Georg Backhaus (1980, 1992, 2005), the NRM works from a careful reinterpretation of Marx's written output. It inflects its reading of Marx with Frankfurt School social theory derived from the work of Adorno, under whom many of its earliest exponents studied (Bellofiore and Riva 2015). As in open Marxism – with which it shares certain personnel, and through the earliest publications of which the likes of Backhaus came to Anglophone prominence – the critique of political economy is read as a critical theory of society rather than an alternative economics per se. It presents 'a Marxism stripped of dogmatic certainties and naturalistic conceptions of society' (Bonefeld 2014: 41–2), radically open to a range of theoretical and empirical applications.

Where the labour theory of value has traditionally held there to be a direct relationship between hours of labour and value, the NRM says, instead, that 'for value *abstract labor* is decisive', as, in the words of Michael Heinrich, 'the result of a social process which validates the concrete, individual labor spent as a part of the total social labor' (Heinrich and Wei 2012: 725). The NRM suggests that value does not consist in the amount of labour-time expended in production by any one labouring individual. It relates to the amount of time 'socially required for its production' (Marx 1976: 301). For the NRM, value is subject to a social validation made after the concrete expenditure of labour (Heinrich 2012). In production, value can thus only be a potential quantity, pending validation in the exchange of commodities. In this respect, a product of labour is not automatically a commodity. By means of its sale it must be validated as such in order to enter into the value relation. For a product of labour to bear value, it must be a commodity. And for a product of labour –

whether a good or a service – to become a commodity, it must be sold (Heinrich and Wei 2012: 727).

For the NRM, the validity of economic categories such as labour and value does not hold in abstraction from society as whole. Rather, their necessity is established socially through the abstract relation of all things with all other things, in monetary exchange. The exchange of money and commodities brings private labours into a social relation with one another by 'establish[ing] the social necessity of the labour expended for the production of a particular commodity' (Bellofiore and Riva 2015: 30–1). By means of money, the formerly *private* labours that take place in production are brought into a *social* relationship with one another. The status of money as universal equivalent mediates all things with all other things. Hence, value rests on the social validation of labour as value-producing via 'exchanging commodities with money as the universal equivalent' (Bellofiore and Riva 2015: 29).

This social aspect is crucial. Labour is only private and pre-social in its doing. As Kicillof and Starosta suggest, '[p]rivate individuals and private labour are the historical predicates of value, not labour per se' (2007; Bellofiore and Riva 2015), insofar as value is the name for the relationship into which they enter in and through market exchange. Value relates to abstract social labour and not its concrete private and individual expenditure (Bonefeld 2010; Kicillof and Starosta 2007: 262). As Bellofiore and Riva assert, 'labour is not immediately social in production as such' (2015: 30). Only concrete, private labour is performed and it is from this private, individual basis that the abstraction of labour proceeds. It is in exchange that previously private labour attains its social form in value. Labour becomes social only through the totality of 'private exchange between independent producers' validated through the market (Bellofiore and Riva 2015: 30). Moreover, this is not one exchange between two things. Value, Marx suggests, is 'purely social' insofar as it exists as the relation between commodities. Indeed, value, Marx writes, 'can only appear in the social relation between commodity and commodity' extended across society as a whole (Marx quoted in Murray 2013: 140). It is this totalising viewpoint that allows Marx to explore the way in which the social organisation of labour within capitalist society is geared towards the commensuration of distinct labours in service of commodity exchange.

The NRM gives a very different reading of the relationship between labour and value than do more traditional and orthodox approaches, seeking the secret of value in the social form assumed by the results of labour rather than in its direct content. For the NRM, the form aspect is the key element of Marx's value theory. As Backhaus writes, the central 'expository motive' of Marx's value theory is the crucial question '*why this content assumes that form*' (1980: 101). It is this that radically destabilises any attempt to recoup Marx for any kind of alternative economics or political economy to pose alongside rather than against their classical cornerstones. Because the central insight of the NRM is that value relates not to expended concrete labour as in orthodox accounts, but to its abstract form, the NRM is therefore an attempt to explain 'the specific social character of commodity-producing labour' (Heinrich 2012: 45–7), i.e. precisely why and how a content should take a certain form. Its focus on form means that, for the NRM, Marx's theory is not 'one "economic theory" beside many others', an alternative 'bundle of sociological and economic hypotheses' to pose against others (Backhaus 1980: 99). In Heinrich's view, stressing Marx's 'labour' theory of value or his theory of exploitation only serves to 'neglect his originality and reduce him to something which was already reached before' in, say, Ricardo (Heinrich and Wei 2012: 722). The specific *monetary* character of Marx's theory distinguishes it from Ricardian value theory, and, moreover, from productivist accounts that centre the content of the labour process writ either small or large, such as in labour process theory and post-operaismo. As Heinrich suggests, it is not any productive activity that renders capitalism a specific and significant kind of social formation, but the purposes to which it is put and the forms in which it results. 'We all produce society' – through time, across places – 'but we do this in certain forms' (Heinrich and Wei 2012: 716). The productive activity of a given society is not sufficient alone to understand it, but rather the forms and purposes under which this productive activity takes place (Murray 2013: 124).

Central to this form-specific analysis of a capitalism that neither political economy nor economics ever truly questions is the value-form. This is the form taken by the wealth by which, as Adorno puts it, life and society are produced and reproduced under capitalism. Thus, the study of what is at bottom an abstract social form always implies the consideration of the specific social relations that it supports and that make it so. But it is only through consideration of this form that the critique of political economy is in any way substantially *historical* (Backhaus 1980: 107). Backhaus quotes Marx, who, in a letter to Engels, wrote that 'already in the most simple form, that of the commodity, the *specific* social, in no way *absolute* character of bourgeois production is analysed' (Marx quoted in Backhaus 1980: 107). Hence, any approach that extrapolates wider historical changes from the immediate content of production or the specificity of capitalist production itself misses what is truly important about capitalism as a social formation.

The understanding of Marx's method is central to the NRM's conceptualisation of social form, and the qualitative sociological side of value that this conceptualisation captures. Marx begins *Capital* with the commodity and goes on to 'elucidate a development that cannot simply be called economic, but rather is really the development of the commodity form as it moves', a development that takes in society as a whole (Postone and Brennan 2009: 313). But although Marx begins from the commodity, and not the social constitution of a society based on the buying and selling of labour power in and through the class antagonism, insofar as the man is the key to the understanding of the ape, he begins from the most developed social form of a set of social relations he progressively unveils as the work goes on. The chapter on primitive accumulation, in which Marx unfolds the historical constitution of the abstract categories covered in early chapters, does not arrive until the very end of the book. As Heinrich writes, history 'does not precede the theoretical development, but rather follow[s] from it', and Marx uses this presentation to show that 'the separation of immediate producers from the means of production is the central historical precondition of the capitalist mode of production' (Heinrich, forthcoming). This demonstrates that for the NRM it is not just the social form assumed by labour that matters, but the constitutive social relations this expresses. However, the NRM does not go far enough in delineating the former, and leaves much of the work required in doing so to its close relative and descendent, open Marxism.

Open Marxism

This OM critique of the NRM provides the theoretical resources to extend the insights of the latter onto the terrain of social reproduction (see Dalla Costa 1995) and the class antagonism by bringing into clearer focus the specificity of the concrete social relations the value-form mediates. Open Marxism works with the same understanding of value as the NRM and intertwines with its Anglophone reception along shared lines of attachment to Frankfurt School critical theory. Open Marxism, for instance in the work of Werner Bonefeld (2014) and John Holloway (2010), describes how abstract labour stems, practically and historically, from antagonistic social relations of production. OM suggests how processes of abstraction, totalisation and socialisation connect with antagonistic relations of domination and resistance.

For OM, the dialectical method of Marx's *Capital* does not counterpose the appearance of value and the reality of labour, or that of social form and social relations. Rather, it suggests that the one is contained within the other – a negative dialectical relationship introduced with critical reference to the NRM tradition most clearly in the recent work of Bonefeld (2016a, 2016b), inspired by Adorno's *Negative Dialectics* (1990). In this respect, the analysis of an abstract social relation arbitrated in exchange is able to open out upon its material undergirding in lived experience and human practice. Here, '[d]omination in capitalism ... is rooted in quasi-objective structures of compulsion constituted by determinate modes of practice, expressed by the categories of commodity and capital' (Postone and Brennan 2009: 316). By dialectically rooting the study of the value-form in the realities of everyday human life, lived experience and practical activity, the OM thus breaks with traditional Marxist accounts inasmuch as the latter purport to 'penetrate' appearances in order to better grasp reality, for which the dive into the 'hidden abode of production' represents the most famous touchstone, and a recurring justification for approaches geared solely around the extrapolation of general laws of capitalism from the labour process and productive relations alone.

As a 'category of social mediation' (Heinrich 2007), value represents a 'non-empirical reality' (Dinerstein 2014) seemingly hard to grasp in such programmes of research or, indeed, struggle. The problem consists in the fact that, as Heinrich puts it, 'the basic notions of *Capital* like value and surplus value are non-empirical notions' not exhausted in the appearances they assume (Heinrich and Wei 2012: 717). They are non-empirical in that, when we say value is a category of social mediation, we mean that a 'mediation', in this instance, constitutes the relation between things via another 'intermediate' thing, in the same way, as in Gunn's apt simile, 'a rope linking two climbers is constitutive of the relation in which they stand' (1987: 57). Value, as such a mediation, is the *mode of existence* of that which it mediates – in other words, its *form*, which takes an appearance in the monetary exchange of commodities (1987: 58). Hence, though non-empirical, it takes on an apparent form. This appearance, contrary to the way Marxist concepts of 'false consciousness' have tended to think it, is not a 'false' overlaying of reality, but itself expresses its essence in a mediated way. This follows Hegel circumnavigation of the dualism between essence and appearance. As Hegel writes, 'essence must appear' (cited in Gunn 1987: 58). Appearance is the 'existence' of essence. And, as Heinrich (forthcoming) suggests, it is precisely those 'non-empirical concepts' – of value and so on – 'that first make possible an understanding of that which appears empirically', rooted as they are in human practice and lived experience.

The dualism between appearance and reality is undermined where, for instance, Marx writes that 'material relations between persons and social relations between things' appear precisely 'as what they are' (1976: 166). Appearance, on this standard, is the *mediation* of those relations (Gunn 1987: 59). The objective appearances assumed by capitalist social relations contain within them the essence of their antagonistic constitution in human practice. And this, for Gunn, opens up the possibility of capturing these antagonisms as 'matters of experience' (1987: 59). It is thus possible to move through form to grasp content. As Heinrich suggests, in '[u]nderstanding the specific forms of society, we can understand the typical action of individuals; but starting with the action of individuals we will not understand the forms. Or we take them for granted, we don't see that such forms have to be explained' (Heinrich and Wei 2012: 716). This captures the assault on 'ticket-thinking' launched by the NRM, and, by extension, OM, through which the social element at the core of economic categories is unpicked.

But it also highlights a tension within the wider NRM tradition addressed by significant thinkers in that tradition including Backhaus and, from an OM perspective, Bonefeld. Heinrich proposes that, from the abstract social form of value, we can logically derive the actions of individuals without any necessary recourse to their study. This suggests that we can infer from the social form the social relations that constitute it. However, as Backhaus contends, '[t]he analysis of the logical structure of the value-form is not to be separated from the analysis of its historical, social content' (1980: 107). Bonefeld, too, in a more recent contribution foundational to the contemporary shape of OM (2014), takes on the NRM's tendency to talk of value as if it unfolds of its own accord, without the antagonistic social basis that makes it historically and continuingly possible, by which one class must be dispossessed of any independent individual or collective means to reproduce the conditions of living without the sale of the one commodity they have at their disposal: labour power. Whilst it might seem, then, that social reproduction and class relations are left out of the NRM's abstract-labour-oriented perspective on value – one in which more traditional concepts like exploitation seldom get a mention – they are, in the hands of open Marxists, made very much present. History, wrote Adorno, 'is the history of class struggles' (2003: 93). He suggests so only insofar as the class antagonism is constitutive of capitalist society, and what went before capitalism is not history, but prehistory (Marx 1970: 22). It is in this same sense that Marx and Engels begin the first section of the *Communist Manifesto* with the immortal words: 'The history of all hitherto existing society is the history of class struggles' (1977: 222). The class antagonism is the precondition of capitalist society, and the way the world is today cannot be explained except with reference to its blood-soaked social constitution.

Indeed, it is in this focus on the 'social constitution' of the value-form in the class antagonism (Bonefeld 2014) that what Murray (2013: 129), quoting Rubin, calls the 'qualitative sociological' consequences of Marx's value theory become most clear, and its complexion as something more than an economic theory is clarified. As Bellofiore and Riva write, 'exchange is the synthetic principle that immanently determines the connection of every social fact' (2015: 25). This, of course, opens out upon an expansive terrain of mediations – 'as modes of existence, or appearances' of the class relation, under capitalism, the capital-labour relation – including 'the commodity-form, the value-form, the money-form, the wage-form, the state-form ... and hence of the struggle in which that relation consists' (Gunn 1987: 60; see also Gunn 1992, and Dinerstein and Pitts 2018). The focus on abstract labour points to social validation as a criterion of validity situated beyond production itself, as Adorno suggests, in 'the form of the relations of production within which production takes place' (2008: 118). In other words: in society at large.

In the hands of OM, Marx's critique of political economy offers a powerful theoretical tool with which to unpack the social core of economic relations. Its object is the systematic development of the specific form of wealth in capitalist society. The historical specificity of capitalism consists in the way that wealth, broadly defined, takes on the social form of value, expressed in money and represented in what Marx opens *Capital* by calling the 'immense accumulation of commodities' (1976; see also Holloway 2015 for a statement of the importance of the first sentence of *Capital*). And this rests on the creation of a society of private property and wage labour through the continued and enforced dispossession of a majority of the world's inhabitants of the independent individual and collective means necessary to reproduce their conditions of living outside of the wage relationship.

In this sense what OM allows us to do is unpick the historical conditions whereby value and measure exert such a hold to begin with. Marx writes that '[a]s soon as men start to work for each other in any way, their labour also assumes a social form' (1976: 164). This social form is value. For it to exist, certain social relations must be in place. As a system of commodity production, capitalist social relations of production have two main dimensions. Ownership of productive resources is dispersed among firms which confront each other as commodity producers in market competition. Under capitalism, labour power itself must become a commodity, and people must have no independent individual or collective ability to reproduce their means of living outside of the wage-money-commodity nexus. Dispossessed of the land and of any means of subsistence, formally free individuals are forced to sell their labour power to capitalists for a wage. Sold on the labour market, their labour power becomes itself a commodity (Marx 1976; Heinrich 2012). In open Marxist hands, Marx's critique of bourgeois political economy clarifies that value must be understood by looking at the underlying relations of production, and not simply as emerging through exchange on the market. Value's existence as a social form is rooted not only in the antagonism of the employment relationship, but in a wider situation of classed and constrained social reproduction and commodification that occupies the social sphere as a whole.

The OM critique of the NRM thus grounds the totalising effect of commodity exchange in the act of dispossession of human beings of any independent individual or collective means to reproduce the conditions of life outside the wage- and commodity-form. Whereas some interpretations of Marx conceptualise primitive accumulation as a pre-capitalistic phenomenon belonging to the 'prehistory' of capitalist society (Heinrich 2012: 92), and others view it as a form of accumulation aimed at resolving capitalist crisis (Harvey 2003), the NRM is among those approaches that sees dispossession as foundational of capitalism in a continuing and constantly reproduced way (see also De Angelis 2004). For trade, exchange and money to be 'transformed into capital, the prerequisites for capitalist production must exist'. That is, 'the owners of the means of production and subsistence [must] meet the free labourer selling his [*sic*] labour power' (Bonefeld 2014: 78 quoting Marx 1976). Primitive accumulation through dispossession induces a state of abstract economic compulsion whereby one class comes to fundamentally depend, for its material existence, on selling its labour for a wage, leading to its domination and alienation, through an ever more completely mediated existence (Bonefeld 2014).

Critically refashioned through an OM appreciation of the class antagonism, the NRM can thus be seen as casting Marx's critique of political economy as '*a theory of historically specific social mediation*' and the misapprehended expression of its 'surface forms' in economic thought (Postone and Brennan 2009: 310; Backhaus 1980). This means that, contrary to approaches that prioritise historical materialism as a kind of economic determinism, Marx's critique of political economy is not an argument for the 'primacy of the economic', but rather concerns the 'social production and reproduction of the life of society as a whole' (Adorno 2000: 141). In this perspective, the critique of political economy captures what classical political economy cannot: that 'human needs, labour and wealth always have specific social form and purpose' (Murray 2013: 131). For Marx, Murray writes, the historically specific forms of capitalist society 'are pervasive and of great consequence', reaching 'all the way down' (2013: 131) into how the things we need to live are produced and how we attain them. This analysis holds a radical potential for the opening out of Marxian value theory beyond labour and into its relationship with life as a whole, with the means by which we reproduce ourselves and others and, in so doing, society itself.

Conclusion

Gaining increasing uptake in recent years for their new way of reading Marx's critique of political economy, and his theory of value, as a radically open, non-dogmatic and unfinished project, the NRM and OM offer new resources of critique to scholars who find little of application or worth in the present array of approaches to the measure of labour and value seen through a Marxist lens. Contrary to the attempts of some to turn it into an alternative economic or political-economic system of thought, Marx's critique of political economy reckons with the question of measure through an understanding of value as form, and it is the value-form theory of the NRM and OM that today offers the most analytically interesting, non-dogmatic and generously accommodating reconstruction of the legacy of that critique, non-deterministically reaching far beyond the workplace as a centre of analysis in order to generate novel empirical and theoretical insights.

References

Adorno, T. W. (1990) *Negative Dialectics*, trans. E. B. Ashton, London: Routledge.

Adorno, T. W. (2000) *Introduction to Sociology*, trans. E. Jephcott, Cambridge: Polity Press.

Adorno, T. W. (2003) 'Reflections on Class Theory', in *Can One Live After Auschwitz? A Philosophical Reader*, ed. R. Tiedemann, trans. R. Livingstone, Stanford: Stanford University Press, 93–110.

Adorno, T. W. (2008) *Lectures on History and Freedom*, ed. R. Tiedemann, trans. R. Livingstone, Cambridge: Polity Press.

Backhaus, H-G. (1980) 'On the Dialectics of the Value-Form', *Thesis Eleven* 1: 94–119.

Backhaus, H-G. (1992) 'Between Philosophy and Science: Marxian Social Economy as Critical Theory', in W. Bonefeld, R. Gunn and K. Psychopedis (eds), *Open Marxism 1*, London: Pluto Press, 54–92.

Backhaus, H-G. (2005) 'Some Aspects of Marx's Concept of Critique in the Context of his Economic-Philosophical Theory', in W. Bonefeld and K. Psychopedis (eds), *Human Dignity: Social Autonomy and the Critique of Capitalism*, Aldershot: Ashgate, 13–30.

Bellofiore, R. and Riva, T. R. (2015) 'The Neue Marx-Lekture: Putting the Critique of Political Economy Back Into the Critique of Society', *Radical Philosophy* 189 (Jan/Feb): 24–36.

Bonefeld, W. (2010) 'Abstract Labour: Against Its Nature and On Its Time', *Capital & Class* 34(2): 257–76.

Bonefeld, W. (2014) *Critical Theory and the Critique of Political Economy: On Subversion and Negative Reason*, London: Bloomsbury.

Bonefeld, W. (2016a) 'Negative Dialectics and Critique of Economic Objectivity', *History of the Human Sciences* 29(2): 60–76.

Bonefeld, W. (2016b) 'Bringing Critical Theory Back in at a Time of Misery: Three Beginnings Without Conclusion', *Capital & Class* 40(2): 233–44.

Dalla Costa, M. (1995) 'Capitalism and Reproduction', in W. Bonefeld, R. Gunn, J. Holloway and K. Psychopedis (eds), *Open Marxism 3*, London: Pluto Press, 7–16.

De Angelis, M. (2004) 'Separating the Doing and the Deed: Capital and the Continuous Character of Enclosures', *Historical Materialism* 12(2): 57–87.

Dinerstein, A. C. (2014) 'Too Bad For the Facts: Confronting Value with Hope (Notes on the Argentine Uprising of 2001)', *South Atlantic Quarterly* 113(2): 367–78.

Dinerstein, A. C. and Pitts, F. H. (2018) 'From Post-work to Post-capitalism? Discussing the Basic Income and Struggles for Alternative Forms of Social Reproduction', *Journal of Labor & Society* 21(4): 471–91.

Elson, D. (1979) 'The Value Theory of Labour', in D. Elson (ed.), *Value: The Representation of Labour in Capitalism*, London: CSE Books, 115–80.

Gunn, R. (1987) 'Marxism and Mediation', *Common Sense* 2: 57–66.

Gunn, R. (1992) 'Against Historical Materialism: Marxism as First-Order Discourse', in W. Bonefeld, R. Gunn and K. Psychopedis (eds), *Open Marxism* 2, London: Pluto Press, 1–45.

Harvey, D. (2003) *The New Imperialism*, Oxford: Oxford University Press.

Heinrich, M. (2007) 'Invaders from Marx: On the Uses of Marxian Theory, and the Difficulties of a Contemporary Reading', *Left Curve* 31, www.oekonomiekritik.de/205Invaders.htm.

Heinrich, M. (2012) *An Introduction to the Three Volumes of Karl Marx's Capital*, New York: Monthly Review Press.

Heinrich, M. and Wei, X. (2012) 'The Interpretation of Capital: An Interview with Michael Heinrich', *World Review of Political Economy* 2(4): 708–28.

Heinrich, M. (forthcoming) *The Science of Value: Marx's Critique of Political Economy Between Scientific Revolution and Classical Tradition*, trans. A. Locasio, Chicago/Leiden: Haymarket/Brill.

Holloway, J. (2010) *Crack Capitalism*, London: Pluto Press.

Holloway, J. (2015) 'Read Capital: The First Sentence of *Capital* Starts with Wealth, Not with the Commodity', *Historical Materialism* 23(3): 3–26.

Kicillof, A. and Starosta, G. (2007) 'Value Form and Class Struggle: A Critique of the Autonomist Theory of Value', *Capital & Class* 92: 13–40.

Marx, K. (1970) *Contribution to the Critique of Political Economy*, London: Lawrence and Wishart.

Marx, K. (1976) *Capital*, Vol. 1, London: Penguin.

Marx, K. and Engels, F. (1977) *The Communist Manifesto*, in D. McLellan (ed.), *Karl Marx: Selected Writings*, Oxford: Oxford University Press, 221–342.

Murray, P. (2013) 'Unavoidable Crises: Reflections on Backhaus and the Development of Marx's Value-Form Theory in the *Grundrisse*', in R. Bellofiore, G. Starosta and P. Thomas (eds), *In Marx's Laboratory: Critical Interpretations of the Grundrisse*, Leiden: Brill, 121–46.

Pitts, F. H. (2017) *Critiquing Capitalism Today: New Ways to Read Marx*, Basingstoke: Palgrave Macmillan.

Pitts, F. H. (2018a) 'A Crisis of Measurability? Critiquing Post-operaismo on Labour, Value and the Basic Income', *Capital & Class* 42(1): 3–21.

Pitts, F. H. (2018b) 'Beyond the Fragment: Postoperaismo, Postcapitalism and Marx's "Notes on Machines", 45 Years On', *Economy and Society* 46(3–4): 324–45.

Postone, M. and Brennan, T. (2009) 'Labor and the Logic of Abstraction', *South Atlantic Quarterly* 108(2): 305–30.

Reichelt, H. (2005) 'Social Reality as Appearance: Some Notes on Marx's Conception of Reality', in W. Bonefeld and K. Psychopedis (eds), *Human Dignity: Social Autonomy and the Critique of Capitalism*, Aldershot: Ashgate, 31–68.

Rubin I. I. (1972) *Essays on Marx's Theory of Value*, Detroit: Black and Red.

5

Is Open Marxism an Offspring of the Frankfurt School? Subversive Critique as Method

Mario Schäbel

When speaking of the legacy of the Frankfurt School, the first names that come to mind are those of Jürgen Habermas and Axel Honneth. However, with the shift of paradigm proposed by the former and continued by the latter, the two theorists left behind what can be called the core of the first generation of this school: Marx's critique of political economy. In this chapter we wish to present Open Marxism (OM) and the New Reading of Marx (NRM) as two theoretical currents which, unlike Habermas and Honneth, did develop the Marxian nucleus of the first generation. To what extent, however, can they be considered successors of the Frankfurt School?

We need not go into more detail on what OM is (see the Introduction to this book); the NRM, however, is not that well-known (see Pitts in this book). In his monumental work, *Marx im Westen: Die neue Marx-Lektüre in der Bundesrepublik seit 1965*, Ingo Elbe (2010) unites under the label 'New Reading of Marx' the works of Alfred Schmidt, Hans-Georg Backhaus and Helmut Reichelt.[1] Elbe's book gave rise to the frequent use of the term 'Neue Marx-Lektüre' (New Reading of Marx) to refer to a new interpretation of the work of Marx on the basis of the critique that different representatives of Western Marxism such as Georg Lukács, Karl Korsch and the Frankfurt School, amongst others, articulated against orthodox interpretations.

Elbe (2010: 67) differentiates a particular variant within the NRM that considers the Frankfurt School relevant. Reichelt (2008: 22), for example, speaks of Critical Theory as a programme of a new reading of Marx. The perspective of these authors is very similar to that of OM, and there are personal as well as professional ties between the representatives of both currents. Hans-Georg Backhaus and Helmut Reichelt, for example, both contributed to the first volume of *Open Marxism*.[2] This proximity between OM and the NRM has also been pointed out by Jan Hoff (2017: 70) and Guido Starosta (2017).

We shall contrast the two currents in order to defend the following thesis: despite their many points of convergence, there is a fundamental difference between the two, namely that the theoretical outlook of OM is of an idealist nature while that of the NRM is materialist. As we shall explain shortly, our use of the term 'idealism' is not pejorative but rather strictly philosophical. With regards to the first generation of the Frankfurt School, we could say that OM is more akin to the approach of Herbert Marcuse, while the NRM is closer to the perspective of Theodor Adorno. The latter is based on the primacy of the object, oddly enough the result of a rigorous critique of the objectivism of orthodox Marxism. Apparently, this critique is also shared by OM; however, unlike OM, Adorno does not succumb to subjectivism. In other words, OM runs the risk of performing an idealist inversion of the materialist interpretation, thus eliminating all materialist elements from Marx's dialectic, just as orthodox Marxism stripped it of all idealist elements.

Admittedly, certain representatives of OM are aware of the danger of succumbing to a subjective idealism that views Man (*Mensch*) as the absolute subject. Bonefeld even writes that the objectification of social relations and the subjectification of the object are 'mutually dependent expressions of a perverted world' (2004b). He also asserts, as Gunn does (1994: 55), that voluntarism can be named 'the other side of determinism'. As a result, our critique might seem irrelevant, for all representatives of OM apparently know that not only are structures a product of struggle but that the opposite is also true: there is no form of struggle untouched by structures. However, there are many reasons to support the thesis that OM is an expression of voluntarism or, rather, of subjective idealism (cf. Dinerstein and Holloway, this volume).

According to Alfred Schmidt, this type of inversion is common amongst many authors who tried to distance themselves from the orthodox interpretation of Marx: 'discontented by the rigid objectivism of orthodoxy, they surely often fell into the trap of its equally false abstract opposite: pure subjectivism' (Schmidt 1977: 285). We will argue here that the NRM tries to rescue Adorno's critically materialist approach, while OM runs the risk of becoming dogmatic on this matter, that is, of sustaining the absolute primacy of the subject. In this sense, it is more akin to the idealism of Marcuse.[3]

The central idea in any form of idealism is the negation of the externality of the object. This is what Holloway does, for example, when he says: 'The essential claim of Marxism, that which distinguishes it from other variants of radical theory, is its intention to dissolve all externality' (1995: 159). Likewise, OM argues that the external existence of the object is to Marx nothing more than appearance. However, Marx does not intend to support a subjective idealism (or even solipsism) that denies the existence of the outside world. On the contrary, the affirmation of the existence of an external, objective world in the sense of a nature that is independent from the subject is a fundamental part of his theorising.

It must be clarified that the present essay is based on what I call *subversive negativism* as a method of thinking. A subversive argumentation, understood as an argumentation taken to the extremes, is a sharpened argumentation that aims at confronting its most negligible problems (which are often the most evident ones) as well as its contradictions. In other words, it is a *self-contradictory* argumentation. How then is critical theory understood from this perspective? For us, it is a theory that is critical not only towards something else but also, at the same time, towards itself: it must be viewed critically. With this understanding of critique we follow Adorno in offering a critique from within or, rather, an *immanent critique*. In the preface of *Negative Dialectics*, Adorno gives an example of such a contradiction: 'To use the strength of the subject to break through the fallacy of constitutive subjectivity – this is what the author felt to be his task ever since he came to trust his own mental impulses' (2004: xx). However, while Adorno shows us how critique and self-critique can be combined in an immanent way, OM is stuck in a subjective idealism of sorts that traces everything back to the creative force of humans. In sum, we argue that OM's *ad hominem* critique does not contain an immanent critique as Adorno's does. However, when the possible future generations of OM dedicate themselves to integrating their *ad hominem* critique with an immanent critique – that is, when they set out to perform a self-criticism of OM – they can become part of the tradition of Adorno. It is arguable whether this is truly a goal of OM or if it should be at some point. Such a project could be titled *opening up the categories of OM*.

The Critique of Historical Materialism: Between Critical Materialism and Subjective Idealism

The critiques of the orthodox interpretation of historical materialism articulated by OM and the NRM are quite similar. All representatives of both currents reject the dogma of the dialectics between transhistorical productive forces and historical relations of production, for this turns Marxian theory into an objectivist science that perceives the development of social relations as equivalent to the 'unfolding [of] a closed logic' (Holloway 2002: 49).

On the contrary, the approach of OM is not based on the fetishist assumption of already constituted forms but conceives them as a product of class struggle and, in this sense, as something open. Therefore, it disagrees with any approach that would turn Marxism into a functional theory interested only in correctly describing existing society. That is, OM rejects the understanding of value as nothing but a law that regulates the reproduction of capitalism.

The NRM has a critical – and not affirmative – understanding of the notion of natural laws in Marx, as well as of his historical materialism in general. Backhaus (2000: 19) contrasts this critical understanding with the ontological, traditional understanding. This interpretation is embraced by Schmidt, who calls Marx's theory 'a theory in retraction [auf Widerruf]. It is not a dogmatic vision of the world but, rather, a diagnostic of a false state that must be abolished' (1976: 104). Reichelt too is convinced that 'materialist dialectics … is a method in retraction [auf Widerruf]' (1973: 264). Consequently, when Marx speaks of the law of value, he does not speak of a universal law of transhistorical validity but rather of something that only has specific historical validity. In other words, the ontological interpretation of the law of value – a product of *natural history* – results in a process of naturalisation of contingent social forms. In this, the representatives of the NRM lean towards Adorno, who strongly criticises orthodox Marxism for considering the law of value a natural law: 'Only to such a perverter of Marxian motives as Diamat … could it occur to falsify Marx's polemical concept of natural legality from a construction of natural history into a scientivistic doctrine of invariants. Yet this does not rob Marx's talk of natural history of any part of its truth content, i.e., its critical content' (2004: 355). Therefore, both OM and the NRM agree that the primacy of material relations must not be understood affirmatively. Schmidt, for example, is well aware that in Marx all objective structures are always mediated by subjective activity; however, he points towards the justification of the structuralist approach and, therefore, does not deny the primacy of material structures. Only when the transformation of men into mere personifications of existing material relations is understood as a neutral truth – rather than a fact expressing the fetishist inversion between subject and object – does structuralism turn into an 'apology for what exists' (Schmidt 1969b: 208). Then, according to Schmidt, the 'structuralist hostility to history' (1981: 134) becomes evident; it is the result of concealing that Marx 'never forgot production in relation to finished products, nor structuring activity in relation to structures' (Schmidt 1969b: 206). Bonefeld too argues that human beings can never be conceived exclusively as the object of given structures for, at the same time, they are subjects who create those very structures. To support this opinion, Bonefeld quotes Horkheimer: 'human beings produce, through their own labour, a reality which increasingly enslaves them' (1995: 184). On the basis of this consideration, Bonefeld wonders about the status of practice and reaches the conclusion that it never reproduces existing structures alone. Although he admits that Horkheimer treats social practice as simultaneously subject and object, he considers its role as subject to prevail. According to Bonefeld, structuralism, which views social practice as nothing more than an executive auxiliary of what exists, also transforms the fetishist inversion between subject and object into an objective truth; therefore, structuralism 'does not recognise appearance as appearance but rather tries to conceive it as an objective reality' (2004a: 126). In other words, structuralism fails to understand social objectivity as something subjectively mediated; it fails to understand it in a dialectical way.

This results in a fundamental difference between the NRM and OM. While the NRM criticises the primacy of existing material relations with regards to social practice, it does not abandon it entirely but rather conserves it (*aufheben*) as a negative fact. OM, by contrast, wholly rejects the primacy of objective structures, for they are viewed as the product of the class struggle that runs through them. Our thesis on this is that, in OM, the dialectic between structure and human practice acquires the form of an idealism based on the absolute primacy of the human being as the central subject. Despite the fact that, in OM, the *unity-in-difference* between base and superstructure or, rather, between subject and object, is accentuated, this dialectic ultimately turns into identity; or, to put it more precisely, *unity-in-difference* turns into *unity-in-identity*. This idealist interpretation thus clashes with the Frankfurt School and its successors, for the latter support a more materialist interpretation: a critically materialist one. It accepts the appearance of the primacy of objective structures as real and, in doing so, assumes that human beings will continue to reproduce the coercions of the social structure, even if it is they who have actually produced them.

Backhaus, just like the other representatives of the NRM, criticises any understanding of the subject-object dialectic that eliminates the object through its dissolution in the subject: 'The common traits of the Hegelian and the "profane" subject-object dialectic apparently consist in the fact that in both cases the "object" vanishes whereas only the "subject" really exists: the object exists by virtue of an "unconscious production" of the "subject"' (1992: 67). On the contrary, in the materialist version of the dialectical correlation on which historical materialism is based, the difference amounts to a real difference: although subject and object form a unit, they are not identical because of it but also remain separated. We shall show this in the following section in relation to the concept of nature in Marx and Adorno. It must be pointed out that, although the demystification of apparently natural relations as a historical occurrence is pivotal in Adorno's theory, the conclusion reached by OM does not concur: 'The inversion of this relation ... that deduces the changing character of relations from their becoming, a conclusion that makes human beings appear as the immediate subjects of their actions, is far from what Adorno intended' (Grenz 1974: 58–9).

The same can be found in Marx, whose critique resembles a theory of action (*Handlungstheorie*) in *Rohentwurf* (*Grundrisse*). In *Capital* too he gives special importance to subjectivity, something that becomes apparent through the introduction of the concept of validity (*Geltung*). Despite this, he understands validity in exclusively objectivist terms, hence Reichelt's assertion that one observes in *Capital* 'a total rupture between an objective processuality and a subjective rationality of action' (2008: 123). The same can be said of fetishism: 'The phrases from the chapter on fetishism, which have been so often quoted and which all theories on the abstraction of value in exchange refer to, only suggest a constituent participation of subjects in the genesis of the economic form. The entire construct "operates", in Marx, without resorting to subjectivity' (Reichelt 2008: 123).

Despite not denying the subjective part of the automation of value, Marx ultimately describes it as a development that cannot be attributed to the intentionality of subjects. Reichelt points out that Marx even criticises 'the action of this process rendered absolute through theory [*handlungstheoretisch*]' (2008: 96) and, in opposition, highlights the importance of the existing structural coercion. Therefore, it is not actually men who produce value as an economic form through their actions, but the opposite: it is value that determines the behaviour of men, and through that behaviour they simply reproduce value.

Interestingly, both Reichelt and Backhaus once again turn to Adorno for this interpretation, an author they have already quoted in relation to his conviction that social relations rendered independent must be derived from behaviour. However, with this assertion, Adorno does not intend to 'subjectivise society and negate its "real predominance", that is, he does not try to render the true object of critique, both of Marx as well as of the Frankfurtians, invisible' (Backhaus 2000: 73). Adorno clearly argues that society and its forms cannot be understood as a 'composite resultant of the actions of the component individuals alone' (1967: 68). Therefore, with regards to Adorno, we observe that the NRM position definitely does not eradicate all objective moments from Marx's theory, thereby succumbing to a subjective idealism. On the contrary, its intention is to illustrate Marx's oscillation between a subjective and an objective conception of his categories. Marx's insistence on the fact that social structure can be understood as the outcome of human practice is not questioned. However, at the same time, the NRM insists on the reality of the autonomisation of the social structure or, rather, of the relations of production vis-à-vis human beings as their producers. This 'excess of objectivity [*Überhang an Objektivität*]' (Reichelt 2008: 19) in Marx is what OM does not accept; this differentiates it from the NRM on this matter.

That said, the following must be specified: it is not that OM does not accept the real force of existing structures on human practice. It is, however, convinced that the fetishism of the alleged autonomisation of social relations in relation too human practice can one day be abolished. Unlike, we believe, the representatives of the NRM, who are closer to Adorno and his conviction that fetishism – and with it the fact that human beings will always be determined by what they themselves have created – is an invariant of human life: this is precisely where Adornian pessimism lies.

The Absolutisation of Constitutive Subjectivity
Versus the (Critical) Primacy of the Object

We shall begin to explain the difference between the idealism of OM and the materialism of the NRM by contrasting two passages from Marcuse and Adorno on historical materialism and its orthodox interpretation. In his 'Ad Lukács', Adorno writes: 'the Marxian doctrine on the priority of being over consciousness does not wish to be understood ontologically but as the expression of something negative: of the predominance of reification, of the relations of production into which men enter "involuntarily"' (1986: 252). Considering what Marcuse writes in his *Reason and Revolution*, he does not seem to differ greatly from Adorno on this matter, although their perspectives were otherwise very different.

The materialistic proposition that is the starting point of Marx's theory thus states, first, a historical fact, exposing the materialistic character of the prevailing social order in which an uncontrolled economy legislates over all human relations. At the same time, Marx's proposition is a critical one, implying that the prevailing relation between consciousness and social existence is a false one that must be overcome before the true relation can come to light. The truth of the materialist thesis is thus to be fulfilled in its negation (Marcuse 1941: 273).

Marcuse's words reveal a profound difference between himself and Adorno. In this passage, Marcuse names the relation between subject and object – in which the object prevails – as a false relation; he suggests it should be inverted by the 'true relation', where the subject prevails. Marcuse thus distances himself from the interpretation of historical materialism deployed by Adorno, for he does not conceive the primacy of the subject which opposes the primacy of the object critically, but rather in an absolute fashion. Therefore, it becomes clear that, for Marcuse, idealism as such was not really something to be overcome; it was something to be radicalised.

On this matter, OM is quite akin to Marcuse, to whom Bonefeld resorts at different moments in order to say something similar: 'Idealism is the true realism. Those to whom human emancipation makes sense should not fear being called idealist. They are. Idealism is the true reality of the spectre of communism' (2013: 303). Thus both OM and Marcuse interpret Marx's theory as an idealist philosophy with social practice at its core. Both approaches represent an 'idealism of procreation [*Erzeugungsidealismus*]' (Schmidt 1971: 96).

It is important to clarify that neither Marx nor Adorno claim that the object is not a product of the subject. They rather complete the one-sided idealist approach by stressing that the object is a product of the subject and vice versa. For example, Adorno criticises the fact that idealism considers subjectivity an ultimate principle, endorsing a constitutive subjectivity that 'falsifies the object ideologically, calling it a free act of the absolute subject' (2004: 350). In 'Subject and Object' he writes: 'As truly nonidentical, the object moves the farther from the subject the more the subject "constitutes" the object' (1985: 506). Thus, subjective idealism, according to which all externality is a product of the subject, as OM claims, is only a half-truth with regards to Marx's interpretation. We believe this is why Adorno's aforementioned critique of idealism has not yet been sufficiently assimilated by OM.

In *Negative Dialectics*, Adorno advocates the primacy of the object and, in doing so, leans more towards materialism or, rather, materialist dialectics. Although he concedes there is simultaneous mediation of the subject by the object and of the object by the subject, he insists on the existence of a certain contradiction in the primacy of the object: qualitatively speaking, the object refers to the subject in a way that is different from how the subject refers to the object: 'Not even as an idea can we conceive a subject that is not an object; but we can conceive an object that is not a subject. To be an object also is part of the meaning of subjectivity; but it is not equally part of the meaning of objectivity to be a subject' (Adorno 2004: 183). Arguably, the critical primacy of the object in Adorno, as well as the contradiction or asymmetry he detects in the (non-)dependence between subject and object, do not agree with the subjectivism of OM. The latter is rather based on a primacy of the subject understood in absolute and not critical terms. Furthermore, OM considers it impossible for the object to exist independently from the subject, while Adorno claims the exact opposite. For example, Bonefeld writes: 'Capital exists only in opposition to living labour as the substance of value. However, it is an asymmetric opposition insofar as capital cannot free itself from labour. This can only be done from the position of labour' (2013: 198).

But the relevant passage we consider most revealing in Bonefeld is the following: 'The *reductio ad hominem* that for Adorno ... characterises the critical intent of Marx's work does not entail the replacement of the object by the subject. It means the comprehension of the object as a mode of existence of the subject. Just as objectivity without the subject is nonsense, subjectivity without the object is nothing' (2009: 129). We believe this should be understood as a distorted interpretation of Adorno, for the latter does not share the idealism that Bonefeld attributes to him. Allow us to explain. In the quotation above, Adorno in fact says 'we can conceive an object that is not a subject', while, according to Bonefeld, for Adorno 'objectivity without the subject is nonsense'. The two assertions contradict each other. The idealist reading that Bonefeld proposes is simply not a true reflection of Adorno's words.

We can use this as a backdrop to summarise one of the fundamental differences between OM and the NRM. OM reduces the critical moment of the Marxist method to a *reductio ad hominem*, that is, to a demystification of the apparently objective forms of social relations as the product of the human subject. At this point, we partly disagree with Guido Starosta. We do agree with him that, despite its effort to transcend all externality between the subject and the object, OM is ultimately founded on a subject that is devoid of social determination and, in this sense, abstractly free: 'The postulate of immanence between content and form ultimately thereby remains just a formal declaration which is belied as the argument unfolds. In the end, an element of exteriority to alienated social practice creeps back in as the residual "substance" of revolutionary subjectivity' (Starosta 2017: 373). This results from the fact that German Idealism is the true foundation of OM's theoretical perspective. And the former, mostly with Fichte, bases itself on subjectivity as a creative force that is only *constituens* but not *constitutum*.

However, we do not agree with Starosta's opinion that this applies both to OM and the NRM. One of the crucial differences between these two currents is that the latter rests on Adorno's idea of the critical primacy of the object. This means that, instead of basing itself on a free subjectivity that leads to the conviction that if humans *stopped producing capitalism* and the forms that sustain it, capitalism would cease to exist, it highlights the fact that the subject is mainly a product of its social determination. Schmidt's critique of Lukács – presented by us in detail in 'Idealism and Orthodoxy in John Holloway's OM' (2017) – goes against Starosta's thesis that the representatives of the NRM also embrace the reduction of the critical moment of the Marxist method to a *reductio ad hominem*. Schmidt writes: 'One of the main endeavours of Marxist analysis is no doubt to penetrate the surface of economic reality which has hardened into things in order to get at the essence behind it – the social relations of men. But ... for Marx these relations are not something final and absolute' (1971: 69).

Adorno acknowledges the need to accept the immanence in the respective social form in which each practice that aims at social change moves. From his viewpoint, an *absolute dynamism* that conceives history as nothing more than present history, that is, as the realisation of the will of the subjects, represents an ideology (Adorno 2004: 191). One could even say that to conceive reality, even nature itself, as nothing more than the objectification of man, would be a new myth that replaces that of men being the product of God.

> Enlightenment thus transcends its traditional self-understanding: it is demythologization – no longer merely as a *reductio ad hominem*, but the other way round, as a *reductio hominis*, an insight into the delusion of the subject that will style itself as absolute. The subject is the late form of the myth, and yet the equal of its oldest form (Adorno 2004: 186).

Negative dialectics could be interpreted as a materialist dialectics that criticises idealist dialectics, for it presumably abandons the idealist identity of subject and object and instead advocates its non-identity. However, negative dialectics cannot be reduced to materialism. This also is but 'one aspect, of course, one whose lack of understanding leads to a lack of understanding of other aspects as well' (Schmidt 1983: 14–15). Adorno also praised idealism for having acknowledged the mediation of the object by the subject:

> Idealism was the first to make clear that the reality in which men live is not unvarying and independent of them. Its shape is human and even absolutely extra-human nature is mediated through consciousness. Men cannot break through that. They live in social being, not in nature. Ideology, however, is idealism which merely humanizes reality. In this it is one with naive realism as its reflective justification (Adorno 1982: 28).

Marx, who 'was very deeply indebted to German Idealism for his whole approach' (Schmidt 1971: 113), also commends idealism when he stresses that the world that surrounds us is mediated by the human being. According to Schmidt (1969a: 11), Marx wants to rescue the idealist idea of the mediation of everything immediate in a materialist way. However, although he sees nature as something that is mediated by the social history of the human being, he does not give up on a material substratum that does not dissolve into the historical modes of its social appropriation without a trace. Nature is also an *in-itself* that exists independently from the human being: 'nature never becomes something completely "made" by us, as Marx wrote following Vico' (Schmidt 1971: 158). In this, Schmidt recognises 'the realist moment of Marx's epistemology' (1971: 154).

With his materialism, Adorno wants to reinforce the moment of the non-identical in nature. In his philosophy, nature symbolically represents what cannot be understood and subsumed by human concepts. Adorno too clings to an immediate object that is not merely a product of the mediation of consciousness, even if it is mediated by it modally. This element of his philosophy can be called a 'quasi-ontological element' (Sommer 2016: 59), one that contradicts OM, considering that Gunn claims 'there is no space of immediacy located outside of mediation' (1987: 64). Adorno has a dual concept of the object as: (a) an object mediated subjectively, and (b) an object that is independent from all mediations. The latter, the object that cannot be understood by concepts, is what Adorno calls *something*:

'Something' – as a cogitatively indispensable substrate of any concept, including the concept of Being – is the utmost abstraction of the subject-matter that is not identical with thinking, an abstraction not to be abolished by any further thought process. Without 'something' there is no thinkable formal logic, and there is no way to cleanse this logic of its metalogical rudiment. (2004: 133)

It is quite useful to mention, at this point, the distinction made by Adolfo Sánchez Vázquez (2003: 155) between *Objekt* and *Gegenstand*. Marx uses two German terms for object: the first time he says *Gegenstand*; the second, *Objekt*. In doing so, Marx wants to distinguish the object as objectification from the object in itself. *Objekt* is the object in itself, external to humans and their activity. *Gegenstand* is a product of practical activity, it is the object captured in a subjective mode. To express our critique of OM on the basis of this distinction, we can summarise it as follows: its authors conceive the world exclusively as *Gegenstand* and not as *Objekt*.

Conclusion

In this chapter we have shown that OM and the NRM have more in common than meets the eye; however, there are also profound differences between them. We have argued that the main difference between the two currents is that while the first adopts an idealist theoretical approach, the NRM is more materialist and, therefore, closer to Adorno. The thesis that OM is a successor of the Frankfurt School cannot be refuted; however, it is easier to defend through the theory of Herbert Marcuse. As a result, OM in general risks the same fate as the latter. That is, simply replacing the dogmatic and one-sided materialism of orthodox Marxism with an equally dogmatic and one-sided idealism. In granting the subject absolute primacy in the context of the dialectical unity of subject and object which tries to replace the base-superstructure model, OM ultimately reaches a conclusion that is the idealist inversion of the dogmatic primacy found in orthodox Marxism.

Is there, however, some element that would allow us to defend the thesis that OM is in fact a successor to Adorno's theorising? One possibility could be the concept of *ambivalence*, understood as a central element in Adorno's theorising (Habermas 1975: 148). Adorno always tries to unite two perspectives on one and the same phenomenon that apparently exclude each other, acknowledging that both parts – despite their contradictoriness – can be legitimately defended. The same applies for the separation between subject and object; in other words, for Adorno's understanding of fetishism:

> The separation of subject and object is both real and illusory. True, because in the cognitive realm it serves to express the real separation, the dichotomy of the human condition, a coercive development. False, because the resulting separation must not be hypostasized, not magically transformed into an invariant (Adorno 1985: 498–9).

If we claim, on the one hand, that the NRM takes on the task of interpreting fetishism as a reality (which has not yet been overcome in the natural history of human life), and, on the other, that OM does not want to give up hope that one day fetishism can be overcome (and interprets it as a real illusion), then yes, OM can indeed be designated an heir to Adornian thought. However, this can only be so under the condition that both currents, OM and the NRM, are conceived not only as mutually excluding but also as complementary. In other words, both should be conceived as *unity-in-separation* or *separation-in-unity*. The relation between both currents can be clarified through a brief illustration: OM does not deny the existence of objective structures, such as the fetishism of the commodity, as real illusions. It rather objects to the *primacy* of these structures over practice. That is, OM accepts the dialectic between subject and object and, with it, the fact that the subject is partly also a product of the object. However, compared to the NRM, OM rejects the *primacy* of the object over the subject and assumes the opposite point of view. Ultimately, only if the possible primacy of both parts is assumed within the dialectic between subject and object could OM arrive at a position similar to Adorno's.

References

Adorno, T. W. (1967) 'Sociology and Psychology (Part I)', *New Left Review* 46: 67–80.

Adorno, T. W. (1982) *Against Epistemology: A Metacritique*, trans. W. Domingo, Cambridge: Polity Press.

Adorno, T. W. (1985) 'Subject and Object', in *The Essential Frankfurt School Reader*, ed. A. Arato and E. Gebhardt, New York: Continuum, 497–510.

Adorno, T. W. (1986) 'Ad Lukács', in *Gesammelte Schriften*, Bd. 20.1, ed. R. Tiedemann, Frankfurt am Main: Suhrkamp Verlag, 251–6.

Adorno, T. W. (2004) *Negative Dialectics*, trans. E. B. Ashton, London and New York: Routledge.

Backhaus, H. G. (1992) 'Between Philosophy and Science: Marxian Social Economy as Critical Theory', in W. Bonefeld, R. Gunn and K. Psychopedis (eds), *Open Marxism 1*, London: Pluto Press, 54–92.

Backhaus, H. G. (2000) 'Über den Doppelsinn der Begriffe "politische Ökonomie" und "Kritik" bei Marx und in der Frankfurter Schule', in *Wolfgang Harich zum Gedächtnis. Eine Gedenkschrift in zwei Bänden*, ed. S. Dornuf and R. Pitsch, Munich: Müller & Nerding, 10–213.

Bonefeld, W. (1995) 'Capital as Subject and the Existence of Labour', in W. Bonefeld, R. Gunn, J. Holloway and K. Psychopedis (eds), *Open Marxism 3*, London: Pluto Press, 182–212.

Bonefeld, W. (2004a) 'Bemerkungen zur Kritik der Voraussetzungen', in *Gesellschaft als Verkehrung. Perspektiven einer neuen Marx-Lektüre*, ed. C. Kirchhoff et al., Freiburg: Ca Ira, 123–48.

Bonefeld, W. (2004b) 'The Principle of Hope in Human Emancipation: On Holloway', www.herramienta.com.ar/articulo.php?id=163.

Bonefeld, W. (2009) 'Emancipatory Praxis and Conceptuality in Adorno', in J. Holloway, F. Matamoros and S. Tischler (eds), *Negativity and Revolution: Adorno and Political Activism*, London: Pluto Press, 122–47.

Bonefeld, W. (2013) *La razón corrosiva. Una crítica al Estado y al capital*, Buenos Aires: Herramienta.

Elbe, I. (2010) *Marx im Westen. Die neue Marx-Lektüre in der Bundesrepublik seit 1965* (Marx in the West: The New Reading of Marx in the Federal Republic of Germany Since 1965), Berlin: Akademie.

Grenz, F. (1974) *Adornos Philosophie in Grundbegriffen. Auflösung einiger Deutungsprobleme*, Frankfurt am Main: Suhrkamp.

Gunn, R. (1987) 'Marxism and Mediation', *Common Sense* 2: 57–66.

Gunn, R. (1994) 'Marxism and Contradiction', *Common Sense* 15: 53–8.

Habermas, J. (1975) *Perfiles filosófico-políticos*, Madrid: Taurus.

Hoff, J. (2017) *Marx Worldwide: On the Development of the International Discourse on Marx Since 1965*, Leiden: Brill.

Holloway, J. (2002) *Change the World Without Taking Power: The Meaning of Revolution Today*, London: Pluto Press.

Holloway, J. (1995) 'From Scream of Refusal to Scream of Power: The Centrality of Work', in W. Bonefeld, R. Gunn, J. Holloway and K. Psychopedis (eds), *Open Marxism 3*, London: Pluto Press, 155–81.

Marcuse, H. (1941) *Reason and Revolution: Hegel and the Rise of Social Theory*, London: Routledge.

Reichelt, H. (1973) *Zur logischen Struktur des Kapitalbegriffs*, Frankfurt am Main: Europäische Verlagsanstalt.

Reichelt, H. (2008) *Neue Marx-Lektüre: Zur Kritik sozialwissenschaftlicher Logik*, Hamburg: VSA.

Sánchez Vázquez, A. (2003) *Filosofía de la praxis*, Buenos Aires: Siglo XXI.

Schäbel, M. (2017) 'El idealismo y la ortodoxia en el Marxismo Abierto de John Holloway: un alejamiento de la Escuela de Frankfurt', *Bajo el Volcán* 25: 81–107.

Schmidt, A. (1969a) *Beiträge zur marxistischen Erkenntnistheorie*, Frankfurt am Main: Suhrkamp.

Schmidt, A. (1969b) 'Der strukturalistische Angriff auf die Geschichte', in *Beiträge zur marxistischen Erkenntnistheorie*, Frankfurt am Main: Suhrkamp, 194–265.

Schmidt, A. (1971) *The Concept of Nature in Marx*, trans. Ben Fowkes, London: NLB.

Schmidt, A. (1976) *Die Kritische Theorie als Geschichtsphilosophie*, Munich and Vienna: Carl Hanser.

Schmidt, A. (1977) 'Geschichte als verändernde Praxis', in *Weiterentwicklungen des Marxismus*, ed. W. Oelmüller, Darmstadt: Wissenschaftliche Buchgesellschaft, 280–311.

Schmidt, A. (1981) *History and Structure: An Essay on Hegelian-Marxist and Structuralist Theories of History*, trans. J. Herf, Cambridge, MA: MIT Press.

Schmidt, A. (1983) 'Begriff des Materialismus bei Adorno', in *Adorno-Konferenz 1983*, ed. L. von Friedeburg and J. Habermas, Frankfurt am Main: Suhrkamp, 14–31.

Sommer, M. N. (2016) *Das Konzept einer negativen Dialektik Adorno und Hegel*, Tübingen: Mohr Siebeck.

Starosta, G. (2017) 'Fetishism and Revolution in the Critique of Political Economy: Critical Reflections on some Contemporary Readings of Marx's Capital', *Continental Thought & Theory. A Journal of Intellectual Freedom* 4: 365–98.

Wildcat (1997) 'Open Letter to John Holloway', www.wildcat-www.de/en/zirkular/39/z39e_hol.htm.

Notes

1. To be more precise, referring to the work of the mentioned authors, Elbe speaks of a 'Frankfurt School of the New Reading of Marx' (Frankfurter Schule der Neuen Marx-Lektüre). Both terms are used synonymously here.
2. Furthermore, it can be mentioned that Werner Bonefeld met Hans-Georg Backhaus in person. On his side, John Holloway tells of how Backhaus spent a few days in the house of Richard Gunn in Edinburgh and met both. Kosmas Psychopedis studied in Frankfurt and was a close friend of theirs as well, especially of Helmut Reichelt.
3. For this previously presented argument, see Schäbel 2017.

PART II

STATE, CAPITAL, CRISIS

6

'Terminary' Accumulation or
the Limits of Capitalism

Sagrario Anta Martínez

In Latin America and the rest of the world, transnational enterprises are accumulating land to establish mines, hydroelectric powerplants and monocultures, amongst other projects. Certain Marxist theories refer to this practice as primitive accumulation, breaking with the orthodox notion that identifies the latter concept with a specific moment in time. Representatives of open Marxism, including Werner Bonefeld (2001), Richard Gunn (2018) and John Holloway (2018), revisit this concept with reference to the consequences of our separation from our means of existence – that is, our proletarianisation for subsistence – and giving special importance to the hijacking of our free doing, repeated every day but never guaranteed beforehand. Others take up David Harvey's (2005) proposal that primitive accumulation is not a thing of the past but an ongoing process in the form of a new wave of violent enclosures of common goods. However, Harvey does not consider it correct to speak of 'primitive' accumulation since it is a process occurring today (see Dalla Costa 1995; Bonefeld 2001; De Angelis 2001); he prefers to describe it as accumulation by dispossession. Nevertheless, the above-mentioned categories do not account for the specific characteristics of today's advanced capitalism, caught up since the end of the previous century in a string of economic and ecological crises – crises which reveal how difficult it is to realise surplus value and how profound the contradiction between life and capital is. That is why certain theorists consider capitalism to be in its terminal phase (Wallerstein 1995; Esteva 2009; Kurz 2014; Vela 2018; see also the debate in Ortlieb 2014). If that is so, can today's accumulation still be considered primitive accumulation? Does it share the same characteristics at the time of its emergence, development and decline? If primitive accumulation is a genesis, is today's accumulation also a genesis of something or is it a different thing altogether?

Accumulation is a historical process, its characteristics varying from one century to another, from one space to another, from an act of beginning to one of perduring: change is one of the premises of capitalism. 'Accumulation is the conquest of the world of social wealth. It is the extension of the area of exploited human material and, at the same time, the extension of the direct and indirect sway of the capitalist' (Marx 1976: 739–40). Those who refer to contemporary accumulation as primitive focus solely on the aspect of our separation from the means of production, without considering the 'progress' of the conquest that Marx refers to, globally and individually. Accumulation today is based on the repetition of the primitive act but is not exactly the same. It has evolved. To focus only on the what and ignore the how, where, who, why, and to what end, is to abandon historical materialism. It is to overlook the specific material conditions of life at each given moment, eventually forgetting the historicity of this system of production, of the individual and of space, of how we relate to it and of how we relate to each other. To consider accumulation in all its stages as primitive is an abstraction, positing an identity of different historical moments, an immobility of capital and ourselves which is not the case, which in fact conceals the finite character of nature. That is why I prefer the category of 'terminary accumulation', which is in my opinion more precise. It considers the object not in isolation but in its specific circumstances.

There are elements of continuity in this process such as the use of violence, credit, our separation from the means of existence, the subordination of reproduction to production. However, the intensity and rhythm of the separation and exploitation have evolved, and I consider this to be crucial. As Holloway reminds us, we must not view origin and reconstitution as separate, but neither must we ignore the differences:

If we deny the distinction between constitution and reconstitution, do we not risk falling into a world of amnesia, in which there is no possible accumulation of experience? This is so. The conditions in which the struggle to constitute capital (to separate done from doing) takes place change all the time. The repetition of the process of exploitation changes the conditions in which the struggle to exploit takes place ... There is indeed an accumulation of experience (albeit not a linear accumulation) on both sides of the struggle (Holloway 2010: 101).

To highlight the specific and temporary characteristics of each time renders us visible as subjects and sheds light on our struggles, as well as those of capital for its reconstitution. Each accumulation is forged in the ever-changing margins of the capital-life contradiction; it is also characterised by the fact that we do not accept it, or at least we do not accept it entirely. Capital has become more efficient over time: the exploitation of human beings and of nature takes place at a faster and more effective pace by virtue of technology. Repression, administrative control and propaganda have also increased. The armies, police forces, legal and illegal armed groups are more numerous and more lethal than ever. Classification of the land and of people according to their function or dysfunction is also on the rise, as is indoctrination by institutions and the mass media. However, the violence of the system is also its fragility, which is why nothing guarantees it will always be in place.

In this chapter, in dialogue with Marx and considering the events of the present, we will try to answer the following questions: what do we understand by primitive accumulation on the one hand and by terminary accumulation on the other? What are the similarities and dissimilarities between the two? What are the limits of capitalism? What is the relation between the limits of this form of social organisation and present-day accumulation? To this end, we will review primitive accumulation as it is described in chapter 24 of *Capital*. Then we will look at why today's accumulation is not primitive, taking into account its increased scope and intensity. The exploitation of us and of nature is, today, much more extensive. However, what can seem like a strength is, in fact, the result of the difficulties in realising surplus value. It is the crisis of capital that intensifies the antagonism between life and capital.

Primitive Accumulation as Genesis

In chapter 24 of *Capital*, Marx describes the origins of the capitalist system of production, which can be traced back to the sixteenth century. This phase is characterised by the violent separation of peasants from their means of production through the excessive use of force by the state. Marx's analysis focuses primarily on England, where communal and private land was enclosed by landowners of the aristocracy; this was done so as to use the land to breed sheep and provide the budding manufacturing industry with wool, driving the rural population out of their crop fields. The separation from the means of existence led to the creation of two different types of commodity owners: capitalists, 'owners of money or commodities'; and 'free workers', free of land on which to subsist and free to sell their labour power (Marx 1976: 272). This is how the proletariat is born in Europe: 'Thus were the agricultural folk first forcibly expropriated from the soil, driven from their homes, turned into vagabonds, and then whipped, branded and tortured by grotesquely terroristic laws into accepting the discipline necessary for the system of wage-labour' (Marx 1976: 899).

Meanwhile, the 'discovery' of gold and silver deposits in America, the launching of extensive agriculture, and its exploitation through slavery and servility, allowed for the expansion of money and commodity exchange. Thus, 'the treasures captured outside Europe through undisguised looting, enslavement and murder flowed back to the mother-country and were turned into capital there' (Marx 1976: 918). In fact, 'the veiled slavery of the wage-labourers in Europe needed the unqualified slavery of the New World as its pedestal' (Marx 1976: 925). Trade was also conducted with Asia: great amounts of America's gold and silver ended up in India's temples, and much silver was taken to China to exchange for porcelain, silk and other products (Graeber 2011). Artisan workshops producing commodities were emerging at the time in the cities of Southeast Asia (Hernández Contreras and Zhenheng 2007). Business was controlled mainly by Dutch, German and Italian bankers and merchants (Graeber 2011: 312). Thus, in Europe and Asia capitalism was born through proletarianisation; in America, through the slavery and servility imposed on the autochthonous and African populations. This passing from the feudal to the capitalist system also involved the redisciplining of women: they had to be confined to the domestic sphere so as to guarantee the reproduction of the labour force. The burning of witches for three centuries guaranteed the success of this endeavour (Federici 2004). For this system of production to be set in motion, violence and division in their different modalities had to prevail. The excess use of force shows that this step was neither 'natural' nor easy; it was met with resistance and opposition to the new emerging social order.

Marx calls this process primitive accumulation, in allusion to a beginning of something that was until then unknown:

The whole movement, therefore, seems to turn around in a never-ending circle, which we can only get out of by assuming a primitive accumulation (the 'previous accumulation' of Adam Smith) which precedes capitalist accumulation; an accumulation which is not the result of the capitalist mode of production but its point of departure (Marx 1976: 873).

It was a stage that served as a 'hinge' between the medieval mode of production and the capitalist mode, today in full fledge. Marx speaks of this moment as historically specific, as the 'pre-history of capital', the 'period in which capitalist production was in its infancy', the 'infancy of large-scale industry' (Marx 1976: 874, 914, 922). In the postface to the second edition of *Capital*, he is more specific as to the temporality of this stage: 'large-scale industry itself was only just emerging from its childhood, as is shown by the fact that the periodic cycle of its modern life opens for the first time with the crisis of 1825 ... With the year 1830 came the crisis that was to be decisive, once and for all' (Marx 1976: 97). Rosa Luxemburg (2003) also reflects on this initial stage between the feudal period and the first decades of the nineteenth century; she refers to the accumulation of her times not as primitive but as a continuation of the primitive phase. My intention is not to draw out a timeline of accumulation but, rather, to discern the sociohistorical differences, to understand what Marx speaks of, and to look into what has occurred since the first third of the nineteenth century.

Marx makes a distinction between accumulation and primitive accumulation in the first paragraph of chapter 24, where one is presented as a 'result' and the other as a genesis. The 'result' refers to expanded reproduction: once constituted, capital needs to conduct an expansive reinvestment in order to be competitive; that is, it must grow. According to Harvey (2005), today's primitive accumulation, accumulation by dispossession, bears a specific mark: violence, a mark not borne by expanded reproduction. This is also mentioned by De Angelis (2001), who understands primitive accumulation as historically specific, on the one hand, but with elements of continuity on the other. According to De Angelis, the accumulation of labour power in the factory does not require violence other than the economic; for capital, the very condition of the proletarian guarantees that she will be back to sell her labour power because her subsistence depends on it. On the contrary, primitive accumulation *is* violent (De Angelis 2001: 14). We would have to ask the workers in China's economic miracle whether it was the violence of production in the factories that drove various of Foxconn's workers to suicide in 2010 (Stracke, Lendal and Johannisson 2013). When Harvey (2005) portrays accumulation by dispossession[1] as the capitalist solution to the problem of extended reproduction (which does not succeed in accumulating), he is only considering extended reproduction within the factory. However, 'accumulation by dispossession' is part of expanded reproduction. Commodity production requires labour power as well as raw materials: 'The causes which concentrate masses of labourers under the command of individual capitalists, are the very same that swell the mass of the invested fixed capital, and auxiliary and raw materials, in mounting proportion as compared to the mass of employed living labour' (Marx n.d.: 157–8).

Extreme Exploitation

Why does Marx speak of 1825 as the end of the industry's childhood? What happened? In the eighteenth and nineteenth centuries, a significant shift takes place from manufacture to the factory. With the development of machinery, the capitalists manage to prolong the workday 'to the limit of the natural day'; this was a time when 'capital was celebrating its orgies' (Marx 1976: 389–90). From the first third of the nineteenth century, long-lasting struggles break out demanding a reduction of the workday. The confrontations led to the enactment in the UK of a new Factory Act in 1847 (Marx 1976: 395): an intensive workday of 12, 14, 16 hours or more was reduced to a day of ten hours; absolute surplus value becomes relative. This refers to the way in which capital is valorised: working hours are reduced but the rhythm of exploitation increases due to the machinery. In turn, the increased speed in the factory also requires a rise in the exploitation of nature and a larger quantity of raw materials. The shift from absolute to relative surplus value reveals one of the limitations of the system: the tendency of the rate of profit to fall. The higher the fixed capital, the lower the inversion in variable capital. This is one of the contradictions of capital, for only human labour produces surplus value.[2] There is an effort to compensate for this through the increase of the mass of profit; that is, by increasing the market and extending capitalist relations. Furthermore, in this period, liberal states are consolidated, and England and France turn into reference points for other states. Colonies gain their independence, slavery is – in theory – abolished, and money begins to spread in the form of the salary.

From the viewpoint of accumulation, this is a change of era. Primitive accumulation that 'proceeded without the advance of even a shilling' (Marx 1976: 917) laid the foundations for the monetarisation of social relations. There was barely any money, and the money that did exist was not capitalised. Today money is practically all over the planet to a greater or lesser extent, be it real or fictitious; proletarianisation spread along with money and money spread along with proletarianisation. According to Rosa Luxemburg (2003), capitalism needs to absorb non-capitalist societies in order to maintain itself. But how many societies today are strangers to money? In certain places, such as many indigenous and rural communities in Mexico, we find mixed forms of economy including the partial, direct or indirect sale of labour power, as well as subsistence farming in private or communal plots. In some communities a family member may emigrate to a city in Mexico, the US or Canada (and send remittances back home); in others, men leave to work as seasonal workers in extensive farming plantations, or grow a specific produce to sell on the global market through intermediaries. This does not occur only in Mexico. Silvia Federici (2012) speaks of the 'feminisation of villages' in Africa, where women farm the land alone or form cooperatives because most of the men have emigrated. This state of semi-proletarianisation in certain communities – which protest 'in defense of life and territory' (Navarro 2014) against their dispossession by multinationals – shows that this is no longer primitive accumulation; capitalist relations have already semi-established themselves in our lives. Aid programmes promoted by governments and international economic organisations infuse money into rural areas. This fosters the abandonment of subsistence farming in favour of informal or wage labour, facilitating the access of capital to land and water.

Let us take a look at the recent example of China, where capitalist rationality has intensified to create surplus value through technological and scientific advances, the intensive exploitation of nature, and the exhausting pace of work in the Special Economic Zones (SEZs). These territories are under special legislation and offer great economic and environmental facilitations to transnational corporations out to exploit 'resources' (González García and Meza Lora 2009). As a result, 80 per cent of the country's rivers are contaminated making their water unfit for human consumption. Consequently, crops and fertile land have decreased (Fayanas Escuer 2006), 600 cities in the north suffer from water shortages due to industrialisation, and the air is highly contaminated, causing higher incidence rates of diseases such as cancer (Smith 2015). In 2012, 25 per cent of CO_2 emissions came from China. Most forests have been cut down (Smith 2015) and minerals are scarce. That is why, since 2000, the Chinese government has been urging state mining companies to conduct business abroad, offering low interest rates. On the one hand, the over-exploitation of nature has led to scarcity; on the other, China has an excess of capacity, technology and capital waiting to be realised (Lee 2014: 29).

As for the workers, those in the electronic sector perform between two and 32 movements per minute (Stracke, Lendal and Johannisson 2013). The internet has led to a different modality of accumulation than that of Fordism and Taylorism, based on large networks of global production with a more finely tuned division of labour due to displacement and subcontracts. This results in high turnover rates, wretched salaries, precariousness, a lack of benefits, and overcrowding in factory dormitories as well as in cities. At the time of maximum economic growth in China, salaries equalled 0.57 dollars per hour, forcing workers to work extra hours – which were and still are compulsory – leading to workdays of ten to 16 hours (Smith 2015). This is a case of absolute and relative surplus value combined in order to halt the falling rate of profit. The workers 'live' in the industrial complexes and pay for their poor nutrition and accommodation. Verbal and physical violence through the use of a system of fines and penalties completes the strategies of accumulation. Smith (2015) clearly states that working conditions in China today are not very different from those prevailing in England during the Industrial Revolution. This is only a half-truth: salaries might be similar and the long working hours as well, and we even find the use of the 'warm bed' system between one shift and the next. However, the intensity with which capital appropriates the labour force has grown exponentially. That is why revolts broke out in China the 1990s, followed by major uprisings in 2010 that attained a rise in salaries – even their doubling in certain cases – and certain social improvements (Gongchao 2014).

As for the reproduction of the labour force, women are still those responsible in society for the labour of care, even if many of us are now also selling our labour power, resulting in a double workday. Moreover, we observe an aggravation of violence: the murder, rape and torture of young female workers at the *maquilas* of Ciudad Juarez; the abduction of Yazidi women by the Islamic State; gang rapes such as the case of the 'wolf pack' in Spain or in India; the kidnapping of young girls to be used as sex slaves by armies or by human trafficking networks to be sold on the global market... The internet and advances in communication technology have perfected the trafficking of women and children around the world (Acharya 2013). This points towards a new disciplining, whose purpose is to keep women tied to the reproduction of the labour force and to the home. Violence is exerted for a reason.

The Capital-Life Contradiction

The combination of absolute and relative surplus value requires a greater amount of raw materials. The intensification of the exploitation of humans leads to the intensification of the exploitation of nature, which in turn results in the ecological disaster we all know. Large extensions of land which used to be fertile and fit for farming have become sterile because of intensive and extensive farming, extractivism, industry, the increasing consumption of commodities and the subsequent production of waste. The speed and extent of the exploitation of nature does not allow it to regenerate, producing what Bellamy Foster (2000) calls the 'metabolic rift' between human action and nature. We have been warned of the dangers of this 'natural' imbalance for life ever since the 1970s; and ever since, the rift has been getting deeper and deeper because of market expansion and technological advances. The result? Bad air quality, unfit for breathing in ever more parts of the planet; polluted oceans, rivers, and groundwater; less water for human consumption and farming; increased CO_2 emissions and record-breaking temperatures year after year. The poles are melting at a high speed and the change of seasons is chaotic; there is a rise in floods, droughts, tornadoes and increasingly violent storms; flora and fauna have been vanishing dangerously since the last third of the twentieth century in what has been called the 'sixth massive extinction', the first to be caused by humans (De Pracontal 2015). As money and commodities expand, the land is being depleted, the planet is getting too small.

However, what threatens life also challenges this system of production: the reduction of many minerals – oil and carbon, amongst others – is proof of this. That is why China is accumulating gold and other materials in an unconventional manner, something Lee calls 'encompassing accumulation' (2014: 36), which pursues long- and medium-term control of 'resources' rather than immediate surplus value. Meanwhile, the answer of international economic organisations to the 'scarcity' (of minerals, water, land, etc.) caused by this system of production and consumption is to propose further privatisations. There has been more and more talk recently of putting a price on water so as to avoid its 'waste' and ensure a fairer distribution. However, we already have the experience of the sale of carbon credits from 'green' industries: it did not reduce air contamination, it just put a price on it; it did not reduce pollution nor favour a 'fair' distribution of the necessary elements for life but rather turned them into new niche markets. The latter is a characteristic of terminary accumulation, other examples being the patenting of genetic material and of ancestral practical knowledge. It confirms that this form of social organisation is what limits water, air, land and life. Considering all the above-mentioned factors, can we continue calling this process primitive accumulation?

Let us now take a look at how this relates to the crisis of surplus value. The working-class struggles at the end of the nineteenth century and the beginning of the twentieth, followed by the 1929 stock market crash, forced the emergence of the welfare state. For the proletariat, this meant gaining a series of 'rights' such as pensions, health insurance, free education, the reduction of the workday, higher salaries, etc. Through these measures, capitalism and the states managed to pacify class struggle for 30 years. However, at the end of the 1960s a wave of opposition began which exploded in 1968 and continued into the 1970s. Students, feminists, ecologists, pacifists and antiracists, among others, profoundly challenged the system and revealed the absurdity of a form of social organisation based on destruction, hierarchies, money, commodities, and the false philosophy of economic progress that disregards nature and aims solely at subjugating it. This, along with the crisis of overaccumulation and the excess of fictitious money circulating in the US, led to the cancellation in 1971 of the convertibility of the dollar to gold that had regulated international trade since Bretton Woods in 1944. The crisis launched a period of fierce competition between states wanting to attract more capital. The fiscal, environmental and human advantages of the SEZs encouraged the move of investments from the US and Europe to Asia throughout the 1980s and 1990s. There, multinationals found an abundant and cheap labour force as well as practically unlimited access to natural 'resources'. Around the world, state-owned companies were being privatised, social expenses cut back, salaries stagnated, basic goods became more expensive, and the female labour force was massively incorporated into the labour market. The latter amounted to an increase in the work performed by women, in both the productive and the reproductive spheres. In production, they received lower salaries; in reproduction, none at all. Working and living conditions worsened but credit expansion managed to mitigate social conflict. The 2008 financial crisis once again brought to the surface capital's difficulties in realising surplus value; the lack of proportion between fictitious and real money, and the fallacy of the self-regulation of the market, became obvious. As occurred at the beginning of capitalism, credit played an important role, reflected in the overwhelming debt of many countries. 'Hence the paradox: so much money, so little capital' (Vela 2018: 102). Bank bailouts, redundancies, foreclosures and readjustments of social expenses wiped out the idea of the welfare state for good; not so the economic crisis, whose threat looms larger than ever. That is why states that used to sell gold are now buying it and stockpiling it. The state and capital are in a process of reconfiguration.

Capitalism no longer manifests itself as it did a few decades ago, nor as it did a few centuries ago. The forms of accumulation of labour and of raw materials have evolved at the same pace as the struggles against them have. Capital tries to absorb conflict.[3] However, the crises also reflect an overflowing of antagonism that goes beyond each separate moment of struggle: 'struggles for specific demands have a limit in time, but that does not mean that is the end of it, it does not mean they do not have medium or long-term effects on the structure of capital' (Vela 2018: 218). Our struggles are an attack on surplus value, be it because we break the rhythm of its movement, because capital is forced to pay higher salaries, or because the state has to invest more in social spending. Not everything goes, which is why 'we are the crisis of capital' (Holloway 2014).

What is clear is that the crisis of capital and the ecological crisis make the future increasingly uncertain. The emerging responses are contradictory: on the one hand we have fetishised answers that channel popular discontent towards support for left-wing parties, as happened in Greece, or in the worst cases towards far-right positions, as has happened in the US and Brazil. According to Esteva, we could be witnessing an unprecedented surge in authoritarian forms, worse than the fascisms of the past (2009: 18, 38). The Social Credit System in China – an ongoing government experiment which consists in a point system based on behaviour, consumption habits and the non-critique of the state, creating lists of good and bad citizens who are prized or punished (Chatellier 2018) – also moves in that direction. On the other hand, the catastrophe of terminary accumulation that is leading us into a terrible 'accident' for humanity – which is in fact by no means accidental – calls upon us to radically change our ways. There are many struggles in cities and rural areas to conserve that which makes life possible and imagine worlds beyond money, beyond commodities, beyond what exists. There is a change in sensitivities that becomes manifest in other forms of relating to each other and to nature, which tend to break with economic, sexual and racial hierarchies. In a way, they are the heirs to the struggles of the 1960s and 1970s, putting sensitive intelligence before rational intelligence, quality before quantity, what should be (the full life) before what is (the negated life). However, the time of capital stands against us; its pace is increasingly terrifying, its disasters more and more profound, with some – as we have seen – irreparable. And here lies the dilemma: either we take the path to social change or we go deeper into human tragedy.

References

Acharya, A. (2013) 'Mujeres invisibles y victimización sexual en México. El caso de la trata de mujeres en Monterrey' ('Invisible Women and Sexual Victimisation in Mexico: The Case of Trafficking in Women in Monterrey'), *Estudios Sociales* 21 (42), 233–58, www.redalyc.org/pdf/417/41728341010.pdf.

Anta Martínez, S. (2017) *Zautla y Olintla: la defensa de la vida frente a la acumulación terminaria* (Zautla and Olintla: The Defence of Life against Terminary Accumulation), Doctoral Thesis, ICSyH 'Alfonso Vélez Pliego', Puebla, Mexico.

Bellamy Foster, J. (2000) *Marx's Ecology: Materialism and Nature*, New York: Monthly Review Press.

Bonefeld, W. (2008) 'The Permanence of Primitive Accumulation: Commodity Fetishism and Social Constitution' in Bonefeld, W. (ed), (2008) *Subverting the Present, Imagining the Future*, New York: Autonomedia: 51–66.

Chatellier, R. (2018) 'Le Crédit Social chinoi et le dilemme étique de la confiance par notation' ('The Chinese Social Credit and the Ethical Dilemma of Trust by Rating'), https://linc.cnil.fr/fr/le-credit-social-chinois-et-le-dilemme-ethique-de-la-confiance-par-la-notation.

Dalla Costa, M. (1995) 'Capitalism and Reproduction', in W. Bonefeld, R. Gunn, J. Holloway and K. Psychopedis (eds), *Open Marxism 3*, London: Pluto Press, 7–16.

De Angelis, M. (2001) 'Marx and Primitive Accumulation: The Continuous Character of Capital's "Enclosures"' in Bonefeld, W. (ed), (2008) *Subverting the Present, Imagining the Future*, New York: Autonomedia, 27–50.

De Pracontal, M. (2015) 'La sixième extinction de masse a commencé' ('The Sixth Mass Extinction has Begun'), www.mediapart.fr/journal/international/270615/la-sixieme-extinction-de-masse-commence?onglet=full.

Esteva, G. (2009) 'La crisis como esperanza' ('Crisis as Hope'), *Bajo el Volcán* 14: 17–53.

Fayanas Escuer, E. (2006) 'China y su grave crisis hídrica' (China and its Serious Water Problem), www.rebelion.org/noticia.php?id=25099.

Federici, S. (2004) *Caliban and the Witch: Women, the Body and Primitive Accumulation*, New York: Autonomedia.

Federici, S. (2012) 'The Unfinished Feminist Revolution', *The Commoner* 15, www.commoner.org.uk/wp-content/uploads/2012/02/08-federici.pdf.

Gongchao (2014) 'Revueltas en China. Ataque capitalista y luchas sociales' ('Revolts in China. Capitalist Attack and Social Struggles'), www.gongchao. org.

González García, J. and Meza Lora, J. S. (2009) 'Shenzhen, zona económica especial: bisagra de la apertura económica y el desarrollo regional chino. Problemas del Desarrollo' ('Shenzhen, Special Economic Zone: A Hinge for Economic Openness and Chinese Regional Growth'), *Revista Latinoamericana de Economía* 40(156): 101–24.

Graeber, D. (2011) *Debt: The First 5,000 Years*, New York: Melville House.

Gunn, R. (2018) '¿Qué es el proletariado?' ('What is the Proletariat?'), *Comunizar*, http://comunizar.com.ar/proletariado-richard-gunn.

Harvey, D. (2005) *The New Imperialism*, Oxford: Oxford University Press.

Hernández Contreras, F. and Zhenheng, J. (2007) 'Las Relaciones Comerciales de Mexico y China en la Historia' ('Commercial Relations between Mexico and China Throughout History'), *Observatorio de la Economía y la Sociedad de China* 5, www.eumed.net/rev/china.

Holloway, J. (2010) *Cambiar el mundo sin tomar el poder*, Puebla: Sísifo Ediciones, Bajo Tierra Ediciones and ICSyH-BUAP.

Holloway, J. (2014) 'Communise!', in S. Brincat (ed.), *Communism in the 21st Century*, Vol. 3, Santa Barbara: Praeger.

Holloway, J. (2018) 'Marx, Civilised or Savage?', *Dialogue and Universalism* 28(3): 101–6.

Kurz, R. (2014) 'On the Current Global Economic Crisis: Questions and Answers', in N. Larsen, M. Nilges, J. Robinson and N. Brown (eds), *Marxism and the Critique of Value*, Chicago: MCM', 331–56.

Lee Ching, K. (2014) 'The Spectre of Global China', *New Left Review* 89: 29–65.

Luxemburg, R. (2003) *The Accumulation of Capital*, London: Routledge.

Marx, K. (1976) *Capital*, Vol. 1, London: Penguin.

Marx, K. (n.d.) *Capital*, Vol. 3, New York: International Publishers.

Navarro, M. (2014) *Luchas por lo común. Antagonismo social contra el renovado cercamiento y despojo capitalista de los bienes naturales en México* (Struggles for the Commons: Social Antagonism Against the Renewed Capitalist Enclosure and Appropriation of Natural Resources in Mexico), Doctoral Thesis, ICSyH, Puebla, Mexico.

Ortlieb, C. P. (2014) 'A Contradiction between Matter and Form: On the Significance of the Production of Relative Surplus Value in the Dynamic of Terminal Crisis', in N. Larsen, M. Nilges, J. Robinson and N. Brown (eds), *Marxism and the Critique of Value*, Chicago: MCM', 77–122.

Smith, R. (2015) 'China: "accidentes de trabajo" y desastre ecológico', www.
sinpermiso.info/textos/china-accidentes-de-trabajo-y-desastre-ecolgico.

Stracke S., Lendal N. and Johannisson F. (2013) *Eléctronica low cost. Estudio de
las condiciones laborales de cuatro proveedores de Dell en China* (Electronica
Low Cost. A Study of Working Conditions in Four Suppliers of Dell in China),
Setem Cataluna.

Vela, C. (2018) *Capitalismo terminal. Anotaciones a la sociedad implosiva*
(Terminal Capitalism: Notes on Implosive Society), Madrid, España: Traficantes de sueños.

Wallerstein, I. (1995) *After Liberalism*, New York: The New Press.

Notes

1. Apart from the accumulation of natural spaces and wealth, Harvey also
   includes in this category the speculation of financial capital, intellectual
   property, seed and genetic material patents, the privatisation of public
   services and of water, etc.

2. Value is the socially necessary labour time required to produce a commodity.
   Surplus value is the extra value appropriated by capital once the 'cost' of maintaining the worker is covered. With the reduction of the time the proletariat
   spends in the factories and the increase of the exploitation due to machines,
   the price of the product also goes down, given that less time is required for
   its fabrication. As a result, the price of labour power also decreases. The use
   of machinery also requires less workers, leading to the reduction of the rate
   of profit if the rate of surplus value and the degree of exploitation remain
   constant (Marx n.d.).

3. For example, by incorporating women into the labour market, controlling
   trade unions and education institutions, giving into certain demands for
   social improvements, etc.

7

The State and Global Capital: Revisiting the Debate

Rodrigo Pascual and Luciana Ghiotto

An assertion runs through Marxism, particularly the Marxism that studies international politics and international political economy: state domination is founded on a specific territory and is limited by it, while capital is capable of overcoming such determinations. But is this difference self-evident?

From the viewpoint of the concept of capital, to accept this dichotomy would be to assume that state and capital are separate entities following a completely different logic. As a way of advancing in a critique of this false dichotomy, we suggest the state be understood as a particularised form of the capital relation, one that is constituted on a territorial basis, but whose domination depends on the broader reproduction of capital at a global scale. Its relation with the 'outside' is immanent to it – it is a precondition for its reproduction. It is also the reason why territoriality-deterritoriality, as Clarke (2001) points out, should not be understood as a dichotomous relationship but rather as a contradictory form rooted in the separation between the process of production and that of circulation.

In what follows, we shall show that the territoriality (production) and globality (circulation) that are embedded in capital create a tension in class domination and exploitation that is expressed in state theories and, more specifically, in the debate on the internationalisation of capitalist social relations. We shall also approach this tension as the result of social antagonism and as a mode of deployment that is specific to domination and class exploitation.

In this chapter we embark on a short journey through the literature that has addressed state theory and its ties to the global market; we shall critically revisit the debate on the relation between the state, multinationals and imperialism from the 1970s until today; we will recover the more recent contributions made by the authors of open Marxism to these debates; and, finally, we will reach our conclusions from this perspective, conclusions that aim at breaking with the realism of international relations and, more specifically, with notions of imperialism that ultimately depend on viewing the state as an entity that is fixed to a specific territory (production) as opposed to the deterritorial form of capital (circulation).

Spinning the Wheel: Inter-state Relations,
the Economy and Politics as Fixed Environments

Alongside the cycle of revolutionary struggles of the 1960s, Marxists once again debated the specificity of the capitalist state. One of the aspects of this debate addressed inter-state relationships amidst the increasing internationalisation of production and the emergence of multinational enterprises. The backdrop was shaped by the advances and setbacks of the European Economic Community (EEC) procedures. This debate forged crucial perspectives on the relationship between the state, the international state system, the market, and the global market. Furthermore, the sides taken on this issue are the key to understanding the relation between (state) territoriality and (capital) deterritoriality.

We shall, for lack of space, summarise these postures in three perspectives: politicist, economicist and dialectic. As we cannot be very thorough, our references will focus on the more illustrative authors within each perspective.

According to the economicist approach, the internationalisation of production modifies political superstructures. In this sense, Ernest Mandel (1969) believed the EEC complied with the process of capital concentration and centralisation (which resulted in transnationalisation) that would lead to a change in the legal forms of capital. Supranationality is considered a necessary movement, a 'reflection' of transformations in the forms of property.

Within this perspective but with certain nuances, Robin Murray (1971) argued that capitalist social relations had donned an international guise from the very beginning. However, the expansion of capital had been accompanied by that of the state, leading to the coincidence of state and capital territoriality. This was initially due to the fact that the two observed the same spatiality. The internationalisation of capital broke the historical link between states and capitals; capital was no longer directly related to the state in which it had been born. With its expansion to other territories, capital made receiving states develop functions to help it grow. According to Murray, the tie between capital and the state needed reinstating.

The politicist perspective, on the other hand, considers that (central) states drive the process of internationalisation as representatives of their own bourgeoisies. This viewpoint was adopted by Bill Warren (1971) and it was not long before he initiated a debate with Murray. Warren considered the expansion of capitals beyond their borders as a state-led process. He pointed out that this process reinforced the states insofar as it expanded their activities.

Following a similar line of argumentation, Nicos Poulantzas (1976, 1979) claimed that the process of internationalisation took place under the critical domination of North American capital. He pointed out that the expansion of the latter affected the class structure (structures and processes of hegemonisation) of the states that housed the bourgeoisie of the United Sates. Thus, the thesis supported by Poulantzas opposed that of Mandel. Internationalisation was not an endogenous process but, rather, an effect of the imperialist penetration of the United States into the rest of the metropolises.

During the 1980s and 1990s, the distinction between politicist and economicist perspectives gradually faded and the two coalesced. They were, in a way, viewed as complementary. This is where Gramscian contributions come into play. Author of reference Robert Cox (1981) developed the idea of globalisation as a process launched by the central states and financial capital. The rest of the states operated as transmission belts. Also from a Gramscian point of view, but embracing some of the ideas articulated by Poulantzas, Kees Van der Pijl (1998) understood globalisation as an effect of the transnationalisation of the bourgeoisies. The latter were considered the main promoters of globalisation and the administrators of the supranational tools of the global economy. Indeed, the transnational capitalist class represented capital globally as a cosmopolitan class. This thesis is now being further developed by William Robinson. More recently, a group of German Poulantzian scholars made contributions from a Poulantzian perspective; however, imbued as they are by the derivation debate, they display certain nuances.

Despite their differences, these contributions agree on the following: when thinking of the process of capital internationalisation, one must understand international organisations as second-order condensations (first-order being capital) that express power relations between classes and within classes (Brand, Görg and Wissen 2011). These organisations, they argue, can effectively intervene in class struggle because they are more unstable. This can seem like a weakness at first, but at the same time it strengthens them for they can appear and disappear as needed. Furthermore, the authors claim, the process of globalisation involves the blocking of social demands, disturbing the mechanisms of state legitimation (Hirsch 2010; Hirsch and Wissel 2011; Wissel and Wolff 2017). They also observe that there have been shifts in the forms of territorial domination (Wissel and Wolff 2017; Brand, Görg and Wissen 2011) creating a multi-scaled power which, in turn, involves a process that differs from the idea of deterritorialisation. This originates in the incomplete transnationalisation of the bourgeoisie (Hirsch and Wissel 2011) and in the fact that each state retained the monopoly of violence in its hands (Hirsch 2010; Hirsch and Wissel 2011).

From the beginning of the 1990s until today, Ellen Meiksins Wood (2003), Alex Callinicos (2009) and David Harvey (2005) have also made valuable contributions that can be placed within the politicist perspective. Internationalisation, they argue, is promoted by a certain type of economic imperialism based on the separation of the political and the economic, and expresses an expansionist logic focused on capital accumulation. At the same time, however, it assumes a territorial logic that contradicts the logic of accumulation and leads to a particular type of imperialism. In addition, they point out that the current phase of capitalism is far from overcoming inter-imperialist disputes. In this sense, there is a rivalry between what they call the global triad: the US, Europe and Asia. Panitch and Gindin (2013) support a similar thesis, although with some variations. Unlike the others, they argue that internationalisation is the result of a process promoted by US imperialism.

With a vision that leans towards politicism and follows along the tradition of Robert Brenner – but is strongly influenced by the derivation debate and especially by the work of Claudia von Braunmühl – Benno Teschke (2003) and Hannes Lacher (2006) launched a debate when they argued that the current international state system can be traced back to the birth of capitalism. They pointed out that, from a logical-conceptual perspective, the state is not necessary for the development of capitalist social relations. Furthermore, they claimed that, since the emergence of capitalism and as a result of sovereign powers competing against each other, states have been divided. This led to the exportation of capitalist social relations which, on occasions, were founded on territorial sovereignties. From this point of view, the internationalisation of capital proves that the relation between capital and the state is not a *sine qua non*.

A Few Critical Comments: On Economicism and Politicism

The economicist vision sheds light on the power shifts towards supranational instances while at the same time argues that there cannot be a complete disconnection between the form of appropriation and its legal foundation. In this sense, the territorialisation of production seems to be crucial in understanding the spatiality of domination. However, it fails to explain the link between this in/adequacy and the development of class antagonism. Indeed, the shifts seem to respond to a certain mechanics that goes from capital to the state or towards its supranational substitute.

The politicist viewpoint allows for a better understanding of the transformations of class structures and attends to an issue of relevance: the relation between the metropolises. In this sense, its contribution looks into the persistence of the inter-capitalist dispute and its inter-state continuity (anti-imperialist struggle). Moreover, it stresses the fundamental role of the US in this process. However, just as in the other vision, here too class struggle is absent. In this case, it is concealed behind the nebulous haze of inter-state dispute; when it is present, it remains subordinate to the inter-bourgeois dispute. This results in a realist (Marxist?) approach to the study of international relations (Callinicos 2007). In one of its variations, however, class struggle does make an appearance, albeit in dual form. The German scholars of Poulantzas appear at times to be referring to class struggle as a mediation of a process, while at others they seem to grant it a prevailing role.

To sum up, this perspective links the territoriality of the state to the results of the inter-imperialist dispute. The work of Callinicos, Ellen Meiksins Wood and, more systematically, David Harvey approaches the main problem through this lens: there are two colliding logics of capitalist development. On one hand, an expansionist and therefore deterritorialising logic of accumulation. On the other, the state logic, immobile and tied to one territory. This involves a specific, strictly economic type of imperialism.

Indeed, both visions (the politicist and the economicist) are founded on the same premise: the political and the economic are two autonomous spheres that relate to each other in a relatively autonomous (external) way. This duality makes analyses leap from economic reductionism to political reductionism. Moreover, it includes (or entails) an instrumental vision of the state and, therefore, of inter-state relations, whereby competition (inter-bourgeois/inter-state) subsumes class struggle. Both visions embrace a certain identification of state and bourgeoisie which results in the analysis of strategies rather than an understanding of the mode in which class antagonism unfolds. This leads to sociological views of the process of internationalisation and, as Hugo Radice (2015) points out, in some cases to reformist and idealist visions of Keynesianism. The proposal of a global New Deal made by Harvey (2005) and Callinicos (2009) moves in that direction.

Regarding the matter at hand, the Poulantzian vision developed by the German scholars seems paradigmatic of this perspective. Indeed, supranationality is the result of neoliberal strategy (Wissel and Wolff 2017). This coincides with their idea that international organisations are the most effective means of intervention in class struggle because of their relative capacity to appear and disappear according to how class struggle unfolds. That is why the latter certainly appears to be bound to the rationality of the bourgeoisie and to inter-state policies. Therefore, the in/adequacy of the spatiality between state territoriality and the process of accumulation is subordinated to the result of opposing inter-bourgeois strategies.

Taking this vision to the extreme, Panitch and Gindin – as we have already pointed out – argue that the internationalisation (globalisation) of capitalism is the outcome of US imperial expansion; therefore, in/adequacy is not a problem to the extent that they seem to fall back onto a variant of Kautsky's thesis on 'ultraimperialism'. Furthermore, Lacher and Teschke's proposal on the lack of historical need for a state is very intriguing and allows for an understanding of the continuous in/adequacy between the territoriality of the state and the tendency of capital to deterritorialise. However, this blurs the difference between logical and historical order in the construction of categories. Indeed, if there is an internal relationship between genesis and existence, as Marx seems to suggest in his understanding of primitive accumulation (Bonefeld 2013), then capitalism would be better understood as being reproduced vis-à-vis the division of the world into multiple states. Moreover, this perspective pays little attention to class antagonism and thus seems to conceal an underlying historicist vision, one focused on competition, very much like Brenner's.

When compared to each other, these perspectives seem to share the view that capital and the state follow two different logics. One is territorial; the other is either deterritorial or at least has the capacity to become deterritorialised. As the economicist perspective suggests, this tension lies in the very logic of capitalist accumulation, where the production relation remains crucial. That is, the cause for the shifts can ultimately be found in the transformation of the forms of producing and appropriating surplus value.

From Derivation to Open Marxism

The third perspective, which can be broadly named as dialectic, originates theoretically in the new reading of Marx's *Capital* launched at the end of the 1960s. This reading resonated in the critique of the state that shaped what became known as the German debate or the state derivation theory. A specific discussion was forged within this debate on the link between the state and the global market. Participants included Elmar Altvater, Klaus Busch, Christel Neusüss and Claudia von Braunmühl.

They certainly shared the same starting point: the state and the market should be understood as necessary forms of capitalist social relations. They also coincided in that the international system had to be considered from the viewpoint of the unity of the global market, and they stressed the primacy of this unity in providing an explanation. In this sense, the passages of the *Grundrisse* on the global market served as a common reference point within the debate. However, they differed as to which social relations rendered the existence of the state necessary (competition, exploitation or common interest) (Holloway and Picciotto 1978). As a result, they disagreed on how the state/bourgeoisie relationship was produced. This was also reflected in the way in which they understood inter-state competition.

The legacy of Claudia von Braunmühl (1978) in this debate has been crucial in advancing the Marxist critique of inter-state relations. One of her main contributions, and perhaps the most relevant for our perspective, is her argument that the capitalist world should be understood as constituted by a multiplicity of states competing against each other. The global market (just like the international state system) is not the sum of its parts but rather a fragmented totality. Von Braunmühl also coincided with Heide Gerstenberger (2007) in stressing the importance of giving the debate a historical dimension. She pointed out the role of the inter-imperialist dispute during the transition, even before Lacher and Teschke launched the debate. This dispute tended to structure the dynamic of capitalist inter-state relations. However, von Braunmühl stressed that this dynamic follows a different set of contents, for it is subordinated to accumulation and, therefore, is more of an inter-capitalist competition than a struggle between sovereigns.

The premises that steered the debate – the totality of the global market and the international state system as the starting point, fragmented in statified spaces mediated by competition – lead to the very negation of the term 'imperialism'. Indeed, von Braunmühl considered it a conservative concept; however, none of the participants took the debate far enough so as to question the notion of imperialism itself.

The debate on the global market must be praised for fuelling an interesting discussion on the possibility of deepening European integration in the context of the capitalist crisis of the 1970s; a discussion which, nevertheless, did not flourish and was quickly interrupted. At the end of the 1980s and beginning of the 1990s, Peter Burnham, John Holloway, Werner Bonefeld and Simon Clarke followed in the footsteps of the previous authors. However, Holloway, Picciotto and Clarke had been imbued by the analyses of the derivation debate since the 1970s, forging a particular approach to the state. Their persistence in understanding capitalist reality and its categories as modes of existence of class struggle, therefore open to possibility, led to the name 'open Marxism' and constituted a leap forward in the debate.

The starting point for the authors was the assumption that state and market are forms of the same antagonistic social relations between capital and labour. The emergence of capitalism results from the separation of producers from the means of production. This historical process led to the separation of exploitation and domination and to a logical and historical division between the economic and the political. The existence of a separate instance of labour exploitation is necessary and immanent in the capital relation, but its appearance as a state is the outcome of the historical contingency of class antagonism.

This aspect had been pointed out by Gerstenberger (2007). The fragmented existence of the world in sovereign states was a result of the transition.

Clarke (2001) argued that the transition to capitalism involved a process of subordination of personal sovereignties to the law of property and the movement of money. The forms of impersonal sovereignty (the state) became tied to the movements of capital accumulation or, in other words, to the logic of capital, understood as the unfolding of the antagonism between capital and labour. Therefore, from this viewpoint, the notion of imperialism loses analytical efficacy and, more importantly, reveals its reactionary content. As Marcel Stoetzler (2018) points out, to understand the global expansion of capitalism through a Marxist lens one needs nothing but the concept of capital. And to perceive inter-state relations all one requires is the notion of competition as the mode of existence of class struggle (Bonefeld 1999).

In this sense, Burnham, Bonefeld, Holloway and Clarke pointed out that capital's process of internationalisation is inherent to capitalism and not a novelty. The modality assumed by capitalism after the 1970s is understood as the product of the crisis of relations of domination and exploitation; therefore, it is the result of the bourgeoisie reacting to labour power. Along this line, Werner Bonefeld (2004) showed that the emergence of the European Union following the Maastricht Treaty was an offensive of capital through the imposition of monetary discipline. The attachment of all EU states to the movements of the European Central Bank resulted in the blocking of social demands and in a tendency to impose value at the EU scale. This perspective of internationalisation involves the opening up of the money category (euro), allowing not only for the understanding of processes of inter-state integration – such as the EU – as the outcome and form of development of class antagonism, but also for the rejection of economicist and politicist instrumentalism as well as of any notion such as imperialism. Moreover, the political and economic spatialities linked to these processes of globalisation and regionalisation can and must be understood as modes of existence of the development of class antagonism.

Territoriality, Circulation, Production and Class Antagonism

In the first section we argued that assuming the concept of capital as our starting point allows us to question the dichotomy between the territoriality of state political rule and the deterritoriality of capital. Thus, following Clarke's argumentation, the state is a particular form of the capital relation that is constituted on a territorialised basis but whose rule depends on the large-scale, global reproduction of capital. Insofar as global accumulation is the assumption and ultimate goal of capitalism, not only can no state choose to relate to others, its power actually depends on the power of capital at a global scale. The reproduction of other states is a requirement for its own reproduction. Thus, territoriality-deterritoriality must not be understood as a dichotomous relationship but as a contradiction (Clarke 2001) rooted in class antagonism which, in turn, results in the constitution of capitalist social relations that are fragmented into a multiplicity of states. This tension between territorial *state* and deterritorial *capital* is not immanent in the concept of capital but rather responds to this historical result and is, therefore, subject to class struggle.

However, the latter shows that state territoriality is rooted in the need to territorialise production but is not a matter of reason; state territoriality is the result of class struggle. Indeed, as Lacher and Teschke point out, the division between political rule and economic exploitation does not require territorialisation in the sense of a separation of the world into states. Production, in turn, does, while circulation tends to exceed this territoriality. The separation between production and circulation is founded on a spatiality of rule divided into territories, thus becoming a source of tension for the reproduction of capital mediated by the fragmented existence of territorial states.

The contradiction is not to be found between the territoriality of the political forms of capital and the deterritoriality of capital, but rather in the fact that the deterritoriality of circulation contradicts the territoriality of production insofar as both production and circulation are mediated by states. This contradiction appears on the social surface as territorial state and deterritorial capital. The tension is ingrained in all states and can appear as deficit in trade balances, monetary pressures leading to devaluation, flight of capital, the need to attract foreign investment and at the same time seek to contain the flow of remittances, etc.

Indeed, the territoriality of production is determined by the relative territoriality of the labour force. And we say relative because this relation is attenuated by migratory flows – but it is not eliminated. Production always depends on a moment of fixing capital, of turning money into constant capital and effectively exploiting the labour force. And it is this exploitation of the labour force that is exercised under the rule of capital in a territory that is delimited as a state. But even so, it was not the territoriality of domination that demanded the emergence of the territorial state, it was rather a historical contingency, a result of class struggle. However, as domination was founded on territorial state political forms, the territoriality of production tended to coincide with state spatiality.

The growing internationalisation of capital – more specifically, the internationalisation of productive processes that began in the 1970s – tended to deepen the gap between the territoriality of the state and the deterritoriality of capital, leading to increasing processes of deterritorialisation of political domination. The processes of regional integration and the organisations that regulate global trade and production can be understood this way.

However, none of this is a natural process or an objective logic of capital. As Holloway, Bonefeld, Negri, Caffentzis and others have shown in numerous works, the internationalisation of the productive processes was capital's response to the growing labour power that had emerged through anticapitalist struggles in the postwar era. In other words, the relation between circulation/production and its articulation with territorial political domination is the result of class antagonism and is modified according to it.

Nonetheless, it should be pointed out that production is more fragmented by states than circulation. This is because the exploitation of labour requires a determined territoriality that has assumed the historical form of the state. Thus, surplus value is realised in a fragmented way through state borders, mediated by competition. Once again, however, the internationalisation of productive processes not only tends to attenuate this fragmentation but also exercises pressure, giving way to a new spatiality of domination. A multi-scaled territoriality, insofar as it coexists with state political forms.

Furthermore, one must not lose sight of the fact that production and circulation are a unit, even if they are separated. Production takes place in the sphere of circulation. To approach this unity in relation to its territorial and deterritorial nature is crucial in breaking with the fetish of the territorialised state and deterritorialised capital. Precisely because, as they are both moments of the same social relations, territoriality/deterritoriality is not the result of the existence of the state but is rather inscribed in the logic itself of the reproduction of capital. However, insofar as production is mediated by competition and by the existence of states, the latter appear as if the nature of political forms were determined by the territorial dimension; as if it were attached to them.

In other words, the expansion of the state beyond its own territorial limits has to be understood as what generates the conditions for the large-scale reproduction of capital. And it does so while mediating inter-capitalist competition and partaking in it. This (competition) is the way in which the state goes 'beyond' its borders. In this sense, the process of expansion is inherent in the accumulation of capital mediated by competition.

Indeed, all states need to reproduce the conditions for accumulation within their borders and compete against each other to attain said reproduction. Their relation is one of competition, but the ultimate substratum is the exploitation of labour. This emerges as mere inter-state competition, as realism. In this sense, inter-state relations appear on the social surface as relations of a competitive and also cooperative nature. Insofar as they are mediations, these relations conceal the underlying relations of exploitation. This can even render inter-capitalist competition invisible, precisely due to the very nature of global-scale exploitation mediated by the existence of states.

References

Bonefeld, W. (1999) 'Notes on Competition, Capitalist Crises, and Class', *Historical Materialism* 5(1): 5–28.

Bonefeld, W. (2004) 'Class and EMU', *The Commoner* 5, www.commoner.org.uk/bonefeld05.pdf. 26.06.2004.

Bonefeld, W. (2013) *La razón corrosive*, Buenos Aires: Herramienta.

Brand, U., Görg, C. and Wissen, M. (2011) 'Second-Order Condensations of Societal Power Relations: Environmental Politics and the Internationalization of the State from a Neo-Poulantzian Perspective', *Antipode* 43(1): 149–75.

Braunmühl, C. von (1978) 'On the Analysis of the Bourgeois Nation State within the World Market Context', in J. Holloway and S. Picciotto (eds), *State and Capital: A Marxist Debate*, London: Edward Arnold, 160–78.

Callinicos, A. (2007) 'Does Capitalism Need the State System?', *Cambridge Review of International Affairs* 20(4): 533–49.

Callinicos, A. (2009) *Imperialism and Global Political Economy*, Cambridge: Polity Press.

Clarke, S. (2001) 'Class Struggle and the Global Overaccumulation of Capital', in R. Albritton, M. Itoh, R. Westra and A. Zuege (eds), *Phases of Capitalist Development*, Basingstoke: Palgrave, 1–14.

Cox, R. (1981) 'Social Forces, States, and World Orders: Beyond International Relations Theory', *Millennium: Journal of International Studies* 10(2): 126–52

Gerstenberger, H. (2007) *Impersonal Power*, Chicago: Haymarket.

Harvey, D. (2005) *The New Imperialism*, Oxford: Oxford University Press.

Hirsch, J. (2010) *Teoría materialista do Estado: processos de transformação do sistema capitalista de Estados*, Rio de Janeiro: Editora Revan.

Hirsch, J. and Wissel, J. (2011) 'The Transformation of Contemporary Capitalism and the Concept of a Transnational Capitalist Class: A Critical Review in

Neo-Poulantzian Perspective', *Studies in Political Economy. A Socialist Review* 88(1): 7–22.

Holloway, J. and Picciotto, S. (1978) 'Towards a Materialist Theory of the State', in J. Holloway and S. Picciotto (eds), *State and Capital: A Marxist Debate*, London: Edward Arnold, 1–32.

Lacher, H. (2006) *Beyond Globalization: Capitalism, Territoriality and the International Relations of Modernity*, Abingdon: Routledge.

Mandel, E. (1969) *Ensayos sobre el neocapitalismo*, Mexico City: Era.

Meiksins Wood, E. (2003) *The Empire of Capital*, London: Verso.

Murray, R. (1971) 'The Internationalization of Capital and the Nation State', *New Left Review* 67: 36–62.

Panitch, L. and Gindin, S. (2013) *The Making of Global Capitalism: The Political Economy of American Empire*, London: Verso.

Picciotto, S. (1991) 'The Internationalisation of the State', *Capital & Class* 43: 43–63.

Poulantzas, N. (1976) 'La internacionalización de las relaciones capitalistas y el estado nación', in N. Poulantzas, *Las clases sociales en el capitalismo actual*, Mexico City: Siglo XXI.

Poulantzas, N. (1979) 'The Internationalisation of Capitalist Relations and the Nation State', in *Social Classes in Contemporary Capitalism*, London: Verso.

Radice, H. (2015) *Global Capitalism: Selected Essays*, New York: Routledge.

Stoetzler, M. (2018) 'Critical Theory and the Critique of Anti-Imperialism', in B. Best, W. Bonefeld and C. O'Kane (eds), *The Sage Handbook of Frankfurt School Critical Theory*, London: Sage, 1467–86.

Teschke, B. (2003) *The Myth of 1648: Class, Geopolitics and the Making of Modern International Relations*, London: Verso.

Van der Pijl, K. (1984) *The Making of an Atlantic Ruling Class*, London: Verso.

Warren, B. (1971) 'The Internationalization of Capital and the Nation State: A Comment', *New Left Review* 68: 24–48.

Wissel, J. and Wolff, S. (2017) 'Political Regulation and the Strategic Production of Space: The European Union as a Post-Fordist State Spatial Project', *Antipode* 49(1): 12–27.

PART III

DEMOCRACY, REVOLUTION
AND EMANCIPATION

8

The Proletariat versus the Working Class: Shifts in Class Struggle in the Twenty-first Century

Katerina Nasioka

Revolutionary theory – in all its different variations – explores the possibilities of social emancipation and the overcoming of class society. However, only a few of its variants place *doing* at its core; not individual doing as isolated activity but, more specifically, the *doing* that is inherently social, as social flow.[1] For the Marx of the 1859 Preface (1976: 4), this social character is expressed in the *definite relations* among people *in the social reproduction of their existence*. However, these relations are not controlled directly by them, they 'are independent of their will, namely, relations of production corresponding to a determinate stage of development of their material forces of production' (Marx 1976: 3). Throughout the historical development of capitalism these relations have constituted a world of domination that seems to negate any (future) perspective. The social flow of *doing* appears fragmented, enclosed within the modality of capitalist *producing*, which constantly confirms the divisions of social relations and, therefore, its very domination: property, money, commodity, value. Every single day and in many different ways we become witnesses 'of an untrue world' (Holloway 2002: 2). What can we do to overturn it? The following analysis revolves around and moves within this question.

At the dawn of the twenty-first century, anticapitalist struggle displays two mutually contradicting dynamics which reflect the intensity of the crisis and the sharpening of contradictions in the capital *relation*. On the one hand, the dominant form of political organisation of the labour class during the twentieth century, hegemonised by the labour movement and the Leninist canon, considered the cornerstone of organisation: labour party, trade union, workers' control of the state and society. This form is hard to assert in the present-day context. Neither can the corresponding attachment of the worker to the hegemonic identity of the labour class be confirmed. While the existence of trade unions or workers' organisations around the world can hardly be ignored, the plan of the working class to take over power (or the means of production), and attain a society controlled by the workers that will overturn class society, cannot be considered hegemonic any more. On the other hand, however, the struggles against capital – of an increasingly defensive/demand-placing character in most cases – are still often fought under the slogan 'we are workers', or look for class unity in the categories that have built the identity of the labour movement (nation, state). Therefore, while the potential for organisation on the basis of previous political mediations by the labour class is debilitated, the *political dimension* of revolution as rendered central by the Leninist canon – the idea of *political revolution* through the figure of a new type of party that was activated by the anticapitalist practice of the twentieth century and harshly criticised after the 1970s – is, in a way, still in place.[2] This is a contradiction I shall try to describe further on. The debilitation of the 'worker identity' – which was never completely solid to begin with, not even at the height of the hegemony of the labour movement – and the impossibility of class unity urgently challenge the relation between social struggles and the prospect of revolution.[3] What shifts are observed in class struggle today? Can they be translated into a prospect that goes *against-and-beyond*[4] capitalist society?

Proletariat, the Working Class and Non-Identity

We are still, in the early twenty-first century, dealing with the crisis that broke out in the 1970s and persists until today, a crisis that has been only partially successful in restructuring capitalist accumulation. Its characteristics force us to look for the links or ruptures that it, along with its contradictions and delegitimisations, brings to anticapitalist struggle:[5] there is a huge growth of the productive force, the concentration and centralisation of capital, and the acceleration of accumulation; huge quantities of capital are left un-valorised, immense masses of active labour power are placed on the shelf; exploitation is intensified, and then intensified some more; surplus populations serve as reserve armies, as a 'stagnant' labour force';[6] and the ragged-proletariat is on the rise.[7] This is, certainly, no exceptional circumstance; it is in the 'nature' of the capitalist form of production, as Marx characteristically notes, *for the working class to produce along with capital accumulation* 'the means by which it is itself made relatively superfluous' (1990: 783).

Neither can we insinuate the 'end' of commodity-producing labour, for 'this surplus population also becomes, conversely, the lever of capitalist accumulation, indeed it becomes a condition for the existence of the capitalist mode of production' (Marx 1990: 784). However, the frequent manifestations of the crisis after the 1970s – its intensity, especially since 2008, which has led to it being considered one of the most profound crises since the Great Depression; the slow pace of capital accumulation; the 'long-term slowdown in economic growth rates' (Endnotes 2013);[8] the fierce competition unleashed between private capitals – all these factors render this crisis (or its more recent subsequent appearances) particularly vehement as to its dynamic to reform social relations. Nevertheless, this is, above all, the crisis of our times.

During the twentieth century, the struggle against exploitation had been indissolubly linked to the organised workers' movement which, throughout the centuries, had acquired the identity of a unified revolutionary subject: 'the working class'. An emancipatory vision was forged on the basis of the unifying class condition ('wage labour') and with factory machines working at full capacity. This vision was not the only existing one,[9] but it was the one that became dominant amongst the proletariat: the construction of a fair society of workers, where the deprived producers of social wealth – the vital force of this world – would gain control of the means of production and the wealth they produce. This twentieth-century image of emancipated society sealed the state-centred character of revolution as well as the corresponding acknowledgement of a common culture and experience of struggle as the tangible everyday reality of the proletariat both in and out of the workplace.

Today's surplus labour, the redundant working population, makes it clear that this relation – class belonging – can no longer be confirmed.[10] Of course, the armies of the unemployed do not cease to be part of the proletariat. However, they continue to be so in a way that, in today's context, cannot validate its unity as 'working class' but exists as a reserve army that continually highlights the separations of the proletariat by capital. The deconstruction of the foundations on which working-class unity was built in the twentieth century practically amounts to the loss of the material reality through which the proletariat was reproduced in the past, and entails, therefore, the increasing exclusion of the proletariat from the produced wealth in its present-day social form (commodities).

However, it is not only these surplus populations that are excluded from all the practices and processes that previously allowed them to identify with a 'normal' working life (a salary, full-time, permanent employment, etc.). Workers who have not been excluded from the labour market experience equally precarious conditions. In this sense, a paradox is created in which *exclusion*[11] is not a condition outside labour and capital, one which would allow us to consider that labour itself has been overcome. The labour form that has become consolidated all around the world today involves incorporation in the capitalist system through the exclusion from all that this incorporation meant in the past, from all that supported the united interests of the working class: work becomes precarious, its relation with the proletariat becomes blurred, the dividing lines between employment and unemployment disappear, the mechanisms that ensure the reproduction of the proletariat are destructured.

Today, proletarianisation is universalised but relates to labour in a negative way. *Proletarianisation-without-labour* means that the proletariat is increasing in number, but as a cursed and unwanted surplus that stands with one foot in the mire of poverty (Marx 1990). Armies of unemployed workers, displaced populations, masses of refugees and economic migrants on the move, and a continuous de-ruralisation of the remaining rural communities through the dispossession of land and vital natural resources – all make up the global flow of a cheap labour force. One could claim that capital simply does not care about all this. As Marx says, 'the more or less favourable circumstances in which the wage labourers support and multiply themselves in no way alter the fundamental character of capitalist production' (1990: 763). On the part of labour, this grey zone of social production and reproduction does not prefigure anything positive; it rather speaks of a future with which none of us can identify. And the struggles to defend it reflect the ruthless coercion of survival within the labour market, not a political programme to overcome capitalist society.

If the labour movement managed to organise itself and articulate a political plan on the basis of class unity, it was because under the specific historical conditions of the late nineteenth and early twentieth centuries this plan was based on a class identity that could be affirmed (Endnotes 2015);[12] that is, it could constitute itself and acquire consciousness as the unity of the 'collective' or 'massive' worker. It also reflected a unity of class interests, the common identity of the labour class which was constructed on a faith in the ethics and fairness of the working-class struggle, and led to an effort (not always successful) to reduce competition between workers in the labour market for the satisfaction of their immediate personal interests and, thus, promote the collective goal. However, this turned class into an *abstraction* that tried to unite workers divided by capital within a 'community' created by a common labour interest. This 'community' firmly believed – as did Marx – that the abolition of capitalism and of classes would necessarily pass through the development of capitalism and of the productive forces. On this conviction, relations of collective culture, labour solidarity, dignity and pride were built in neighbourhoods and workplaces. In this way, however, the category of 'class' remained an abstract idea of a moral community that envisioned social emancipation and changing the world without going beyond 'rational production and equitable distribution' (Endnotes 2015: 102).

With the crisis of capital after the 1960s – the dismantling of the welfare state, the attack on salaries and the crisis of wage labour – the real subsumption of labour to capital showed that the 'liberation of labour' envisioned and propagated by the labour movement (at least as an intermediate stage on the way to communism) had come up against the very incorporation of the labour class into capital's circuit of reproduction. Of course, as we mentioned earlier, the struggle against capital is not and has never been that unified and solid. However, the struggle against everything that constitutes the labour form within the historical capital relation (liberation from labour itself) is fought at a different level than that of the labour movement against capital (liberation of labour from capital). I believe it is through this analytical lens that Holloway asserts that 'The labour movement is the movement of abstract labour' (2010: 151), the affirmation of the positiveness of labour. Today, this positive element around which class unity had been organised is lost, and the labour movement is dead. There is a dramatic increase in the number of people subsisting on underpaid and precarious employment, participating in irregular and illegal employment networks where gender- and race-based discrimination, violence and exploitation prevail. In other words, the mechanism of capitalist production and accumulation that continually adapts the number of workers to its employment needs (Marx 1990) leads to an ever-intensifying impoverishment of the proletarianised social strata and an increase of the *dead weight of poverty* (Marx 1990); that is, of the segment of the proletariat that has been stripped of its terms of existence and is vegetating. In the inclusion through exclusion that defines the labour norm today, labour finds no positive affirmation; once a pivot around which the labour class was organised as a unified subject, it is now a dividing and defining line within struggles, between those who can find regular employment in the labour market and those who enter and exit the ranks of the reserve army. Thus, class *belonging* is no longer a basis for unity, a cause for proletarians united in struggle. Competition to access the labour market and to keep a job is a matter of life and death for the worker.[13] Very recently in Greece (January 2019), the announcement of a meagre increase in the minimum wage by the Syriza government infuriated not only employers, who argued that this would force them to make redundancies, but also part of the active labour force who used the exact same argument. At the moment of struggle, today's proletarians do not come closer as members of the same class; they do not even recognise themselves as workers. This, however, does not mean that there are no moments in which the proletariat tries (with greater or lesser success) to overcome the divisions of capital. Such unity was attempted by the movements after 2011, but it proved to be weak.[14] Why?

In the Sweet Embrace of State and Nation

The collapse of the 'world of labour' as we came to know it during the twentieth century has clearly led to theoretical debates on the category of class (already from the 1970s).[15] However, the process of de-identification with the content and forms of struggle of the old labour movement can hardly – even less than before – be interpreted as the 'abolition of class' or even as the 'end of class struggle'. The accumulation of capital amounts to the reproduction of the class relation: capital on one side, wage labour on the other. Capital reproduces a proletariat that is divided but at the same time dependant on the totalising labour form that homogenises it.[16] The existence of the capitalist requires and reproduces the separation of the worker from the means of production and the capitalisation of the labour of the worker as the private property of the capitalist.[17] Therefore, for Marx, the proletariat must be identified not with a specific social group but with this circumstance of separation that is at the basis of the social relation, the unity for capital.

Historically speaking, the twentieth-century movement of the 'working class' did not provide an answer to the issue of abolishing the social form of labour in capitalism, that is, commodity-producing labour. Instead of struggling against-and-beyond, it often swore by the maximisation of productivity, a defining element in the development of the particular form of capitalist production that increases competition amongst workers in the labour market and constitutes the social bond on the basis of quantifiable performance, homogeneous linear time and the production of the body as a physical accessory of labour. The figure of the 'collective (industrial) worker' became tantamount to that of the 'consumer' rather than the revolutionary, accentuating divisions within the proletariat, whose unity, for the time being, lies only in the unity of capital. The rhythm of money and the markets might not be the only one, but it is certainly the one that rules; it makes the world go round it, gasping for breath. The victories of the labour movement in the twentieth century indeed led to the *empowerment of the labour class* as a class within capital, but they also signalled its incorporation into capital's circuit of reproduction. We cannot, however, speak of the abolition of 'class'; what we have is a transformation of class struggle, one that is making it hard for the proletariat to affirm its identity as a class of capital. The latter, of course, must be considered not as something given a priori but as a dynamic process of historical transformation and a condition that has created tension throughout history.

The labour movement has been historically linked to the state; to a great extent, it has also been connected to the nation. According to Endnotes (2015): 'If the accumulation of capital was the multiplication of the proletariat, then the strength of the nation was the degree of organisation of its working class.' Its initial survival, but also its expansion, have been built on national discourse as a counterweight to the increasing internationalisation of capital and interdependence of states. Needless to say, the reinforcement of the 'labour class' also meant the reinforcement of the 'national labour class', insofar as it exists within the geographical boundaries of a state. In the *Communist Manifesto*, Marx and Engels say that class struggle, in 'form' if not in substance, is national (1969: 20). This is not what we are referring to here, of course. Or maybe it is, if this is a matter of definitions. When we define the working class as national, we immediately place the state at the centre of the transformation of social relations. It is no coincidence that the historical action of the official labour movement was posited by nations in a way that the national character prevailed and came up against the internationalist character of proletarian struggle, thus leading to its defeat.[18] Furthermore, the internationalist movements of the nineteenth and twentieth centuries (such as the anti-imperialist movements in the third world) did not 'do away with their country's bourgeoisie' (Marx and Engels 1969: 20); in many cases – as many as the movements of liberation themselves – they actually sided with it after coming to power, leading to the consolidation of capitalism and the worsening of living conditions for the majority of the population.[19] To say that what begins as a bourgeois form turns into content would be an understatement, if not outright deceptiveness. The issue is that the bourgeois form *is* a constituent element of the labour movement form and of a revolution that becomes a state and, in doing so, reproduces bourgeois categories. However, the idea of internationalisation is not a matter of altruism, it is an inseparable part of the *potential* for liberation of all proletarian struggles.

The foundations of the hegemonic identity of the *worker* have been laid with faith in technology, industrialisation, mass production, national progress and the full and centralised planning of society through the state. The role of the state, a fundamental element for the reproduction of the class relation, also remained dominant in the socialist imaginary. The Leninist canon imposed the statification of the economy, the concentration of all the means of production-circulation-distribution in the hands of the state as the sole owner, as well as the statification of political power, that is, the monopolisation of political power by the party-state. It is in these two elements, the state and the nation, that one can appreciate the conflicts that grew within the movement around the dilemma: *nationalisation or socialisation of the economy*? Regardless the divisions that this dilemma created, it never ceased to reflect faith in (national) progress and the development of the national economy. This anticapitalism, systematised during the twentieth century, did not directly question the capitalist mode of production. Its theoretical avowals went only as far as to defend the bourgeois perception of exploitation[20] (that is, the understanding of exploitation from the viewpoint of political economy), speaking of the appropriation of part of the worker's labour, that is, the appropriation of the wealth that the worker produces for the benefit of the capitalists; or, even, of part of her labour remaining unpaid (that is, the worker is not paid the entire value of her labour). This perspective turned exploitation into a moral category, at the same time justifying the central role of the state in regulating and promoting the collective interest of the working class. While, in both cases, the aim was to strike down exploitation, this was pursued through the reform of exchange relations and not the abolition of the mode of production. Marx spoke of communist society as a 'co-operative society', without giving any role to the state:

> Within the co-operative society based on common ownership of the means of production, the producers do not exchange their products; just as little does the labor employed on the products appear here as the value of these products, as a material quality possessed by them, since now, in contrast to capitalist society, individual labor no longer exists in an indirect fashion but directly as a component part of total labor. (1970)

Of course, Marx spoke of many things, including that the state will not disappear from one day to the next but will continue to exist during the revolutionary dictatorship of the proletariat (1970). In arguing that Marx grants no role to the state, we mean that he claims it will no longer be needed in communist society. He also maintains that the 'co-operative society' will not produce value.[21] However, the theory of transition was crucial for the labour movement in organising the taking of power. Therefore, be it as generalised statism (Leninist canon), or as a critique thereof (council communism) and a self-management of production (transitional stages),[22] in its struggle for emancipation the twentieth-century working class remained trapped within the capitalist mode of production and glorified the need to universalise labour and, therefore, the law of value itself. Workers, of course, remained attached to trade unions and workers' organisations until the 1970s, when the restructuring of the class relation signalled the attack of capital against the wage relation, and national labour movements were left in a position of disadvantage. Instead of prefiguring the hegemony of the labour movement, de-industrialisation and the deceleration of growth rates signalled its decline and defeat.

The recent movements of 2011–12 (including all that falls under the name of Occupy) rallied behind the ideas of anti-austerity and (direct) democracy, and on these two categories they tried to constitute class unity. A connection was created between an ideal community of friends (majority) that had to confront and defeat certain (external) enemies. Sometimes the enemy takes the form of the global financial elites and their transnational governments, and class struggle is expressed in terms of state versus state. In other, reactionary forms, the enemy appears in the shape of the dirty and repulsive immigrant who has come to 'steal' the scant social benefits. In this case, the elements of nation and state – on which the organised labour movement had founded its massive character – return to their conservative expression. However, in their totality and through their contradictions, these movements attacked the state (and the lack of democracy) while at the same time demanded a solution from the state (anti-austerity and more democracy). The practices deployed (street clashes, occupations) were similar to those adopted by more militant segments of the far-left or the anarchists, but it was mostly political corruption and the crippled democracy of the representatives and their voters that remained in the line of fire. The movements of 2011–12 basically went against the decline of the labour movement and the absence of all that it meant to belong to the working class in the twentieth century: full and stable employment, social security, national sovereignty. This also revealed why class unity was weak, that is, why proletarians were not able to overcome their interclassness as a sign of division within the struggle.

As the dynamic of the movements of the squares weakened, the struggles returned to the 'worker' as the figure of the organised labour movement, albeit with no success so far. The delegitimised and incorporated political mediations of the past (trade unions, cooperatives or parties) are having trouble expressing a perspective focused on overturning capitalist society. On the one hand, the political projects deployed by different segments of the left who insist on the reconstruction of labour identity and the revival of the terms and perspectives of the – already deceased – old labour movement assert a dead-end of sorts which confirms the 'statification' of the anticapitalist imaginary, or, simply, a nostalgia of times past. On the other hand, the wager within the struggles themselves is whether the debilitation of the 'working-class identity' will lead to a questioning of the content that the hegemonic labour movement form – without ever being unified – had given to revolution and social emancipation during the previous century. The reassertion from parts of the far-left of the need to acquire class consciousness through forms of political organisation which, even if they are not a party or the state, inevitably require the central control of society, cast doubt on whether these segments of the movement are capable of escaping the Leninist canon. It is hard to speak of or anticipate class consciousness 'in itself' as the unity of working-class interests. In any case, the process of de-identification with previous collective subjectifications must not be constructed theoretically as a negative teleology of class struggle with a happy ending, one that comes to replace the positive teleology of the twentieth-century labour movement.

The lack of institutions of solidarity – and the normalisation of that lack – is a dominant feature in the labour form and the labour condition. The system of reciprocity that had been established between organised workers (through their representatives) and the employers, as well as the power of negotiation of trade unions to define all new elements in the working process (on the basis of mutual agreement), is now in the past. The worker stands alone against the employer, vulnerable and subjugated. The ground on which the social safety net and the forms of mediation were constructed in the era of the Keynesian state proved to be 'quicksand'. From the 1970s onwards, it became clear that the Keynesian state was no longer working, and the neoliberal management regime was depleted. On the contrary, there was a rise in what Marx, in his few references to it, names the ragged proletariat or the lumpenproletariat. Through social marginalisation, irregular/illegal employment and illegal networks, class 'dignity' and labour ethics were continually undermined. The lumpenproletariat was the 'anti-revolutionary' side of the movement and stood at the opposite pole of the 'class consciousness' which characterised the organised segments of the working class. This degeneration was a bogeyman of sorts for the labour movement, a sign that its struggles would not be victorious. What about today? Does the defeat of the labour movement signal the lumpenisation of the proletariat, that is, the constitution of its dark, anti-revolutionary side?

Beyond the Working Class?

Agamben links the proletariat to a non-identity. He argues that Marx's idea of the working class did not refer to a 'specific' class but rather to a non-class that would overturn another class. Agamben considers Benjamin's messianic motive on revolution to be linked to Marx's idea that the proletariat does not acquire a specific identity. 'We cannot identify the proletariat with the worker', Agamben (2011) argues. 'The proletarian is not the worker, the proletarian is an almost metaphysical figure: someone who is not identifiable and, because of this lack of identity, will overthrow and eliminate all classes.' On the contrary, according to the author, whenever the proletarian claims a class identity, as has occurred historically, she turns into the working class; as a result, she can potentially be incorporated into the capitalist system and does not wish to change

it anymore. This metaphysical dimension of the non-identity of the proletariat claimed by Agamben is a 'purified' – and therefore 'innocent'
– category and is probably, because of this purity, able to maintain its rev-
olutionariness. From a different analytical approach, Gunn (1987) agrees
in his notes on 'class' with the opinion that Marx does not consider class
to be a specific group of people. On the other hand, he stresses that the
category of class refers to a relation of struggle, and that the proletarian
is not a 'pure' being but rather a self-contradictory being that struggles
both within and against her fragmentation. For Gunn (1992) this can
occur only because existence is perceived as an ecstatic dynamic process.
The proletarian *is* and *is not* a worker, and exists within the struggle
which may (or may not) succeed in breaking definitions.

The proletarian condition is universalised. Social war is all-pervasive
and competition is universal, sundering the existence of proletarians
in all spaces and moments of everyday experience. Going against what
exists is hard to identify with class unity and the narrative of a unified
working-class identity anymore; it is, rather, the result of a negative
connotation in the world of labour. Class hatred and hate-for-class boil
over in ways that assert class as a 'category of division', underlining the
class divisions of the proletariat. The figure of the obedient, ethical
and responsible worker who enjoys work-related or political privileges
(Holloway 1987) is a distant memory for most of the proletariat. In terms
of a 'labour movement', the working class is lumpenised; misery and destitution bring the figure of the lumpen closer and closer, a figure whose
instability and incapacity to struggle have been repeatedly underlined
and criticised in Marxist theory, which focuses mostly on the organised
segments of labour. However, as Gunn (2018a) points out, today, images
of immigrants and the precariously employed make us think more of the
initial meaning of the term proletarian as conceived by Marx: a residue,
capable only of spawning. For Gunn, the use of the term proletariat by
Marx aimed at shocking us with the revelation that there is so much
'propertylessness at the centre of the richest society that the world has
known' (Gunn 2018a). It is easier for us today to return to this version,
that is, to the concept of the proletarian as a 'reject and outsider', rather
than that of the 'worker' organised on the basis of her labour. For Gunn,
'Marx's well-known distinction between a "proletariat" and a "lumpenproletariat" ... has become problematic to say the least' (2018b).

Two clarifications: To claim that the working class has become
lumpenised and at the same time accept its anti-revolutionary consti-

tution as opposed to some other revolutionary nature of the organised labour movement is, to say the least, a paradox. No subject is innocent and there is no revolutionary nature within the proletariat. Furthermore, to stress the increase of surplus labour is by no means to say that we imagine the armies of the unemployed as the new subject of struggle. However, if the working class of the so-called Fordist struggles expressed the positiveness of class and of labour, the proletariat takes up a broader space as a category of constant tension, a dynamic process of identification/de-identification. The working class, linked to a historically specific form of class struggle during the twentieth century, has also been a specific *form of struggle of the proletariat* aiming at the hegemony of one class that would abolish both hegemony and classes. Initially, however, it aimed at emancipating labour as a way of *emancipating an alternative identity*.[23] Naturally, we are not speaking of crystallised identities whose breaking depends on *contingency*, that is, on the contradictions of capital during a specific period of its development, but rather of dynamic processes of movement (identification/de-identification, fetishisation/de-fetishisation), understood as flows of struggle. The contribution of open Marxism to the analysis of this posture is crucial. In 1992, at a time when neoliberalism was on the rise, Holloway wrote:

> Seeing fetishism as a process of defetishisation/refetishisation has important consequences, theoretically and politically. The understanding of fetishism as established fact, as blanket fog, leads to a concept of revolution as event, an exogenous event which is either virtually impossible (the pessimistic position) or will be the triumphal conclusion of the growth of the party. (1992: 157)

This specific analytical approach to capitalist forms (not as economic forms but as the continuous struggle to constitute them) allows us to think that the two poles of capital and labour are mutually and inherently connected and, therefore, display internal ruptures. Thus, the *proletariat* can be perceived not only as the contradiction of the capital-labour relation but also as the contradiction of *labour-within-capital*, that is, as the self-contradiction of labour that pushes beyond its form of constitution (self-denial). The proletariat becomes the movement-against class definition and, therefore, the rupture with the working class, the emancipation of a non-identity. It is the ecstatic denial *against and beyond* the labour class, against and beyond any definition that classifies. It is the twofold dimension of the ecstatic scream (Holloway 2002), the projection beyond the self towards a desired future, a projection that is completely real.

The elements that can potentially appear in the struggles of the proletariat – nationalism, populism, competition in the labour market, individualism, militarism, authoritarianism, gender- and race-related discrimination, etc. – are not external obstacles that must be overcome by the revolutionary movement. They are components of the proletariat itself, they are the forms of its division by capital, forms it ruthlessly comes up against time and time again, either reinforcing them or undermining them. Therefore, true unity cannot be sought in an autonomous subject. There can be hope only within social revolution, when accumulated repression explodes. It is the transformative force of struggle that leaves nobody and nothing untouched and can create new forms of interaction between us.

References

Agamben, G. (1998) *Sovereign Power and Bare Life*, Stanford: Stanford University Press.

Agamben, G. (2005) *State of Exception*, Chicago: Chicago University Press.

Agamben, G. (2011) 'Giorgio Agamben on Biopolitics', interview with Akis Gavriilidis for the Greek public TV channel ET3, Athens, October, https://nomadicuniversality.com/2015/10/30/giorgio-agamben-on-biopolitics-the-greek-tv-interview-2.

Bonefeld, W. (2016) 'Science, Hegemony and Action: On the Elements of Governmentality', *Journal of Social Sciences*, http://eprints.whiterose.ac.uk/114319/1/Science_Hegemony_and_Action.pdf 19–41.

Bonefeld, W. and S. Tischler (2002) *What Is To Be Done?*, Aldershot: Ashgate.

Endnotes (2013) 'The Holding Pattern: The Ongoing Crisis and the Class Struggles of 2011–2013', *Endnotes* 3 (September 2013), https://endnotes.org.uk/issues/3/en/endnotes-the-holding-pattern.

Endnotes (2015) 'A History of Separation: The Rise and Fall of Workers' Movements, 1883–1982', *Endnotes* 4 (October 2015), https://endnotes.org.uk/issues/4/en/endnotes-the-defeat-of-the-workers-movement.

Gunn, R. (1987) 'Notes on Class', *Common Sense* 2 (July), 15–25.

Gunn, R. (1992) 'Against Historical Materialism: Marxism as First-Order Discourse', in W. Bonefeld, R. Gunn and K. Psychopedis (eds), *Open Marxism* 2, London: Pluto Press, 1–46.

Gunn, R. (2018a) '¿Qué es el proletariado' ('What is the Proletariat?'), *Herramienta*, http://comunizar.com.ar/proletariado-richard-gunn.

Gunn, R. (2018b) 'La negación de la negación' ('The Negation of Negation'), trans. A. Bonnet, *Herramienta*, http://comunizar.com.ar/la-negacion-la-negacion.

Holloway, J. (1987) 'The Red Rose of Nissan', *Capital & Class* 11(2): 142–64.

Holloway, J. (1992) *Crisis, Fetishism, Class Composition*, London: Pluto Press.

Holloway, J. (2002) *Change the World Without Taking Power: The Meaning of Revolution Today*, London: Pluto Press.

Holloway, J. (2010) *Crack Capitalism*, London: Pluto Press.

Holloway, J. (2015) 'Read Capital: The First Sentence of *Capital* Starts with Wealth, Not with the Commodity', *Historical Materialism* 23(3): 3–26.

Holloway, J. (2016) *In, Against and Beyond Capitalism. The San Francisco Lectures*, San Francisco: PM Press.

Marx, K. (1937) *The Eighteenth Brumaire of Louis Bonaparte*, Moscow: Progress Publishers, www.marxists.org/archive/marx/works/download/pdf/18th-Brumaire.pdf.

Marx, K. (1970) *Critique of the Gotha Programme*, www.marxists.org/archive/marx/works/download/Marx_Critque_of_the_Gotha_Programme.pdf

Marx, K. (1976) *Preface and Introduction to A Contribution to the Critique of Political Economy*, Peking: Foreign Languages Press, 1976.

Marx, K. (1981) *Capital*, Vol. 3, London: Penguin.

Marx, K. (1990) *Capital*, Vol. 1, London: Penguin.

Marx, K. (1993) *Grundrisse: Foundations of the Critique of Political Economy*, London: Penguin.

Marx, K. and Engels (1969) 'Manifesto of the Communist Party', in Marx and Engels, *Selected Works*, Vol. 1, Moscow: Progress Publishers.

Nasioka, K. (2014) 'Communities of Crisis: Ruptures as Common Ties during Class Struggles in Greece, 2011–2012', *South Atlantic Quarterly* 113: 285–97.

Nasioka, K. (2017) *Ciudades en insurrección. Oaxaca 2006 / Atenas 2008*, Guadalajara: Universidad de Guadalajara-CIESAS-Cátedra Jorge Alonso.

Nasioka, K. (2018) 'Crisis and Negativity: On the Revolutionary Subject in Times of Crisis', in J. Holloway, K. Nasioka and P. Doulos (eds), *Beyond Crisis: After the Collapse of the Institutional Hope, What?* trans. Anna Holloway, San Francisco: PM Press.

Rolan, S. (2003) 'Le Pen et la disparition de l' identité ouvrière' ('Le Pen and the Disappearing of the Worker's Identity), *Théorie Communiste* 18 (February).

Rubin, I. I. (1972 [1928]) *Essays on Marx's Theory of Value*, Detroit: Black & Red.

Tischler, S. (2012) 'Revolution and Detotalization: An Approach to John Holloway's Crack Capitalism', *Journal of Classical Sociology* 12(2): 267–80.

Tischler, S. and A. García Vela (2017) 'Teoría crítica y nuevas interpretaciones sobre la emancipación' ('Critical Theory and New Interpretations on Emancipation'), *Nueva Época*, year 11, no. 42 (April–September): 187–207.

Théorie Communiste (2009) 'Communisation in the Present Tense', in B. Noys (ed), *Communisation and its Discontents: Contestation, Critique, and Contemporary Struggles*, Nueva York: Minor Compositions, 41–60.

Notes

1. 'Doing is practical negation' (Holloway 2002: 23), that is, it is the practical movement of negation and therefore a defining element of struggle. That is, it is not reproductive doing, but a pushing-beyond (Holloway 2002: 152). The notion of *doing* in the work of John Holloway is a critical/prefigurative category of social practice or human activity that aims at a *beyond* the separation of abstract and concrete labour.
2. On this, see the analysis in Tischler and García Vela 2017.
3. In the same way – truth be told – that they were posed in the nineteenth century. See Marx 1937.
4. The dialectic category of *in-against-and-beyond* has been posited and analysed in detail in Holloway 2016.
5. On this, see the analysis of Greek reality in Nasioka 2017.
6. According to Marx it is the category of relative overpopulation, as a segment of the active reserve army, with a completely unregulated employment: 'It calls to mind the boundless reproduction of animals individually weak and constantly hunted down' (1990: 797).
7. Marx distinguishes three categories within the ragged proletariat: those who are capable of labour, the destitute, and the 'decayed roués' incapable of performing labour (Marx 1990: 797). In the *Eighteenth Brumaire* he refers to this in derogatory terms: 'Alongside decayed roués with dubious means of subsistence and of dubious origin, alongside ruined and adventurous offshoots of the bourgeoisie, were vagabonds, discharged soldiers, discharged jailbirds, escaped galleyslaves, swindlers, mountebanks, lazzaroni, pickpockets, tricksters, gamblers, maquereaux [pimps], brothel keepers, porters, literati, organgrinders, ragpickers, knifegrinders, tinkers, beggars in short, the whole indefinite, disintegrated mass, thrown hither and thither, which the French call la bohème' (1937: 38).
8. Endnotes (2013) refer to this with the term 'holding pattern'.
9. From the 1960s or even earlier, autonomous working-class struggles and struggles 'against labour' have been questioning this interpretation, both in theory and in practice. New subjects (e.g. students) appear in the struggles. Even during the nineteenth century relevant perceptions were being criticised. See, for example, Marx's critique of the Gotha Programme or, at the beginning of the twentieth century, the critique of communists against social democracy (e.g. Luxemburg), of the left against Lenin, etc.
10. The thesis on the disappearance of the working-class identity has been analysed in detail (and variety) by large parts of the theoretical current of *communisation*. On this, see Théorie Communiste 2009, Rolan 2003, Endnotes 2015.
11. In his philosophical analysis on the state of exception and bare life, Agamben (1998, 2005) speaks of such exclusion, one that can simultaneously include. He speaks of the 'oxymoron ecstasy-belonging' as the topological structure of the state of exception that is 'outside and yet belonging' (2005: 35). Its

main characteristic is the lack of distinction between the 'inside' and the 'outside' which thus creates the space in which deviation is legitimised. Although Agamben's analyses have to do with law and the state, the nature of this exclusion lies, I believe, very close to today's labour norm.

12. Endnotes mention in reference to workers that 'To say that they affirmed a shared identity is to say that the movement succeeded in convincing workers to suspend their interests as isolated sellers in a competitive labour market, and, instead, to act out of a commitment to the collective project of the labour movement' (2015: 100).

13. On this, see the analysis in Bonefeld 2016.

14. On the occupy movement in Greece, see Nasioka 2014. Today, this text seems quite optimistic.

15. For a reference to the major ones, see Nasioka 2017, 2018.

16. For the relation between totalisation and detotalisation, see the detailed analysis in the work of Sergio Tischler (2012; Bonefeld and Tischler 2002). Wage labour is a totalising condition in the sense that it entirely transforms and shapes the life of the worker.

17. On this, see Marx 1981.

18. A few events that give an idea of the ideological framework in which the labour movement was constituted during the twentieth century: The capitulation of the SPD in Germany in favour of the war and the alliance of the official labour movement with the Freikorps in order to suppress the Spartacist uprising in 1919 (who also executed Rosa Luxemburg). In Greece, the signing of the Varkiza Agreement by the official leadership of the Greek Communist Party in 1945, considered to have ended the civil war.

19. The case of Vietnam is reference enough.

20. See Rubin (1972) on the theory of money in Marx and the critique of the bourgeois foundations of the classic understanding of exploitation.

21. One must examine the consequences of such a claim in relation to the currently widespread anticapitalist *theory of the commons*. Of course, the desired goal is a communist version of the commons, one of communal ownership without the mediation of value.

22. Marx clearly states in relation to this that, 'In joint-stock companies, the function is separated from capital ownership, so labour is also completely separated from ownership of means of production and of surplus-labour. This result of capitalist production in its highest development is a necessary point of transition towards the transformation of capital back into the property of individual producers, though no longer as the private property of individual producers, but rather as their property as associated producers, as directly social property. It is furthermore a point of transition toward the transformation of all functions formerly bound up with capital ownership in the production process into simple functions of the associated producers, into social functions' (1981: 568).

23. On this, see Holloway 2002.

9

A New Grammar or an Anti-Grammar of Revolution? On Zapatismo and Open Marxism

Sergio Tischler

Struggles and 'Elective Affinities'

If there is a point where the political perspective of Zapatismo and the theorising of open Marxism converge,[1] it is in the urgent need to change the existing world that is dominated by capital and in the realisation that anticapitalist struggle for this change involves breaking with the traditional grammar of revolution. In other words, this affinity can be understood as a common perception of anticapitalist struggle as a process that reinvents the very term 'revolution'.

From the moment of their uprising, at the dawn of 1994, the Zapatista Army of National Liberation (*Ejército Zapatista de Liberación Nacional,* EZLN) gave signs of bringing something new into revolutionary politics. In time, this became clearer. Their idea of revolution is not only different to the classic Leninist canon, it is actually profoundly critical of it. They do not fight to take power; theirs is a revolution that 'makes revolution possible', for taking power does not guarantee a revolutionary transformation of social relations. Theirs is a revolution 'from below and to the left', one that focuses on autonomy. It is a political process that revolves around the experience of struggle to eliminate the relations of domination entrenched in the 'above' of the rulers and the 'below' of the ruled; and it is one expressed in a language that challenges the rigid forms of power, both of capital and of the power involved in the classic forms of organisation of the left. In other words, Zapatista politics embraces a revolution against the grain, one that rejects the idea of a vanguard – so vital in the classic canon – as well as of political homogeneity.

For its part, open Marxism has been characterised by its criticism of orthodox Marxism in its different variants, as well as of the theoretical perspective deployed by structuralist Marxism. One of the central aspects of this critique is directly related to the state and to the idea of anticapitalist revolution. According to the theoretical argumentation of open Marxism, there are many reasons why official communism failed to become a revolution that would emancipate humanity. The most significant, however, is its state-centred nature, which determined the authoritarian traits of the social transformation that took place in countries where a Leninist-inspired revolutionary vanguard was successful in taking power. At the same time, Marxism suffered a fundamental mutation: it went from being a critical theory of capital, providing a solid conceptual ground for a radical perspective on human emancipation, to being a state ideology. The main political thesis of open Marxism is that a true anticapitalist revolution cannot take place through the occupation of the state and its preservation as the fundamental political instance, an assertion based on the theoretical argument that the state is a form of capitalist social relations. The category of *form* is crucial in this approach for the analysis both of capital and of the state. It involves the need to radically rethink the concept of revolutionary politics and what we imagine as anticapitalist change.

Although the two are not directly related, for all the above-mentioned reasons we consider there is a 'selective affinity' between the political practice of Zapatismo and the theorising of open Marxism. While each retains its specificity (each in its own 'way', as the Zapatistas like to say), this affinity builds bridges and can, on occasions, create sparks that illuminate the path of 'Asking We Walk'. However, the question remains whether stories so different can converge at a specific moment. I believe the answer lies in class struggle. The focal point of the stories is revolution, in particular its updating. And this updating is based on the awareness that the traditional grammar of revolution has been a grammar of power that has negated the verb of emancipation. Are we then on the verge of a new grammar of revolution or of something different, of revolution as the anti-grammar of power? We have chosen to highlight these two stories for the reasons already explained, but we are well aware that many different stories converge in the field that Zapatismo has opened up.

The Jungle and the Thunderbolt

How do we see Zapatismo? How do we avoid the trap of a subjective perspective or, even worse, of one that objectivises or positivises it? It is a complex matter, one hard to tackle. Perhaps one way forward is to see ourselves within its experience, to use it as a mirror for our own reflection: What does it tell us and how does it call to us in relation to the fundamental question of the struggle to change the world?

The starting point for Zapatismo is *digna rabia* – dignified rage. Two words that sum up the pain of this world of oppression and the anger we carry within, transformed by the Zapatistas into an organised will for change under the specific conditions prevailing in Chiapas. In fact, *digna rabia* is the driving force, the elementary flame of any transformation in an unfair world;[2] it is what fuels revolutionary theory. It is not rhetoric. Is there dignified rage in *Capital*? Without it, without the negative drift, this work might have been an objectivist treatise on capitalist reality and never a critique thereof. In this sense, Holloway (2002) is right in rejecting objectivist interpretations of Marx's work and defending the perspective of the *negated scream* of humanity in the categories of political economy. That said, we believe that to assume dignified rage as our starting point is, essentially, to say that the struggle does not begin from the concept but from something more basic that does not require theoretical legitimisation. At its centre lies the experience of specific struggles fought by ordinary men and women which generates an empirically critical knowledge, one that is not necessarily mediated by theory and has memory at its core.

This was understood by the members of the National Liberation Forces (*Fuerzas de Liberación Nacional*, FLN) when they entered the jungle of Chiapas and made first contact with the indigenous communities living there. As Marcos said in interviews held after the 1994 uprising, they had to 'learn to listen'. And they learned how to listen to the dignified rage that came from the beginning of time; in doing so, they changed their mental habits, habits that had been shaped by the tradition of leading they had learned through urban revolutionary experience and theoretical knowledge.

They had to understand that this was a revolution of the indigenous and the peasants and that they, the non-natives, should learn how to swim in the waters of this experience of resistance, how to comprehend its key elements, its codes. They had to admit that this *other* knowledge called the arrogance of the concept into question, demonstrating that if the latter wants to converse and go beyond abstractions it must descend from its hierarchic pedestal and take a critical look at itself. In sum, it must learn. This challenged – and thrust into crisis – the idea of revolu-

tion as a universal model to be replicated, as an idea that subsumes the
diversity of concrete struggles to a superior unity of a synthetic nature. It
shook the perception of myth and of (totalising) abstraction[3] as symbolic
and conceptual tools for revolutionary thought.[4]

However, to learn is not to strip oneself of certain content and fill
oneself with another, just as we empty a glass of water so as to fill it
with another liquid. In this specific case, learning to listen is part of an
attitude of mutual recognition[5] that opens up a process of exchange and
transformation and takes a critical approach to the relatively closed codification of particular experiences of struggle. This has been the 'method'
of Zapatismo to date, spanning from that encounter in the Lacandon
Jungle to how it relates to other struggles, constituting a fundamental
part of the idea and the process of constructing a we from 'below and
to the left' which rejects any pretension of hegemony and homogeneity.

What have they learned? What is the content of this learning? Many
things can be said, of course, such as learning how to learn by forgetting
what has been learned already. As we cannot make detailed reference to
this knowledge in all its variety, we will focus on a fundamental element
of Zapatista practice and thought which, in a way, encompasses the rest.
We will speak of the anti-vanguardist idea of revolution and of some of
its plans.

Through their spokespersons, and mostly Subcomandante Marcos
(now Galeano), the EZLN have asserted that they are not a model to be
replicated and that the notion of a revolutionary vanguard has no place
in their idea of politics and revolution. Beyond their communiqués, the
significance of this anti-vanguardist idea of anticapitalist change can also
be traced to the practice of Zapatismo, to instances such as the Other
Campaign (Otra Campaña), the autonomic process of the Caracoles and
the Good Government Councils (Juntas de Buen Gobierno), and the
Little Zapatista School (Escuelita Zapatista), amongst others. All this is
well known. What is less well known is all that relates to the specific core
of the experience expressed in the Zapatista way of doing-knowing.

How does anticapitalist struggle unfold as anti-vanguardist struggle
through this doing-knowing? Clearly, Zapatista anti-vanguardism is not
derived from an abstract theoretical formulation or from an idea that is
one-sidedly articulated in the field of theory and aspires to guide practice.
At the centre of this concept lies a resignified community experience that
is expressed in the fundamental guiding principles of Zapatismo.[6]

This experience is in itself very complex, and perhaps its intimacy
renders it inaccessible to those of us who are not at the heart of it.

However, to serve the purpose of this chapter – and having expressed our caution – we shall highlight two aspects that we consider fundamental. Firstly: the understanding that community revolves around the axis of resistance and struggle against oppression. From this perspective, the community is no longer viewed as a continuum of shared practices of resistance in times of domination but as the conscious production of a temporality of rupture of domination, one that feeds off the memory of ancestral struggles and involves the *resignifying* of practices of resistance.

In addition, it is well known that this process is not the result of one isolated experience, restricted to the field of local resistances. Other struggles and experiences come into play, such as those of the already mentioned FLN. To put it plainly, the members of the FLN were forced to question and shed their vanguardism along the way, and the communities had to do the same with their localism; it was this dialogue and mutual questioning, this *mutual mediation*, that led to the emergence of the anti-vanguardist character of the EZLN and its anticapitalist idea of change. This process also bears testimony to the profound effect of the general crisis of the hegemonic concept and of the classic canon of revolution.

The profoundness of the change brought about by this mutual mediation can be perceived, amongst other things, in the horizontal relation between an experience whose main form of expression is orality and one that is codified in written terms. Within the classic canon of revolution there is a hierarchic connection between the two, with written experience relating to the oral form in terms of hegemony.[7]

However, it would be wrong to positivise this experience. We believe the Zapatista anti-vanguardist idea of revolution must be considered the expression of a politics that emerges from negation: from the negation of capitalism, the negation of vanguard and hegemony, the negation of the patriarchate, among many others. It is a politics that opens up a horizon on the basis of all that is rejected. It posits the opening of the world towards an anticapitalist experience that defies the tendency to homogenisation and the idea of revolutionary political action as producing a new synthesis of power.

This politics is at the same time the negation of the state, considered the expression of the *separation* between the leaders and the led, the rulers and the ruled, hegemony and the subaltern. For Zapatismo, we believe, awareness of this separation is crucial in the understanding of politics as a process of domination and of estrangement from the collective. That is why its main premises create a type of consciousness which aims at avoiding this separation and at creating horizontal processes that tend to eliminate what they call the 'above and the below' in politics and in society.

A movement from 'below and to the left' suggests an anti-synthetic subject made out of multiple struggles which, in dialogue, produce a mutual knowledge of the common. This subject does not fix its rebel flow on one point so as to autonomise itself from it and establish itself as an institution; it is rather part of the flexible updating of the anticapitalist flow in an anti-instrumental perspective of politics. Its goal is not to take state power; its ideas of government and democracy are anchored in a practice that sets out to dissolve the determinations of power that have led to the separation of the above and the below, as one can observe at the local level in the autonomous experience of the Good Government Councils. Generally speaking, in the context of 'a world where many worlds fit', the Zapatista proposal is fuelled by an idea of emancipation in which the government is part of the social flow towards collective self-determination; it does not try to capture it within the political synthesis of the state.

In other words, the anticapitalism of Zapatismo is one that *detotalises*.[8] It does not set out to substitute capital with another totalising form of domination, as occurred with so-called real socialism. It swims against the grain of the classic revolutionary tradition codified in Leninism, for in this tradition the idea of the hegemony of the vanguard entraps the meaning of class struggle within a totalising form of power that ultimately negates social emancipation.

This trait of Zapatismo also manifests itself in the rejection of the 'personality cult' of leaders, fuelled by the subalternity of the ruled, as well as in its criticism of the exaltation and mystification of the sacrifice of emblematic figures. Perhaps one of the most accomplished expressions of this critique can be found in 'Between Light and Shadow', written by Marcos in 2014. Years before, in a magnificent interview with the Subcomandante, Manuel Vázquez Montalbán (1999) also pointed out the significance of the use of masks for the Zapatista revolution.

Class Struggle and the Category of Form

On what points could the Zapatista experience and open Marxism converge? We must not lose sight of the already mentioned obvious differences that arise from the fact that the two are experiences with very different stories to tell, stories that distinguish them from one another. The history of Zapatismo is deeply rooted in the resistance of the indigenous peoples and in armed struggle for socialism in Mexico. Open Marxism, for its part, is a theoretical current especially recreated in critical academic circles, one that aims at updating Marxism as a critical theory and as a core element in the re-elaboration of revolutionary practice. In this sense, its subject matter is anticapitalist revolution and its current existence against the historical backdrop of the failure of the so-called – state-centred – socialist revolution, particularly the criticism of the theoretical weaving of the latter.

However, a broader look at these experiences reveals common features that allow them to enter into dialogue as part of a 'below and to the left'. In fact, many of the more recent reflections of open Marxism have arguably drawn their inspiration from the Zapatista experience, and have been shaped within the context of the failed revolutions in Central America and other parts of Latin America.[9] In this chapter, dialogue will revolve around the conceptual re-elaboration of revolution proposed by open Marxism on the basis of the category of *form*.

The concept of form lies at the centre of Marx's analysis in *Capital* and is the main axis of the critical argumentation of open Marxism on domination and the state. For lack of space, we cannot offer a detailed analysis of this concept in the present essay; such a deconstruction would involve considering the dialectic between form and content, essence and appearance, or the problem of fetishism and reification, amongst others.[10] We shall limit ourselves to certain general considerations leaning towards an issue that is eminently political, that is, the critique of politics and of the state as part of form.

For Marx, capital is not a thing; it is a social relation of domination/ exploitation that necessarily manifests itself through forms (commodity form, money form, factory form, etc.). The latter appear as autonomous but are in fact part of the contradictory movement of value, creating a unity that is mediated by money. Resultantly, forms constitute a totality that is deployed as part of the movement of social reproduction dominated by abstract labour.[11] In a broader sense, forms are 'real abstractions' (Sohn Rethel 1978), and the domination built on them assumes the characteristics of an 'objective domination' (Postone 1996), an impersonal domination inscribed in the object that gives these abstractions a neutral appearance. However, it is quite the opposite: they are a specific

A NEW GRAMMAR OR AN ANTI-GRAMMAR OF REVOLUTION? · 149

historical form of capital domination and, therefore, of the negation of the freedom of human beings, if this is understood as an individual and collective self-determination free of personal or 'objective' coercion. A negation that appears as formal freedom in the commercial – wage – relationship established between those who sell their labour force and those who buy it.

According to Holloway, forms are 'frozen or rigidified modes of existence of social relations' (2002: 51) that cut off or negate the doing of people by transforming it into labour through the wage relationship, that is, by the force of objective compulsion to which people are submitted in order to sell their labour force. This compulsion is part of a social relation that is based on the *separation* of the workers from the means of production as analysed by Marx in the process of primitive accumulation of capital, reproduced in the capitalist relation once this has been established (Bonefeld 2014).

The process of reification that manifests itself in 'objective domination' and in the forms is not limited to the economy. As we have seen, this process is a social totality that does not leave politics or the state untouched. The very separation of the economic and the political that characterises bourgeois domination involves a type of relationship that is understood based on forms. The categories of 'civil society' or 'citizenship', for example, cannot be perceived if not on the basis of the separation of the economy and politics; however, when the separation is positivised it implies a process of fetishisation. The concept of form breaks with this process in that it unveils the relation that exists in the separation of the economic and the political, and reveals this separation as a constituent element of capital domination. Thus, the concept of form allows for an understanding of the state as a form of social relations and, more specifically, as the political form of capital (Bonefeld 2014).

It is clear that this perspective involves a critique directed against the liberal conceptions of the state. However, the critique is aimed mainly at orthodox and structuralist Marxist conceptions of the state which consider the latter to be relatively autonomous from capital. This idea is either supported by a perception of the state as part of a superstructure 'ultimately determined by the economy' or by a more complex and sophisticated structuralist approach that interprets it as a specific structure that is relatively autonomous from the economic structure. Both perspectives lead to a state-centred politics and a view of social transformation that is determined by this centrality. In this sense, they embrace grammars of power and not languages of emancipation.

On the contrary, open Marxism regards revolution as a challenge for humanity to dissolve all forms, the state included, given that they are specific expressions of the rule of capital. According to this perspective, class struggle is not outside forms, it is one of their constituent elements. The state-centred versions of social change interpreted class struggle as the struggle to establish a new power, the power of the workers represented by the party. This led to the enclosure of the concept of class struggle within *forms* and to its taking an ideological and instrumental turn; in practical terms, it translated as a politics that, far from expressing social emancipation, constituted its negation.

A New Grammar or an Anti-grammar?

In our case, the terms grammar and anti-grammar are in no way related to deconstructionism and to its 'decentring' of texts as an individualist act (Buck-Morss 1981). The terms are suggested in Angel Rama's *The Lettered City* (1996). In his work, Rama posits the idea that, ever since the colonial period, grammar and written language in Latin America have been the legacy of scholars in the service of power. While there have been significant changes, such as those caused by revolutionary changes, this has been a constant that has determined the vertical codification of language, creating a true antinomy between a language from above and a language from below, a written and an oral culture, a dominant culture and a subaltern one. In other words, Rama argues that the 'grammarisation' of language and culture has been pivotal in the weave of power and hegemony. However, he does not deny the importance of written language; he rather questions its placement at the service of domination and, therefore, of the production of subalternity.

How to transform it into a language of life and break the abstract carcass of a grammar that is at the service of power? This is the question that Rama asks, leading us, in turn, to the question of the language of revolution. Should it be codified in terms of a (new) grammar or should the *flow of rebelliousness* against the system invent a language that goes against the grain of this codification? Should theory be the grammar of practice or should it emancipate it from the 'imperialism of the concept' (Adorno 1990)?

Decades ago, in their critical analysis of enlightenment, Horkheimer and Adorno (1972) untangled the relation between identity and the domination that hides under the neutral guise of the concept, and showed that the latter is part of the 'conceptual grammar' of the 'system'; that is, of the set of social relations that are dominant in an antagonistic society. By antagonistic society they meant specifically the capitalist one, but the critique also involved the ongoing ideological and political process taking place in the Soviet Union. The lesson that emerged from that critique was that an identitarian concept is a damaged concept – an idea analysed by Adorno in *Negative Dialectics* – and cannot be revolutionary for it is part of a process of homogenising the world and bringing about the universal domination of instrumental reason (Horkheimer 1974) that resembles capital valorisation.

This theorising spoke of the effects of a process of conceptual positivisation of Marxism which was already underway during the years of the Second International and which concluded in the conversion of Marxism-Leninism into a state ideology. Through this cultural and ideological process, Marxism was transformed into a science, a positive science, the so-called science of the proletariat, adopting the conceptual parameters of a markedly positivist materialism.[12] Somewhere along the way it lost its critical edge and went from critical theory to positive theory, traditional theory according to Horkheimer's definition (1972). Part of this critique had already been formulated by Walter Benjamin (2006).[13]

We could go on with more arguments like those above. However, what interests us here is to highlight all that creates a shared conceptual field between the cited authors, the concept of form that is at the centre of open Marxism, and the Zapatista experience. It seems to us that here there is a point of convergence resembling a constellation, in search of a language of emancipation.

One could say that this 'constellation' encourages the breaking of grammar as a language of power in revealing it as the expression of a homogenising and totalising practice, as a form of social relations. Language imprisoned within a grammar of power cannot be the expression of a process of social emancipation, for it is part of its negation. In this sense, there is an urgent need to emancipate language from the form that turns it into a grammar of power and domination. Walter Benjamin possibly had a similar problem in mind when he spoke of the language of Adam as opposed to the language of men. The latter is a damaged language, one that cannot name the process of human emancipation for it presupposes the separation between subject and object and, therefore, constitutes a mere instrument and not a means of redemption. This language is incapable of being a means for true expression, for a politics in the *here and now* that could open up time.[14]

In any case, to name revolution today is to name it in another language. This language must arise from the breaking of form as the expression of capital domination, and it must have an anti-instrumental and detotalising character. It must interrupt the flow of domination that turns it into an instrument of yet another process of totalising social relations. The Zapatista's experience and its modes of expression have paved the way in this regard.

Grammar or anti-grammar? This is an open question. Our chapter wants only to ask this question, following in the footsteps of Zapatismo's 'Asking We Walk'.

References

Adorno, T. W. (1990) *Negative Dialectics*, London: Routledge.

Bakhtin, M. (2009) *Rabelais and His World*, Bloomington: Indiana University Press.

Benjamin, W. (2006) 'Eduard Fuchs: Collector and Historian', in *Walter Benjamin: Selected Writings, Vol. 3: 1935–1938*, Cambridge, MA: Belknap Press.

Berger, J. (2009) *Hold Everything Dear: Dispatches on Survival and Resistance*, New York: Pantheon Books.

Bonefeld, W. (2002) '¿Dignidad versus respetabilidad? Marx y la ciencia', *Revista Bajo el Volcán* 5, Puebla.

Bonefeld, W. (2014) *Critical Theory and the Critique of Political Economy: On Subversion and Negative Reason*, London: Bloomsbury.

Bröcker, M. (2014) 'Lenguaje', in M. Opitz and E. Wizisla (eds), *Conceptos de Walter Benjamin*, Buenos Aires: Editorial Las Cuarenta.

Buck-Morss, S. (1981) 'Walter Benjamin, Revolutionary Writer', *New Left Review* I/128, July–August.

García Vela, A. (2014), *Forma, trabajo y lucha de clases: derivación del Estado capitalista a partir del antagonismo de clase*, unpublished PhD thesis, Benemérita Universidad Autónoma de Puebla, México.

Gunn, R. (1992) 'Against Historical Materialism: Marxism as a First-order Discourse', in W. Bonefeld, R. Gunn and K. Psychopedis (eds), *Open Marxism 2*, London: Pluto Press.

Gunn, R. (2015) *Lo que usted siempre quiso saber sobre Hegel y no se atrevió a preguntar* (What You Always Wanted to Know About Hegel and Never Dared to Ask), Puebla, Buenos Aires: Benemérita Universidad Autónoma de Puebla (BUAP)/Herramienta Ediciones.

Gunn, R. (2017) 'On Open Marxism', Lecture given at the International Colloquium '25 Years of Open Marxism: Reflections on Critical Theory and Revolutionary Praxis', Benemérita Universidad Autónoma de Puebla, Mexico, 16–20 October.

Gunn, R. (2019) *Five Lectures on Hegel*, San Francisco: PM Press.

Holloway, J. (1998) 'Dignity's Revolt', in J. Holloway and E. Peláez (eds), *Zapatista! Reinventing Revolution in Mexico*, London: Pluto Press, 159–98.

Holloway, J. (2002) *Change the World Without Taking Power: The Meaning of Revolution Today*, London: Pluto Press.

Holloway J. (2015) 'Read Capital: The First Sentence of *Capital* starts with Wealth, Not with the Commodity', *Historical Materialism* 23(3): 3–26.

Horkheimer, M. (1972) 'Traditional and Critical Theory', in *Critical Theory: Selected Essays*, New York: Seabury Press.

Horkheimer, M. (1974) *Critique of Instrumental Reason*, New York: Continuum.

Horkheimer, M. and T. W. Adorno (1972) *Dialectic of Enlightenment*, New York: Herder and Herder.

Lukács, G. (1971) *History and Class Consciousness*, Cambridge, MA: MIT Press, 1971.

Postone, M. (1996) *Time, Labour, and Social Domination: A Reinterpretation of Marx's Critical Theory*, Cambridge: Cambridge University Press.

Rama, A. (1996) *The Lettered City*, Durham, NC: Duke University Press.

Sohn Rethel, A. (1978) *Intellectual and Manual Labour*, London: Macmillan.

Subcomandante Marcos (2014) 'Between Light and Shadow', https://enlace zapatista.ezln.org.mx/2014/05/27/between-light-and-shadow.

Tischler, S. (2008) *Tiempo y emancipación. Mijaíl Bajtín y Walter Benjamin en el Selva Lacandona* (Time and Emancipation. Mijaíl Bajtín and Walter Benjamin in the Lacandon Jungle), Guatemala: *Cuadernos del Presente Imperfecto*, F&G Editores.

Tischler, S. (2012) 'Revolution and Detotalization', *Journal of Classical Sociology* 12(2): 267–80.

Vázquez Montalbán, M. (1999) *Marcos: el señor de los espejos* (Marcos: the Lord of the Mirrors), Madrid: Aguilar.

Notes

1. By 'open Marxism' we understand a critical theorising that is founded on Marx and, according to Gunn (2017), can be generally formulated as follows: 'Open Marxism is not a doctrine or "line" that a formal political party might espouse. It is not a view which might be endorsed, as "Leninism" might be endorsed, in the days when "Marxism-Leninism-Stalinism" ruled the roost. It is, much more, an approach or attitude – albeit one which is present or absent depending on what claims are made.'

2. One author who has best highlighted the relation between pain, rage and hope in the struggle for transforming the world is John Berger, in his *Hold Everything Dear: Dispatches on Survival and Resistance* (2009). Holloway

(1998), for his part, reflects on Zapatismo and posits the idea of dignity as the revolutionary subject, while Bonefeld (2002) stresses the existing antagonism between dignity and respectability. Dignity is subversive, while respectability belongs to the weave of the mediations of capital (also Dinerstein, this volume).

3. We refer to the abstraction that is part of dominant thought, characterised by the autonomisation of the concept from the subject. In this type of abstraction, the object is reduced and homogenised in its identification with the concept (see Adorno 1990). Traditional theory is based on this type of abstraction (Horkheimer 1972), and the latter is linked to power and domination.

4. The relation between the production of the revolutionary myth and the theorising that leads to an abstraction of the concrete processes of struggle is highlighted by Angel Rama (1996) when he speaks of the Cuban Revolution.

5. On 'mutual recognition' as a critical notion, see Gunn 2015.

6. The general principles of Zapatismo are: 1) To serve others, not serve oneself. 2) To represent, not supplant. 3) To construct, not destroy. 4) To obey, not command. 5) To propose, not impose. 6) To convince, not conquer. 7) To work from below, not seek to rise.

7. On this, see Rama 1996. It was probably Bakhtin (2009) who, in his interpretation of carnival in the Middle Ages, best revealed the wealth of popular culture and the oral character of its expressions. For an approach to certain aspects of Zapatismo from a viewpoint that adopts Bakhtin's perspective, see Tischler 2008.

8. On this concept, see Tischler 2012.

9. We refer especially to the history of the Permanent Subjectivity and Critical Theory Seminar of the Institute of Postgraduate Studies on Sociology of the Benemérita Universidad Autónoma de Puebla.

10. See Holloway 2002; Gunn 1992; Bonefeld 2014; and García Vela 2014.

11. On this, see Holloway 2002, 2015.

12. These features are present in Lukács' (1969) critique of the theorists of German social democracy in *History and Class Consciousness*.

13. Benjamin believed that the historical materialism of his era had an erroneous vision of culture. Culture, he argued, cannot be appropriated in a positive and instrumental manner by the proletariat as if it were an object, an attitude derived from the positivist perspective of Marxism within German social democracy. On the contrary, for works of culture to turn into a heritage of humanity, the bourgeois code in which they are inscribed must be set on fire, these works must be liberated through the destructive act of dialectics. For Benjamin (2006), theoretical positivisation was not a superficial ideological phenomenon but rather an element of the process of reification of culture.

14. On this, see Brocker 2014; Buck-Morss 1981.

10

From Revolution to Democracy: The Loss of the Emancipatory Perspective

Edith González

Any concept that eliminates the division or does not speak of class division between the exploiters and the exploited, allowing them all to live together, this transversality, as you call it, between capital and labour, is good for nothing, it explains nothing and leads us into a perverse coexistence of the exploited and the exploiters who for a moment appear to be one and the same but are not (Sub Galeano 2018).

Nineteen-sixty-eight was the year that opened up the abyss, causing the concept of revolution that had characterised traditional Marxism to enter into crisis.[1] The new organisational practices and new language revealed a shift in the meaning of anticapitalist struggle that overflowed the image of hegemony, the taking over of the state, the party as the only form of organisation and the proletariat as the historical subject. However, in this process of reconsideration of the left, a movement was consolidated in which the concept of revolution was gradually replaced by that of democracy as the goal of the struggle. Ellen Meiksins Wood (1995: 12) has pointed out that if there is one unifying element in all struggles taking place during the last decades, it would be democracy. During the last 30 years, the drive towards *self-determination* or *prefigurative* moments of an emancipated world have become more and more identified with democracy. This theoretical shift can also be found in the major works of certain authors who have – directly or indirectly – played an important role in the construction of a concept of democracy that suggests an alternative form of organisation; that is, they have shaped a new utopia based on the concept of democracy. Such are the works by Laclau and Mouffe (2001), Hardt and Negri (2000, 2004, 2009), or Graeber (2013, 2014).

This becomes clear through the experience of contemporary struggles such as Occupy Wall Street (OWS). However, we have witnessed the consequences of such a change of direction. While democracy is the new utopia, it is increasingly difficult to think of emancipation. With the movement focusing on the affirmation of democracy, the concept of capital is set aside and with it the possibility of creating a society that is not based on the expansion of value. Theoretical interpretations do not question the rise of democracy as the purpose of struggle or how this affects emancipation. In this chapter, I argue that anticapitalist struggle that does not criticise capital reproduces the logic of the latter and contributes to the loss of the emancipating perspective.

I

¡Ya basta! (Enough!) In November 2011, this was the *scream* (see Holloway 2002) of pain and rage. It didn't matter if the financial firms were there physically or not; Wall Street is the metonymy of the financial markets or, to be more precise, the metonymy of the rule of capital. Although a call to take over the world's major financial district can be seen as a symbolic move, it should be perceived as something more than that. Unlike the struggles in the European South or Latin America, the most important aspect of OWS was that, in calling for an occupation of Wall Street, it displaced the centrality of the state. The absence of demands acknowledged the fact that the state and financial institutions formed 'an apparently seamless social and economic order', capable of absorbing any demand and of containing the force of a movement that was just emerging (Schrager Lang and Lang 2012: 18). To make demands would be to acknowledge that the state and Wall Street had the power and, therefore, to assume our role as victims. However, it became commonplace in theoretical interpretations to understand the OWS mobilisations as protests against the concentration of wealth in the hands of the world's wealthiest 1 per cent, against its practices of bribery and corruption and the financialisation of the economy. That is, as a social movement that enclosed itself in protests and goals that did not challenge capitalist relations. The opportunity was not seized to interpret OWS as an expression of the critique of capitalist social relations, as the rejection of the power of money, as a *form* of *class struggle*.

In the 2008 elections in the United States, rage against republican economic policies and the financial elite eased the way for the triumph of the democrats. Barack Obama came to power through an electoral strategy that combined the massive mobilisation of the country's youth and of the more progressive sectors of US society, using a language that was unusual in political discourse (Graeber 2013: 102). Obama's discourse was built on change and hope. The high levels of citizen engagement that year, when many young people participated in the country's political life for the first time, suggested a trust in the electoral system and, above all, support for the promise of change. According to David Graeber (2013: 104–5), at some point the idea prevailed that Obama's government would lead to a socialism of sorts; he was expected to carry out nationalisations, as well as introduce reforms in the health system and more controls on financial corporations. However, when the state stepped in to bail out the banks, a process of disillusionment in representative democracy was soon triggered.

Those who had voted for the platform of change took to the streets in search of the hope they had been stripped of: unemployed youth who could not afford the rise in the debts they had contracted to complete their higher education; sons and daughters of Latino migrants, African Americans or single mothers, turned into easy prey for financial and mortgage speculation by the 'American dream'; employed and underemployed workers with precarious salaries, insufficient to cover the costs of their means of subsistence; pensioners who, affected by the cutbacks in pensions, had been forced to re-enter wage labour in order to cover their healthcare and basic expenses; men and women weighed down by discourses sanctioning unemployment and poverty as the result of individual failure. In this sense, the occupying of the public space was liberating. It revealed to society as a whole that 'the US [was] a nation of debtors' (Sitrin and Azzelini 2014: 155). Once indignation became politicised and individual blame boiled over, people began 'to organize and fight back' (Sitrin and Azzelini 2014: 154).

Three months of marches, blockades, multitudinous general assemblies and camp-outs led to the creation of an alternative space. The occupations allowed for the restitution of the sense of collectivity negated by the dynamic of individualisation that characterises capitalist relations, as well as the experience of a time filled with experience and personal interaction. Graeber has referred to this time as the unveiling of the 'communism' that already exists in everyday life and is expressed in love, friendship and solidarity, 'the ability to all agree to arrange things in a different way' (2014: 390). This is the experience of men and women who discover themselves through participating in a movement that is constructed and organised collectively. The success of OWS, in Graeber's terms (2013: 188), is attributed to the unfolding of its horizontal forms of organisation, steered by direct action, mutual aid, assembly practices and 'the principle of full and equal participation': *the democracy project.*

Unlike representative democracy, the importance that the squatters and social struggles in general give to assembly is not 'decision-making' per se, based on the instrumentalised rationality of counting votes for practical purposes, but the very process of a discussion that is open to all who participate in it. The assembly is presented as the meeting point and time where alternative subjectivities are promoted and the goal of building a democratic consensus and community is pursued (van Gelder 2011). The occupations and the reinvention of radical democracy as a form of organisation, operation, decision-making and discussion eventually led to the radicalisation of society. 'We are the 99 percent' became the slogan for all those struggles that rejected the accumulation of wealth as the other side of the production and accumulation of social misery. Struggles without demands, parties or representatives sooner or later occupied the main squares of different parts of the world.

However, three months later, economic compulsion and the systematic exercise of violence forced OWS to take a radical turn towards political realism. The crushing of the collective work that had been undertaken during those months intensified the movement's internal contradictions and led it to elaborate specific demands focused on the abolition of debt, while the flow of radicalisation was channelled towards the construction of a democratic culture. So, what is it about democracy?

II

The primacy of democracy is largely due to events that took place in the 1960s and 1970s. This was the beginning of a new era, not only for struggle but for the overall critical thinking of the left. While the struggles of that time interrupted the relative harmony and social peace that had prevailed in industrialised countries, and challenged the content of social justice defended by liberalism (Day 2005), the wave of national liberation movements in Latin America and Africa contributed to the exposure of the threads that interweave the accumulation of capital with racism, colonialism and the patriarchate. This explosion of movements, resistances and social struggles reflected the great polyphony existing within class struggle.

The image of the welfarist democracy – combined with an increased wealth distribution and the recognition of social rights – while very limited, was enough for it to become a threat for capital. This democracy suggested the possibility of a radical transformation in that it became 'possible to think and do things that were not possible before' (Holloway 2019: 224). The utopian content of freedom and equality that remained concealed in the concept of democracy was now tangible in real life. Struggles rendered this content explicit, thrusting capitalist social relations into crisis. If Keynesian policies pursued the containment of antagonism, the struggles of that time showed that the situation was no longer sustainable (Holloway 2019: 91). Democracy was transfigured, turned into freedom and equality. That is, it expressed the very contradictions of democracy as a form of capitalist social relations.

At the same time, the convulsions of that period led to a schism in left-wing theorising. The struggles triggered a great number of theoretical interpretations that tried to account for this 'wide range of antagonisms' (Day 2005: 69) that overflowed the traditional canons of critical thought, particularly those of traditional Marxism. According to Hardt and Negri (2000), the new theories were highly influential for decades because of the sensibility they displayed towards issues such as difference and the affirmation of identities, until then ignored by modern theorising, but also because they represented an effort to overcome the crisis of the critical thinking of the left. The radicalisation of struggles 'opened the door to a change in the world, a change in the rules of anti-capitalist conflict, a change in the meaning of anticapitalist revolution' (Holloway 2019: 220).

Laclau and Mouffe's *Hegemony and Socialist Strategy* is indicative of the changes that were taking place at that moment.[2] In this work, the authors argued that the plurality expressed by the so-called new social movements had in fact already been present since the Second and Third Internationals, even though in Marxism it was always class unity, the plan, the historical 'necessity' or 'Revolution' that prevailed (2001: 166). It was a process that concealed the plurality of antagonisms, one that undermined the coherence of Marxist categories in their interpretation of the events of 1968 that attacked the hegemonic image of revolution. In this sense, *Hegemony and Socialist Strategy* was a call to revisit left-wing thinking theoretically and politically, in terms of the 'democratic revolution' that was taking place at the time. According to Laclau and Mouffe, the emergence of a 'new left' in fact represented a break with Marxism as a revolutionary theory:

> At this point we should state quite plainly that we are now situated in a post-Marxist terrain. It is no longer possible to maintain the concep-tion of subjectivity and classes elaborated by Marxism, nor its vision of the historical course of capitalist development, nor, of course, the conception of communism as a transparent society from which antag-onisms have disappeared. (Laclau and Mouffe 2001: 4)

The political repercussion of this rupture was the abandonment of the communist utopia that had inspired the struggles and the critique of capitalist social relations; that is, the possibility of imagining a classless and stateless society. Laclau and Mouffe (2001: 2) argued that radical and plural democracy expressed the profound rejection of the Marxist 'ontological centrality' of the working class and economic determin-ism. Thus, the sphere of the political was granted a central role as the locus for the recognition of social antagonisms. It is not surprising that Conway and Singh pointed out that radical and plural democracy is 'a "conservative utopia" – that is, a utopian project that identifies itself with present-day reality and derives its utopian dimension from the radical-isation or complete fulfilment of the present' (2011: 692). For Meiksins Wood (2000: 1–2) it was clear that the new left of 'post-Marxism' did not point towards the destruction of capitalism but rather towards making a space for itself within it.

Even if we perceive this theoretical shift within left-wing thought as related to the global reorganisation of the relations of production, to the attacks from the right aimed at stripping democracy of all content, and to the fall of socialism, the result remains the same: the need to destroy capitalism becomes ever more distant. Terms such as class struggle, communism and even capital, at the centre of the struggle for decades, became gradually displaced, replaced by democracy as the main goal. The critique of capital has dissolved into a critique of globalisation, neo-liberalism or the financialisation of the economy.[3] But what can be the meaning of an anticapitalism that makes no reference to capital?

III

This theoretical shift is still in place and is being reinforced through the major works of certain authors who have played an important role in the construction of a concept of democracy that suggests an alternative form of organisation other than capitalism. While these interpretations attend to a concern for creating knowledge from struggles, we cannot ignore the underlying problematics. Namely, that the movement that positivises democracy (as real, radical, direct, true, etc.) as a new concrete utopia is limiting the horizon and displacing the emancipatory perspective.

Experiences such as the occupations of public spaces or the struggles against the commodification of common land and water are presented as prefigurative moments of emancipation in the present. From anti-globalisation movements in Seattle and the insurrections in Greece and Oaxaca, to the Arab Spring and OWS, a wide variety of possibilities and questions in relation to emancipation have emerged, contributing to the development of a concept of democracy viewed as an alternative to the capitalist form of organisation. This is what has been happening in the last 30 years, especially after the Zapatista uprising. The latter opened up a new cycle of anticapitalist struggles and resistances around the world, and revealed the existence of a drive towards radical transformation when everything seemed to be lost. This cycle of struggles has emerged as an expression of generalised discontent against representative democracy, the normalisation of violence, the reality of everyday life and the fetishisation of social relations. However, we can also see that struggles remain trapped within the contradiction that identifies emancipation with democracy.

The economic crisis and the answer of struggle through the occupation of public spaces sped up the debate on the operations and contradictions of capitalism. According to Heinrich, 'Even beyond traditionally left circles, discussions about the destructive consequences of capitalism [were] taking place' (2012: 7). However, there were fundamental limits to this discussion. On this score, Clinical Wasteman (2012) pointed out that 'the notion of the "unsustainability" of capitalism slips easily into capitalist media when everything specific to capital as such is left out of the question.' Despite their different perspectives, the works of Wolf (2014), Stiglitz (2010 and 2011) and the signatories of DiEM25 reached the same conclusion: the logic of capital can be domesticated. It was argued that, left to its own logic, capital would lead to the irreversible destruction of the *social fabric*,[4] but the direct or indirect goal was to save capitalism from itself. The main idea of the debate was to provide 'theoretical tools' that would justify the regulation of the flows of capital, or to create democratic mechanisms that would impose controls on the financialisation of the markets.

That said, Graeber's contribution to this discussion is important, and not only because of the impact of his work on debt or his participation in OWS. Graeber is also relevant because one of the characteristics of recent debates is that the distinction between anarchism and Marxism is becoming increasingly blurred in the struggles.[5] Graeber's *Debt: The First 5,000 Years* (2014) offers a comprehensive historical analysis of the conceptual transformation of debt and money. It is an alternative history of these concepts that demystifies the economic determinism of social relations. In this work, Graeber describes world history as an alternating sequence of cycles of domination. That is, of social modes of existence based on credit and debt that involved the recomposition of relations of trust and honour through mechanisms that prevented social rupture, particularly periodical debt jubilees. This cyclic movement of history was radically transformed with the emergence of capitalism, which Graeber conceives as a system of infinite growth that subordinates social relations to the economic dimension. The economic collapse of 2008 and the subsequent bank bailout confirmed Graeber's hypothesis and marked the beginning of a permanent dialogue with OWS.

This work is also a critique of two central ideas that prevailed in traditional Marxism: revolution and communism. Rather than communism conceived as a new *totality* of social relations, Graeber tries to shed light on the 'already existing communism' in everyday life that is expressed in relations of love, friendship or solidarity. Graeber eventually suggests that the celebration of life and love with family and friends is what led to the 2008 financial crisis. That is, the crisis of capitalism is linked to the subversive potential of this communism that already exists, albeit in the *form-of-being-denied* (see Gunn 1992). It is not surprising that this dimension of reality is being criminalised and that debt is portrayed as a symbol of excess and pleasure (Graeber 2014). In other words, Graeber's reading suggests there is a potential in the antagonism that is inherent in capitalist social relations. That is why, beyond a protest against the inequalities and consequences of the economic crisis, we should understand the movement of OWS as the rejection of a society based on the accumulation of value.

However, one of the main problems in Graeber's alternative history of debt and money is his lack of interest in discussing the value-labour theory. The parallelism he draws between capitalism and debt servitude ignores the fact that capitalism is a form of social organisation unknown to any other type of society he analyses. His refusal to reduce social relations to the economic dimension results in an indifference to analysing the specific character of value in the capitalist mode of production, as well as its relation to money and debt. While we cannot reduce social relations to their economic dimension, neither can we ignore the fact that a society dominated by the capitalist mode of production is based on the expansion of value. This indifference is apparent in the passages where Graeber reduces the category of value to a myth that the critique of political economy never abandoned (see Clinical Wasteman 2012). To assert that the theory of value is a myth is to leave aside important questions as to what produces it, what are the true consequences of this myth and why we continue to reproduce it. It is a critique by halves: it scratches the wall but does not *crack it*.[6] Both debt jubilee and the positivisation of democracy – while committed to the square uprisings – reproduce the problematic underlying the interpretations that try to regulate and discipline capital. In abolishing debts, 'one might just as well abolish the Pope while leaving Catholicism in existence' (Marx 1990: 181, fn. 4). Once again, we find ourselves facing the same question: What is it about democracy?

IV

Although the economic crisis of 2007–8 hurled millions of people into unemployment and destitution, fictitious capital today is growing even more than during the period that preceded the financial breakdown. There is a lot of talk on the possibility of a much more severe crisis, although no one knows when and where it will strike. And yet this threat and the disenchantment caused by the governments of hope and change has propelled the most conservative forces around the world – Bolsonaro in Brazil, Macri in Argentina, Trump in the US, the Brexit debate in the UK and the rise of the far right in Europe. The images of rebelliousness that inspired so many writings on emancipation seem to languish. That is why we should take a moment to analyse what has been happening in the discussions of the left in the last thirty years. My argument is that the rise of democracy as the goal of struggle is shifting the critique against capital and causing the loss of the emancipatory perspective.

In this sense, there is a tendency to minimise the analysis of contradictions within our experiments through avoiding a false dilemma between political commitment and the need to engage critically with the categories through which we analyse reality. I have tried to approach this issue in the present chapter through the concept of democracy and the example of OWS. The few debates that have emerged within the struggles for democracy have focused on emphasising the rupture with the notion of representation that characterises state democracy (including real, direct, radical or true).[7] While the occupation of space, the radicalisation of society and the reinvention of radical democracy as a form of organisation, operation, decision-making and discussion against the state was impressive, the urgent need to analyse capital was never on the table or, rather, was reduced to a critique of neoliberalism and the financialisation of the economy, as occurred with Graeber's interpretation of OWS.

The resignification of democracy as a positivisation of our experiments wipes the possibility of creating a society that is not based on the expansion of capital off the map. This movement of positivisation abstracts democracy from all relation with the capitalist mode of organisation and suppresses the analysis of its contradictions. That is, it creates a pure category of democracy, whose main political consequence is the loss of the emancipatory perspective. The same occurs with other concepts that try to account for the dynamics of anticapitalist struggles. I refer specifically to the concepts of *autonomy* and *the commons* that have caught the attention of many authors in the last years, such as Federici, and Hardt and Negri.[8] I often find it hard to establish differences between radical democracy and the theories on autonomy and the commons. Most times it seems to me they are interchangeable, in the sense that they are pure categories or models of emancipation. While I acknowledge that these theoretical interpretations ultimately originate in the crisis of the idea of revolution and express the concern for – and importance of – creating knowledge from the experience of these struggles, I believe there are still problematic contradictions at their core, as I have already mentioned.

One of the results of the fetishism of the commodity is the separation of the political and the economic. It is possible that these anticapitalist experiments are breaking – or beginning to break – this separation. However, it remains unclear to what extent thinking in terms of a radical democracy (the rule of the people) entails a critique of capital in the way the term *class struggle* did.[9] It might. Nevertheless, what is more likely is that, as we have witnessed during the last thirty years, democracy is the *form* in which political relations present themselves to us in capitalist society;[10] the form in which, for a moment, the exploited and the exploiters appear to be one and the same but are not, in the words of the Zapatistas. The equality that democracy offers is the abstraction of inequality. 'Democracy, they say, is the rule of the people. But in capitalism there is no people, only classes' (Pannekoek 1969: 136). The drive towards emancipation that shines through the experiences of horizontality and rebelliousness is not indicative of a straight road from democracy to emancipation. To what extent, therefore, does democracy contribute to the critique of the class divisions of this society, where the capitalist mode of production prevails? And, if it doesn't, to what extent does it make us perpetuate the 'perverse coexistence of the exploiters and the exploited'? Is it possible to think of radical democracy as a form of class struggle? To imagine an emancipated society is to imagine a classless society beyond democracy.

References

Boron, A. (2000) *Tras el Búho de Minerva. Mercado contra democracia en el capitalismo de fin de siglo* (Following Minerva's Owl: The Market Against Democracy at End-of-the-Century Capitalism), Buenos Aires: Fondo de Cultura Económica.

Borón, A. (2001) 'La Selva y la Polis, Interrogantes en torno a la teoría política del zapatismo' ('The Jungle and the Polis: Questions on the Political Theory of Zapatismo'), *Revista Chiapas* 12, ERA-IIEc, Mexico.

Clinical Wasteman (2012) 'No Interest But the Interest of Breathing', *Mute* 3(3), www.metamute.org/editorial/articles/no-interest-interest-breathing.

Conway, J. and Singh, J. (2011) 'Radical Democracy in Global Perspective: Notes from the Pluriverse', *Third World Quarterly* 32(4): 689–706.

Day, R. (2005) *Gramsci is Dead: Anarchist Currents in the Newest Social Movements*, London: Pluto Press.

Democracy in Europe Movement 2025, DiEM-25, https://diem25.org/manifiesto.

González Cruz, E. (2018) *De la Revolución a la Democracia* (From Revolution to Democracy), ICSyH 'Alfonso Vélez Pliego', Puebla, Mexico.

Graeber, D. (2013) *Somos el 99%. Una historia, una crisis, un movimiento* (The Demcoracy Project: A History, a Crisis, a Movement), Madrid: Capitán Swing Libros.

Graeber, D. (2014) *Debt: The First 5,000 Years*, New York: Melville House.

Grollios, V. (2017) *Negativity and Democracy: Marxism and the Critical Theory Tradition*, New York: Routledge.

Gunn, R. (1992) 'Against Historical Materialism: Marxism as First-Order Discourse', in W. Bonefeld, R. Gunn and K. Psychopedis (eds), *Open Marxism* 2, London: Pluto Press.

Gunn, R. (2017) 'On Open Marxism', Lecture given at the International Colloquium '25 Years of Open Marxism: Reflections on Critical Theory and

Revolutionary Praxis', Benemérita Universidad Autónoma de Puebla, Mexico, 16–20 October.

Hardt, M. and Negri, A. (2000) *Empire*, Cambridge, MA: Harvard University Press.

Hardt, M. and Negri, A. (2004) *Multitude: War and Democracy in the Age of Empire*, New York: Penguin.

Hardt, M. and Negri, A. (2009) *Commonwealth*, Cambridge, MA: Harvard University Press.

Heinrich, M. (2012) *An Introduction to the Three Volumes of Karl Marx's Capital*, New York: Monthly Review Press.

Holloway, J. (2002) *Change the World Without Taking Power: The Meaning of Revolution Today*, London: Pluto Press.

Holloway, J. (2010) *Crack Capitalism*, London: Pluto Press.

Holloway, J. (2019) *We are the Crisis of Capital*, San Francisco: PM Press.

Laclau, E. and Mouffe, C. (2001) *Hegemony and Socialist Strategy: Towards a Radical Democratic Politics*, London: Verso.

Marx, K. (1990) *Capital*, Vol. 1, London: Penguin.

Meiksins Wood, E. (2000) *Democracy Against Capitalism: Renewing Historical Materialism*, Cambridge: Cambridge University Press.

Pannekoek, A. (1969) 'Bolchevisme et democratie' (Bolshevism and Democracy), in S. Bricianier (ed.), *Pannekoek et les Conseils Ouvriers* (Pannekoek and the Workers' Councils), Paris: EDI.

Ross, K. (2015) *Communal Luxury: The Political Imaginary of the Paris Commune*, London: Verso.

Schrager Lang, A. and Lang/Levitsky D. (eds) (2012) *Dreaming in Public: Building the Occupy Movement*, Oxford: New Internationalist.

Sitrin, M. and Azzelini, D. (2014) *They Can't Represent Us! Reinventing Democracy from Greece to Occupy*, London: Verso.

Stiglitz, J. (2010) *Freefall: America, Free Markets, and the Sinking of the World Economy*, New York: W. W. Norton & Company.

Stiglitz, J. (2011) 'Of the 1%, By the 1%, For the 1%', *Vanity Fair*, www.vanityfair.com/news/2011/05/top-one-percent-201105.

Sub Galeano (2018) 'Comunicado Palabras del Sub Moisés y el Sub Galeano' (Comunique Sub Mosies and Sub Galeano) *Clausura del Encuentro de Redes de Apoyo al #CIG y su Vocera*, en El Caracol de Morelia, Chiapas, 5 August.

van Gelder, S. R. (ed.) (2011) *This Changes Everything: Occupy Wall Street and the 99% Movement*, San Francisco: Berrett-Koehler Publishers.

Wolf, M. (2014) *The Shifts and the Shocks: What We've Learned – And Have Still to Learn – from the Financial Crisis*, New York: Penguin.

Notes

1. This chapter includes some of the main ideas of my doctoral thesis (González Cruz 2018). Many thanks to Ana C. Dinerstein, John Holloway and Panagiotis Doulos for their detailed reading, observations on and critique of a draft version of this text.

2. The publication of this book opened up a powerful debate in Latin America on the state and its relation to struggles (see Borón 2000, 2001). However, further on, Laclau supported the government of Néstor Kirchner in Argentina (2003–7).

3. Holloway argues that the category of Fordism had the advantage of calling attention to the way everyday activity was organised: massive production, relatively high salaries and a welfare state. On the contrary, the category of *financialisation* refers mostly to the precarisation of labour, the absence of the welfare state and the expansion of fictitious capital. While these categories are analytical tools, they invite us to section capitalism 'as one of a series of modes of regulation ... as a series of restructurings or syntheses or closures', that is, they naturalise capitalism and avoid understanding where its crisis lies (Holloway 2019: 221).

4. What did they refer to by *social fabric*? It can only be capitalist relations.

5. In relation to the dissolution of identities between communists and anarchists in the Paris Commune, see Ross 2015. The preservation of this division has had fatal consequences for anticapitalist struggle.

6. On cracks and their implications, see Holloway 2010.

7. On this, see Graeber 2013.

8. Let us recall the work that Hardt and Negri co-authored, in which they conclude that democracy is the mode of organisation of the collective will of the multitude. Or the version of the commons to which Silvia Federici, amongst others, has dedicated her work in the past years. In Federici, particularly, we find a concept of the commons that tends to evoke a world that is not dominated by the individualism or rational pursuit of self-interest that characterises capitalist social relations; that is, a world based on horizontal relations grounded on cooperation, mutual care and inclusive democracy.

9. I believe that texts such as those by Vasilis Grollios (2017) or Richard Gunn (2017), which make reference to the relation between negativity and democracy, are important contributions, but there is no space here for a more in-depth review.

10. Even more conservative and liberal theorists are aware of the dangers involved in the financialisation of the economy, or, more precisely, the dangers of the totalisation of the logic of value. In this sense, they struggle to revitalise democracy and respect for public spaces in order to preserve the social fabric. Theorists such as Martin Wolf (2014), for example, acknowledge the importance of a certain level of wealth distribution and a democracy that is legitimised in the eyes of society for the stability of capitalism.

11

The Train

John Holloway

I

The train rushes forward into the night, faster, faster.[1] Where is it going? To the concentration camps? Or to nuclear war? Or to annihilation by global warming and ecological disaster? To extinction?

Some of us sit comfortably, with our professorships or our student grants. We see only what is in the train, worry only about how to improve the seats, do not ask where the train is going. We live in institutions dedicated to improving the decorations in the carriages: these institutions are called universities.

Others, we know, are less comfortable. That is a euphemism: they are actually being thrown, one after another, into the engine of the train and burned up. Human sacrifice provides the energy that drives the train forward. The train is accelerating, fuelled by more and more sacrifice, an ever-intensifying subordination of human life to the dictates of the train.

But there is a restlessness. Even those of us who are relatively comfortable know that all is not well. We feel our seats becoming more uncomfortable, realise that we too are part of the fuel of the train, that the fierce engine that drives the train faster and faster is all-devouring.

We start to think 'how do we get out of here? How can we stop the train or change its direction?' We seize control of the engine room, but it makes no difference, the engine is more powerful than any driver. We grow more and more desperate. How do we get out? How do we stop the terrible destruction of human life? How do we stop the train before it reaches its destination of total annihilation? Where is the emergency brake?

We organise protests, rebellions, even revolutions. We walk in the opposite direction, hoping that this might affect the forward rush of the train. We organise spaces within the carriages where we try to take control over our lives on a harmonious, non-hierarchical basis. We even rush from one side of the carriage to the other, thinking this might derail the train.

Impervious to our protests, the train rushes forward into the dark night of destruction. No: not entirely impervious. Sometimes it slows down, sometimes it stutters, we even think it might stop. But each time it gathers strength again, rushes forward. The Russian Revolution, the Chinese, Vietnamese, Cuban revolutions, the uprisings and revolutions in Africa and Latin America in the seventies, the Zapatistas, the alter-globalisation movements, the Occupy movement – but still the train rushes on with a terrible, destructive power. And we see that its name is written on one side of the engine in big bold letters: ACCUMULATE, ACCUMULATE! THAT IS MOSES AND THE PROPHETS! And we know that this is the principle that rules the world, today just as much as in the time of Marx, probably much more.

The object gets stronger, the train's dynamic makes it harder to stop, makes it harder to even imagine stopping it. We examine the train and see how its different parts fit together, how one part can be derived from another, how there is such a tight concatenation of forms that it is impossible just to dismantle it bit by bit. The terrible force of the train lies in its totality, the system as a whole. There is a logic here, the logic of capital. At its centre is abstract labour, which constitutes value, which is inseparable from money, which leads us on to capital, which is constituted by the exploitation of labour, and so on and on: a tightly woven totality of forms of social relations driven by capital's werewolf hunger for surplus value.

The concept of capital is crucial to understanding our situation, the terrible dynamic in which we are entrapped. In this sense, the work of those associated with the so-called New Reading of Marx discussed in Mario Schäbel's and Harry Pitts' chapters in this book, of people like Backhaus, Reichelt, Postone, Heinrich, Kurz, Krisis and so on, is very important. They help us to understand the movement of the engine and where the train tracks are heading. If we lose the concept of capital, we lose all sense of the social dynamic and the urgency of our present predicament. Capital, an antagonistic movement with an all-devouring dynamic, becomes replaced by vaguer concepts such as 'empire', 'the 1 per cent', 'injustice', 'neoliberalism', and then the remedy is simply more or more genuine democracy, as Edith González analyses in her chapter. The problem is that more human rights, more democracy, more equal distribution of income may be important in making the carriages more comfortable but will do little or nothing to halt or even slow the train. More than that, the abandonment or tabooing of the concepts of capital and revolution make it even harder to imagine a world beyond the train. The name of the train is capital and its principle is Accumulate! Accumulate!

The concept of capital, then, is all-important. But there is a problem here. If we understand capital simply as a form of domination (as capital-logicians and New Readers of Marx tend to do), then we come to the conclusion that we must get out of the train, that we need a revolution. And we cry 'yes, yes, yes' with enthusiasm, and then we add 'But that was not the question. We know that we must get out, the question is how.'

We do not know how to stop the train, we do not even know how to open the doors and jump. There is no revolutionary party to take up the challenge, and certainly the experience of revolutionary parties does not suggest that that is where the answer lies. Then how, how, how!?! The desperate torment of the subjects trapped in the train grows louder. We scream.

II

'We scream' is a subjective point of departure. It lays down the primacy of the subject, not in the sense that the subject rules, but in the sense that the subject is the starting point for our thinking. As Alfonso García Vela puts it (correctly, albeit critically) in his chapter, 'from this viewpoint, the subject is the epicentre of the theoretical perspective and the starting point for thinking of emancipation'.

But our subject is not a pure subject. Her vision, her ideas, her conception of the possibility of action are penetrated by the fact that she is inside the train. The object penetrates the subject. The object cripples the subject, desubjectifies her. And yet never totally. The fact that I write this, the fact that you read it, the fact that the world is full of struggles against the deadly dynamic of accumulation and full of dreams of how the world might be – all this suggests that there is a misfit between the train and us passengers, that in our aspirations and our actions, we break and break through the rhythms of the train. There is, in other words, a non-identity between the train and us who live inside it, between the objective force of accumulation and the subjective misfitting of ourselves.

However, this relation between us and the train, between damaged subject and terrifying object, is not a stable one. That is what is so frightening about the world today. The train is speeding up, gaining force: neoliberalism, as it is sometimes called, or 'terminary accumulation', to use Sagrario Anta's much more helpful term. This has two effects on the subject: the train penetrates more and more deeply into our minds, bodies, imaginations, damaging us ever more profoundly; and also it forces from us a scream that grows louder and louder, a scream of desperation. A scream of desperation that throws us back to the subject, however damaged. The caravans of Central American migrants camp just around the corner from where I live, on their way north towards the US border, where, subjectively-desperately-absurdly, they hurl themselves often quite literally against the objective frontier, sometimes climbing five-metre-high fences with their children and then throwing themselves down to the other side.

Alfonso García is right then, when, referring to Adorno, he says 'the more anonymous and alien the relations of domination are, the more unbearable it is for the subject to experience its own impotence. Therefore, thinking will tend towards a higher subjectivity. At the same time, the desperate self-exaltation of the subject stands in the way of its self-reflection. Generally speaking, the rise of subjectivity in theorising and the reification of the world are correlated.'

Yes, but where else do we go? The more overwhelming the weight of capitalist domination, the more like those Central American migrants we become, throwing ourselves subjectively-desperately-absurdly against objective frontiers. Perhaps there is now no other way to go. The situation itself pushes us towards being more idealist, more subjectivist.

Both Alfonso and Mario Schäbel, in slightly different ways, criticise our approach for being blind to the 'primacy of the object'. They both strengthen their argument by reference to Adorno's beautiful and enigmatic comment in his Preface to *Negative Dialectics*, that his ambition is 'to use the strength of the subject to break through the fallacy of constitutive subjectivity'. Mario, in an earlier work (2018), even sees in the scream an echo not of Marx or even Hegel, but of Fichte and the young Schelling.

In responding to their arguments, it seems important to distinguish between two senses of the 'object' and of the 'objective'.

The first sense of the object is nature, the natural object. In this sense, to recognise the primacy of the object is to respect the natural limits on human action, to accept that humans are just part of a totality of natural conditions in which they constantly intervene, but which they do not control. The non-conceptual is then that which goes beyond human control and indeed human understanding. Understood in this way, the primacy of the object is an important antidote to anthropocentrism.

But there is a second and quite distinct understanding of the object: that the object is simply the totality of social relations. It is a socially constituted object, with a force that leads to it sometimes being referred to as a 'second nature'. This distinction between the two meanings of 'object' is akin to the distinction that Marcuse makes in his discussion of Freud's Reality Principle between a reality that is valid beyond any social constitution (the fact, for example, that however tall we are we cannot reach out and touch the moon) and a socially constituted reality, which he calls the performance principle. In this case, the primacy of the object still retains force, but it is a very different force. It is the force of the totality of existing social relations. Mario Schäbel, drawing on Adolfo Sánchez Vázquez's reading of Marx, makes a similar distinction between *Objekt* and *Gegenstand*: '*Objekt* is the object in itself, external to humans and their activity. *Gegenstand* is a product of practical activity, it is the object captured in a subjective mode. To express our critique of OM on the basis of this distinction made by Sánchez Vázquez, we can summarise it as follows: its authors conceive the world exclusively as *Gegenstand* and not as *Objekt*.' In terms of our train example, the train is clearly a *Gegenstand*, a socially constituted object, while what we see outside (the sky, hills, rivers) may be an Objekt (if, of course, we leave out of consideration what the train and other human-made objects do to the sky, hills, rivers, not to mention our perception of them). Whatever the validity of the objectivity of nature, which we leave aside for the moment, what interests us here is the force of the objectivity of the train, a *Gegenstand*, an object constituted by the totality of capitalist social relations.

If we understand the object as the totality of social relations, then the train is a metaphor for the primacy of the object. The primacy of the object is destroying us and hurtling us towards total annihilation and we, the screaming subjects, cannot accept that. Mario is quite right when he says: 'Therefore, this idealist interpretation [by which he refers to open Marxism] clashes with the Frankfurt School and its successors, for the latter support a more materialist interpretation: a critically materialist one. It accepts the appearance of the primacy of objective structures as real and, in doing so, assumes that human beings will continue to reproduce the coercions of the social structure, even if it is they who have actually produced them.' The problem is that by reproducing 'the coercions of the social structure', we are not reproducing a stable system of domination but rather a dynamic of death and destruction. That, surely, is why, while we recognise the primacy of the object, we can hardly accept it. If we look again at the engine of the train, we see that on the other side is written in equally big bold letters: THE PRIMACY OF THE OBJECT. It is simply a more abstract reformulation of Marx's 'Accumulate! Accumulate! That is Moses and the Prophets.'

We are in a tragic situation, in which there is an increasing primacy of the object, and that object is carrying us towards our destruction. At the same time, the object is penetrating the subject ever more deeply, crippling us, making it harder and harder even to imagine a different world. It is also true that the primacy of the object is pushing the desperate subject into an ever more unrealistic 'fallacy of constitutive subjectivity', an exaggerated idea of what can be achieved by pure subjective effort, Hollywood-style. Adorno is right, as is the New Reading of Marx, and Mario, and Alfonso and this post-2011 realism (if that's what it is).

Better give up then, better stop writing here, better not bother to send the book off to the publisher. But we can't do that, can we? (At which point the intelligent reader cries 'No, of course not! These people are right and they are wrong.' An intelligent and dialectical reader.)

III

'Not enough, not enough, not enough', puffs the train complacently, 'all your struggles against me are not enough. The Object rules. I am who am, I am Identity!'

Behind the complacency of the train is our terror. The train rushes forward, proclaiming on the one side 'The Primacy of the Object' and on the other the terrible, frightening 'Accumulate! Accumulate! That is Moses and the Prophets'. Terrible and frightening because it shows the dynamic of the primacy of the object, because the accumulate-accumulate is so obviously the force that rules the world, that shapes what governments left-or-right actually do, that shapes the details of our daily lives.

We cannot start from the object. Whatever comes out of our mouth or from our fingers on to the screen is inevitably part of our subjective scream. Nevertheless, we must look carefully at this terrible object that dominates us. We must have a concept of capital. The train is a human-made object, a *Gegenstand*. It is the totality of social relations and that totality is made by us: not freely or consciously, but it is the social inter-action that we humans have produced. And continue to produce. This is surely the key to the fragility of the train.

It is clear that we have produced the train. Capitalism (the train) is a social construct. Through bloody struggles, capital was created as the dominant form of social relations, a system was created which has its own logic (accumulate! accumulate!), its own laws of movement. Once constituted, the system appears to run automatically, as an automatic subject, like a train. Its existence is separate from its constitution: it was constituted, now it exists. As Alfonso García Vela puts it: 'Adorno (2007) acknowledges that, in capitalism, human practice has produced a social objectivity that is independent from particular subjects to a certain extent and rules over them universally, preventing their becoming subjects.' Everything depends, of course, on this 'a certain extent': if it is a real independence, if, therefore, the existence of capitalism really is independent of its constitution, then the train really is an independent force and it is difficult to see how we can get out of here. In this case, the subject constituted the object in the past, but the object is now indepen-dent and enjoys primacy. Capitalism depended on human action for its creation, but that is no longer the case.

This we cannot accept. Capital depends on human action not just for its original creation but for its continued existence. That is surely the significance of Marx's labour theory of value: capital depends for its exis-tence on labour, that is, on the constantly repeated conversion of human activity into abstract labour. It is the channelling of human activity into labour that constantly re-constitutes capital, that constantly re-consti-tutes the apparently autonomous existence of the train. It is perhaps not accurate to say that there is no separation between constitution and exis-tence; rather, that separation is always a fragile, momentary separating of existence from its constituting. Capital exists as an autonomous force to the extent that we constantly re-constitute it as an autonomous force. Capital exists to the extent that the subject reproduces the object as sep-arate from itself, alien from itself. This is not the identity of subject and object that Alfonso claims to see.

It might be objected that the weight of the object and its penetration of the subject is so great that the constant reproduction of the object (the train, capital) by the subject is simply an automatic process, that the dull compulsion of economic forces leaves no other possibility. In that case, the subject would indeed be an identity (as Alfonso, citing Adorno, claims) and there would be no way out of the train. But if that were so, why are you reading this article and why am I writing it? And I do not think that we (you, dear reader, and I) are so special (forgive me): we are rather part of a great world of resistance and refusal and rebellion, part of a world of confused No's saying 'take control of the engine', 'pull the emergency brake', 'jump out through the door', 'climb out through the windows', and our own preferred 'stop making the train, stop them from throwing us into the engine furnace'.

We are no identity. We are Hegel's 'sheer unrest of life', however weakened and maimed. We are Marx's 'absolute movement of becoming', entrapped, but not entirely entrapped, in that other terrible movement of Accumulate! Accumulate! We are a misfitting, an overflowing, a constant movement in-against-and-beyond capital. Capital depends on the containment of our misfittings and overflowings, its capacity to channel them into labour, the labour that produces and reproduces capital, that produces and reproduces the train.

The excitement of a paragraph like the last one almost convinces us that we are free. But no: we are still in the train and the train is charging forward towards the destruction of life on this planet. We have perhaps taken a step forward: the problem is not to conquer the capitalist beast, but to stop creating it. To stop creating the world of capital and do something sensible instead.

How do we stop creating the society that is destroying us now and threatens to annihilate us completely? By creating other worlds, by inventing other ways of living. Not easy, but there are millions and millions of people doing it already, by choice or necessity or both. And all these experiments-inventions are supported, must be supported, by another grammar, or anti-grammar: not the tight derivations of the train analysed and criticised by Marx, those tight connections wrought by abstract labour, but a looser series of connections – a world of many worlds, as the Zapatistas put it. It is not a question of building a train that will go in a different, happier direction (as in images of socialist progress), but of dissolving the train altogether. There is an anti-grammar that is being elaborated in practice by many different movements and experiments, most articulately and brilliantly by the Zapatistas, as Sergio Tischler shows in his chapter of this volume. It is the anti-grammar of an anti-world, an anti-world that does not yet exist but exists not-yet as a scream against the primacy of the object. This anti-grammar is very present but clumsily expressed in Marx's *Capital*, with its awkward and neglected or distorted categories of wealth, use value, concrete labour, forces of production; it is present too in Bloch's latent world of the Not Yet, in Adorno's shadowy non-identity, in Marcuse's return of the repressed, in Richard Gunn and Adrian Wilding's mutual recognition (also in this volume), in Arundhati Roy's beautiful world that is on her way ('Another world is not only possible, she is on her way. On a quiet day, I can hear her breathing'), in the Zapatistas' dignity, in Raoul Vaneigem's idea that ours is a revolution without name. This anti-grammar is what we discover when we open up the categories to see what is inside, or rather to see what it is that is overflowing from them.

And yet. Always this dreadful 'and yet'. Always we can hear the self-satisfied puffing of the train: it is not enough, not enough! We have to make explicit the subject's penetration of the object. It is easy to see how the object penetrates the subject, more difficult to see how the subject penetrates the object and constitutes its crisis. That capital is in crisis is clear, but often we see our struggles as being the consequence of the crisis rather than the other way around. We have to make explicit how our struggles are the crisis of capital, the crisis of its capacity to channel our activity into the labour that creates and re-creates it.

The relation between subject and object, far from being an identity, is a dissonance that is present within both subject and object. The presence of the object within the subject has been much emphasised, but what interests us more is the destructive force of the subject within the object, the presence of the subject in-against-and-beyond the object as its crisis. As long as we see our struggles as being external to (or even unrelated to) capital, the engine will puff happily 'not enough, not enough'. And we respond in desperation, in fury, 'Not enough! Not enough!'

References

Adorno, T. W. (2007) *Negative Dialectics*, London: Continuum.

Schäbel, M. (2018) *El Marxismo Abierto y la herencia de la Escuela de Frankfurt*, unpublished PhD Thesis, Benemérita Universidad Autónoma de Puebla, Puebla.

Notes

1. With many thanks to Ana Cecilia Dinerstein, Panagiotis Doulos, Alfonso García Vela, Edith González and Sergio Tischler for their comments on an earlier version of this chapter.

Notes on Contributors

Sagrario Anta Martínez has a degree in French Philology, a Master's degree in Romance Languages and a PhD in Sociology from the Benemérita Universidad Autónoma de Puebla, Mexico. Her topics of interest are ecology, the crisis of capitalism and the possibilities of emancipation.

Werner Bonefeld studied at the University of Marburg, the Free University of Berlin and the University of Edinburgh, where he received his doctorate. Before working at the University of York, UK, he taught at the Universities of Frankfurt and Edinburgh. He is a co-editor of the three first OM volumes published by Pluto Press in the 1990s. Recent book publications include *Critical Theory and the Critique of Political Economy* (Bloomsbury, 2014) and *The Strong State and the Free Economy* (Rowman & Littlefield, 2017). With Beverly Best and Chris O'Kane he is co-editor of *The Sage Handbook of Frankfurt School Critical Theory* (Sage, 2018).

Ana Cecilia Dinerstein is a Reader in Sociology. She studied at the University of Buenos Aires, and the University of Warwick, where she received her doctorate. She teaches political sociology, global political economy and critical theory at the University of Bath, UK. Her research on the global politics of hope connects critical theory with movements' autonomous praxis. Her publications include *The Politics of Autonomy in Latin America: The Art of Organising Hope* (Palgrave Macmillan, 2015), *Social Sciences for An-Other Politics: Women Theorising without Parachutes* (Palgrave Macmillan, 2016, editor), and *The Labour Debate: An Investigation into the Theory and Reality of Capitalist Work* (Routledge, 2002, co-edited with M. Neary). Her co-authored books *A World Beyond Work? Automation, Basic Income and Bad Utopias* (Emerald, with F. H. Pitts) and *Opening Fronts of Political Possibility* (Kairos, PM Press, with S. Amsler), are forthcoming.

Alfonso García Vela is Professor and researcher at the Instituto de Ciencias Sociales y Humanidades, at the Benemérita Universidad Autónoma de Puebla, Mexico. In 2017, he was a Visiting Scholar in the

Department of History at the University of Chicago. His fields of research and teaching are sociology, theories of the state, Frankfurt School critical theory, modern social theory and Western Marxism. His latest publications, both co-authored with S. Tischler, are 'On Emancipation', in Beverly Best et al. (eds), *The Sage Handbook of Frankfurt School Critical Theory* (Sage, 2018), and 'Teoría crítica y nuevas interpretaciones sobre la emancipación', *Tla-melaua: Revista de Ciencias Sociales* 11:42 (2017).

Luciana Ghiotto teaches International Relations in the School of Politics and Government at the Universidad Nacional de San Martín, Argentina. She holds a MREs and a PhD in Social Sciences from the Universidad de Buenos Aires. Her research addresses the problem of globalisation, international economic relations, and the social resistance against Free Trade Processes, with a focus on the Free Trade Area of the Americas. She is co-author of 'Las empresas transnacionales: un punto de encuentro para la Economía Política Internacional de América Latina' (*Desafíos*, 2018, with M. Saguier), and 'Brasil y la nueva generación de Acuerdos de Cooperación y Facilitación de Inversiones: un análisis del Tratado con México' (*Revista de Relaciones Internacionales*, 2017, with A. Arroyo).

Edith González holds a PhD in Sociology from the Benemérita Universidad Autónoma de Puebla (BUAP). She is a Lecturer in Sociology in the Department of Humanities at the Universidad de Oriente, Puebla, Mexico, teaching courses on international relations, communication sciences and research methods. Since 2012 she has been a teaching assistant in the Master's courses on 'Capital' and 'The Storm', with focus on debt crisis and revolution, convened by John Holloway. Her research offers a critical approach to democracy, social movements and emancipation, as well as the relationship between the institutional left and the autonomy projects.

Richard Gunn lectured in political theory at the University of Edinburgh until he retired in 2011. He was a member of the editorial collective of *Common Sense*. Since he retired, he has been an independent researcher and has published several articles, most notably articles co-authored with Adrian Wilding, e.g. 'Revolutionary or Less-than-Revolutionary Recognition?', published online by Heathwood Institute and Press (www. heathwoodpress.com) on 13 November 2013, and 'Recognition Contradicted', *South Atlantic Quarterly* 2 (Spring 2014). Gunn and Wilding are currently at work on a book-length statement of their views. Richard gave a paper at the conference on Open Marxism and Critical Theory held at Puebla, Mexico in October 2017.

John Holloway is Professor and researcher at the Instituto de Ciencias Sociales y Humanidades, at the Benemérita Universidad Autónoma de Puebla, Mexico. His best-known books are *Change the World Without taking Power* (Pluto, 2002) and *Crack Capitalism* (Pluto, 2010).

Katerina Nasioka completed her doctoral studies in sociology in the Instituto de Ciencias Sociales y Humanidades, Benemérita Universidad Autónoma de Puebla, Mexico. Her research interests address issues related to urban space, critical theory and social insurrections. She participates in self-organised collectives and projects in Greece and published and presented articles and papers on recent Greek social struggles. She is co-author of *Gender and Journalism in Greece* (2008), author of *Ciudades en Insurrección, Oaxaca 2006 / Atenas 2008* (2017), and co-editor of *Beyond Crisis: After the Collapse of the Institutional Hope in Greece, What?* (PM Press, 2018).

Rodrigo F. Pascual holds a BA in Political Science and a PhD in Social Sciences from the University of Buenos Aires. He is an Associate Professor and researcher at the National University of Tierra del Fuego, a Fellow of CONICET-Argentina and of the Universidad Nacional de Quilmes. His research interests are critical theories of the state, the critique of international relations, and globalisation. He is co-editor of *Integrados: Debates sobre las relaciones internacionales y la integración regional latinoamericana y Europea* (Imago Mundi, 2013).

Frederick Harry Pitts is a Lecturer in Management at the University of Bristol and leads the Faculty Research Group for Perspectives on Work. He holds a PhD in Global Political Economy from the University of Bath. He is co-editor of *Futures of Work*, and a member of the Associate Board of *Work, Employment & Society*. He is the author of *Critiquing Capitalism Today: New Ways to Read Marx* (Palgrave, 2018) and, with Matt Bolton, *Corbynism: A Critical Approach* (Emerald, 2018). Engaged in debates about how the changing workplace is conceived in thought and practice through contributions to journals such as *Economy & Society*, he has been described by the *Guardian* as 'perhaps the sharpest outside judge of the post-work movement'.

Mario Schäbel concluded his Master in Politics, Philosophy and Media Studies at the Ludwig-Maximilians-Universität München (Germany) and has just completed a PhD in sociology in the Institute of Social Sciences and Humanities 'Alfonso Vélez Pliego', at the Benemérita Autonomous University of Puebla. His research topic is Open Marxism and the heritage of Frankfurt School. His publications include 'El Idealismo y la Ortodoxia en el Marxismo Abierto de John Holloway: un alejamiento de la Escuela de Frankfurt' (*Bajo el Volcán*, 2016), 'La Importancia de la Escuela de Frankfurt para una nueva Lectura de Marx' (*Constelaciones*, 2017), and 'Die Bedeutung der Frankfurter Schule für eine neue Marx-Lektüre' (Kassel University Press, 2018).

Sergio Tischler is Professor and researcher at the Instituto de Ciencias Sociales y Humanidades, at the Benemérita Universidad Autónoma de Puebla, Mexico. He is the author and editor of several books, among them *Imagen y dialéctica. Mario Payeras y los interiores de una constelación revolucionaria* (FyG editores, 2009); *Revolución y destotalización* (Grietas Editores, 2013), co-author with John Holloway and Fernando Matamoros of *Zapatismo. Reflexión teórica y subjetividades emergentes* (Herramienta, 2015), co-editor with Werner Bonefeld of *What Is To Be Done? Leninism, Anti-Leninist Marxism and the Question of Revolution Today* (Ashgate, 2002), and, with John Holloway and Fernando Matamoros, of *Negativity and Revolution: Adorno and Political Activism* (Pluto, 2008).

Adrian Wilding studied Politics and Philosophy at the universities of Edinburgh and Warwick. He has taught at Edinburgh University, the Open University and the Friedrich-Schiller-Universität Jena, and is currently a Fellow at the Großbritannien-Zentrum, Humboldt Universität zu Berlin. He is the author of 'The Complicity of Post-History', in *Open Marxism 3* (Pluto, 1995), 'Pied Pipers and Polymaths: Adorno's Critique of Praxisism', in John Holloway et al. (eds), *Negativity and Revolution* (Pluto, 2008) and more recently, with Richard Gunn, 'Critical Theory and Recognition', in Beverly Best et al. (eds), *The Sage Handbook of Frankfurt School Critical Theory* (Sage, 2018). Various of his recent writings and translations can be found on the websites of Heathwood Press, Grundrisse and Verso.

Index

abstract Utopia. See Utopia, abstract
accumulation, 8, 42, 106, 107, 108,
    109, 110, 112, 113, 114, 115, 116,
    117, 118, 120, 126–7, 129, 130,
    131, 162, 170
    of commodities, 71
    by dispossession, 106, 110
    primitive accumulation, 7, 21, 68,
    72–3, 95, 97, 97–100, 101, 104,
    106, 107, 108, 109, 110, 112, 115,
    117, 118
    rejection of, 158
    terminary accumulation, 4, 7, 21,
    95–108, 106, 107, 108, 114, 116,
    117, 171, 182
Acharya, Arun, 113, 117
Adorno, Theodor W., 5, 6, 7, 36–7, 39,
    47–62, 61n4, 62n7, 62n8, 62n9,
    62n10, 65, 67, 69, 71, 76–91, 151,
    171, 173, 174, 175, 176 See also
    dialectics
affirmation, 59, 78, 129–30, 156, 159
    critical affirmation, 5, 33–46
Africa, 98, 101, 158, 169
African Americans, 157
Agamben, Giorgio, 135–6, 140–41n11
Agnoli, Johannes, 2
alienation, 5, 22, 28, 29, 73
Altvater, Elmar, 115
Amsler, Sarah, 2, 38, 40
Anderson, K.L., 4
Anta Martínez, Sagrario, 4, 7, 21, 106,
    117, 188
antagonism, 7, 70, 72, 97, 109, 159, 160
    class, 8, 68, 71, 113, 114, 116, 117,
    119
anti-capitalism, 37, 47, 134, 142, 146,
    147
    practice, 4, 125, 126

revolution, 143, 148, 159
struggles, 5, 9, 119, 145, 155, 156,
    161
transformation, 8
anticipatory consciousness, 38, 39,
    42
anti-grammar, 142–54, 175–6
anti-identitarianism, 47, 48, 54
anti-imperialist movements, 113,
    133
anti-vanguardism, 145, 146
Asking We Walk, 143, 152
Aubry, A., 56, 57
Azzelini, D., 157

Backhaus, Hans-Georg, 65, 67–8, 70,
    73, 76, 79, 81, 82, 91n2, 169
Bakhtin, Mikhail, 154n7
barbarism, 3, 5, 35, 36
Bauer, Edgar, 27
Bellamy Foster, J., 103, 114, 117
Bellofiore, R., 65, 66, 71
belonging, 72, 127, 130, 140–41n11
Benjamin, Walter, 34, 151
Berger, John, 153–4n2
Bhattacharya, Tithi, 57
Bloch, Ernst, 2, 5, 33–46, 176
Boldyrev, I., 36, 38
Bolsonaro, Jair, 163
Bonefeld, Werner, 2–13, 33, 34, 36,
    41, 50–51, 54, 61n3, 61n6, 69, 70,
    77, 80, 83–5, 91n2, 95, 106, 116,
    117, 119
bourgeois society, 54, 55
Burnham, Peter, 116, 117
Busch, Klaus, 115

Caffentzis, George, 119
Callinicos, Alex, 112, 113, 114

means of production, 25, 68, 72–3, 96,
97, 116, 126, 127, 130, 132, 133,
141n22, 149
mediation, 41, 58, 69, 70, 71, 73, 84,
86–7, 113, 120, 126, 134, 135,
141n21, 146, 154n2
Meiksins Wood, Ellen, 112, 113, 155,
160
Meza Lora José Salvador, 101, 112,
118
migrants, 32n22, 128, 133–4136, 157,
171
mode of production, 68, 99, 127, 132,
133, 163, 165
Moir, C., 38, 39, 42
money, 2, 3, 23, 24, 36, 37, 41, 98,
116–18, 125, 131, 156, 162
as command, 6
exploitation, 100–106
labour, 66, 72, 169
money-capital, 34, 40
money-form, 148, 71, 148
Mouffe, Chantal, 155, 159, 160
Murray, P., 66, 67, 71, 73
Murray, Robin, 110–11
mutual recognition, 4–5, 17–32, 176

Nasioka, Katerina, 2, 8
nation, 130–35, 148
nationalisation, 119, 132
Navarro, Mina, 101, 112, 118
negation, 35–6, 40–41, 47, 48, 49, 52,
59, 77, 83, 116, 140n1, 146, 149,
150, 151
negative dialectics. *See* dialectics
Negri, Antonio, 32n3, 50, 119, 155,
159, 167n8
Neupert-Doppler, A., 41
Neusüss, Christel, 115
new left, 160
New Reading of Marx (NRM), 5–7,
63–75, 76–91, 169, 173
non-identity, 42, 54, 86, 126–30, 135,
136, 137, 170, 176
Not Yet, 176
Novum, 36, 40

object, primacy of, 6, 7, 9, 58, 59, 77,
82–9, 171–5
objective coercion, 149
objective domination, 50, 59, 148
objectivism, 6, 48, 51, 53, 54, 57, 59,
77, 79, 81, 144
objectivity, 47–62, 80, 82, 84–5, 172,
174
Occupy Wall Street (OWS), 9, 155
ontology, 38, 49, 55, 56
open Marxism (OM), 1–13, 17, 35,
39, 47–62, 63–75, 76–91, 95, 106,
110, 115–17, 137, 142–54. *See
also* Marxism
Ortlieb, C. P., 7, 95
Otra Campaña, 145
overpopulation, 126–7, 140n6

Panitch, L., 112, 114
Paris Manuscripts (Marx), 23
Pascual, Rodrigo, 7, 8
personification, 25, 26, 79
Phenomenology of Spirit (Hegel), 5,
17, 22, 61n4
Picciotto, Sol, 115
Pitts, Frederick Harry, 5, 6, 7, 34, 35,
64, 65, 71, 76, 169
political economy, 2, 23, 24, 25, 27,
65, 67, 71, 72, 73, 76, 109, 132,
144, 163
Ponce de León, J., 42, 45
positive science, 50, 151
positivisation, 5, 41–3, 163, 164
fear of, 36
positivism, 49, 55–6, 62n8
possibility, 4, 33–46
post-Marxism, 160
Postone, Moishe, 33, 50, 58–9, 64, 68,
69, 73, 148, 169
Poulantzas, Nicos, 111, 113
power, 9, 22, 40, 48, 49, 52, 53, 54,
56, 57
labour-power, 25, 34, 68, 71–3,
98–102, 108n2
prefiguration, 9, 28
pre-history of capital, 99